Directors' Duties and Insider Dealing

Philip L R Mitchell LLB
Solicitor of the Supreme Court

London
Butterworths
1982

England London — Butterworth & Co (Publishers) Ltd
88 Kingsway, WC2B 6AB

Australia Sydney — Butterworths Pty Ltd
271–273 Lane Cove Road, North Ryde, NSW 2113
Also at Melbourne, Brisbane, Adelaide and Perth

Canada Toronto — Butterworth & Co (Canada) Ltd
2265 Midland Avenue, Scarborough, M1P 4S1

New Zealand Wellington — Butterworths of New Zealand Ltd
33–35 Cumberland Place

South Africa Durban — Butterworth & Co (South Africa) (Pty) Ltd
152–154 Gale Street

USA Boston — Butterworth (Publishers) Inc
10 Tower Office Park, Woburn, Mass. 01801

ISBN 0 406 29580 8

Printed and bound in Singapore by
Singapore National Printers (Pte) Ltd

Directors' Duties and Insider Dealing

Preface

The present work had its origins in Parts IV and V of the Companies Bill 1978. For the first time the legislature was attempting a general restatement of the law about directors, coupled with provisions aimed at stamping out the abuse of securities dealings on the basis of confidential information. A committee of lawyers and accountants on which I served advised Members of the Parliamentary Standing Committee on possible amendments as the Bill slowly advanced through its various stages. It became clear, however, that the Government had been over-optimistic in supposing that directors' duties could be codified in a few short clauses, and Part IV was still in flux when political events intervened and the whole Bill fell in February 1979. The present Government has contented itself in the Companies Act 1980 with a passing reference to duties owed to employees, and to the implementation of criminal sanctions against 'insiders'. Civil remedies for recovery of profits were not adopted. The present framework is therefore a mixture of common law and statute together with input from the City self-regulatory bodies. Rationalisation may be expected and it was thought timely to produce an elementary account of the present rules and to consider the context in which further reforms could be made.

Apart from their legislative proximity, directors' duties and insider dealing are obvious candidates for common treatment, not because directors are more likely to abuse confidentiality than any other 'insiders', but because both topics are founded on the equitable obligation of a fiduciary not to exploit his position to his own advantage. As research for this book progressed, I found that in reality one was looking at the same problem from different sides of the glass; and it is hoped that the continuity of the subject matter makes Part II more accessible than if it were treated in isolation.

My aim throughout has been to present a readable, up-to-date account to the hard-pressed company secretary and non-specialist legal adviser, of an important area of law and practice where legislation bids fair to outrun comprehension and highly technical rules, e g as regards disclosure of interests, have to be transformed for the benefit of impatient boards of directors into simple memoranda of guidance for actual situations. Where the law is mostly precedent, I have let the nineteenth-century judges do their own talking; where it is statutory, and no case law gloss exists, I have attempted to bring the subject to life by numerous illustrations and examples. On the other hand, there is sufficient citation of authority to enable the more serious researcher to pursue his problem, although in no sense is this a scholarly treatise. In adopting this dual approach I hope not to have fallen between two stools.

The debt owed by myself and by company lawyers generally to Professor L C B Gower, both for his authorship and his work at the Department of Trade will be obvious in the text. I have also drawn on the massive work of Rider and Ffrench, *The Regulation of Insider Trading*, published on behalf of the British Institute of Securities Laws. More particularly, I am most grateful to Dr Richard Prior of Lloyds of London for his comments on chapter 3 and to Dr Richard Buckley of Mansfield College, Oxford for his more general review of Part I. Where I have made assumptions or questionable value-judgments I have not done so without due warning. The errors are all mine. I am happy to acknowledge the help and forbearance of my publishers. My thanks are also due to Mrs Janet Harris and Miss Trudi Billsberry who laboured cheerfully in their off-duty hours to produce an elegant typescript.

The law is stated as at 1 October 1981.

P L R Mitchell
London
October 1981

Contents

Table of statutes

References in this Table to *Statutes* are to Halsbury's Statutes of England (Third Edition) showing the volume and page at which the annotated text of the Act will be found. Page references printed in bold type indicate where the Act is set out in part or in full.

Table of cases

PAGE

S

T

V

PAGE

W

Y

Part one

Directors' duties

1 The position of directors

1 As organs of the company

THE THEORY OF INCORPORATION

The cornerstone of English company law remains that a corporation, whether statutory, registered or chartered, is a distinct legal persona from its promoters or members. This secures the advantages of limited liability, a common seal, and perpetual succession. But the legal entity so created is of a highly artificial kind. It can only countenance the performance of functions or the exercise of powers which are conferred by its statutes, memorandum of association, or charter. In the case of a company registered under the Companies Acts 1948 – 1980 these will fall short of the capabilities of a natural person, since the promoters cannot hope for investors' support for other than specific commercial ventures or well-defined charitable objects. The widely-drawn objects clauses of modern 'off-the-shelf' companies are hardly exceptional, since they will either be construed as ancillary to the main objects,[1] or else, even if expressed as independent main objects,[2] be acquired into a group of companies already operating along particular lines. While there is no objection of legal principle to the formation of a company for any lawful purposes,[3] however widely conceived, in practice most incorporations involve the defining of certain trading objectives which, if exceeded, and subject to statutory alteration of the memorandum,[4] are ultra vires the company and beyond its powers to pursue.

A further practical limitation is that a company cannot think or act by itself. The power of decision rests with the shareholders in general meeting. The power of execution is assigned to servants or operatives employed for that purpose. It would, however, be unduly cumbersome for the 'thinking' or decision-making process

1 *Ashbury Railway Carriage and Iron Co v Riche* (1875) LR 7 HL 653.
2 *Cotman v Brougham* [1918] AC 514.
3 Companies Act 1948, s. 1 (1). Statutory references are to this Act throughout the text, unless otherwise stated.
4 S. 5.

to proceed throughout by resolutions of members. Only in the smallest family concern can this occur. The law has therefore shifted from its nineteenth-century posture whereby the general meeting was regarded as the company's ultimate authority,[5] to one where such authority is shared with the persons to whom the members choose to delegate the management and direction of the business. This duality of function corresponds in broad terms with that of the executive and the legislature in Parliament: foreign affairs or economic policy could never be conducted simply by passing enabling Acts. Thus, today, directors are a primary organ of the company and capable of exercising all its given powers on its behalf. As Cairns LJ pointed out in *Ferguson v Wilson*:[6]

> The company itself cannot act in its own person, for it has no person; it can only act through directors, and the case is, as regards those directors, merely the ordinary case of principal and agent. Wherever an agent is liable those directors would be liable; where the liability would attach to the principal, and the principal only, the liability is the liability of the company.

The duties owed by agents generally therefore form the basis of the law of directors' liabilities to their companies.[7] The duties are owed to the company alone and not to the shareholders as individuals or as a body.[8] Exceptionally the directors may assume a direct relationship in particular circumstances, e g where they negotiate for the sale of the issued shares in the company,[9] but this is not the normal case.

Since the directors are given control of the company's affairs and property, their position in fact exceeds that of ordinary agents. A link with managing partners of an unincorporated firm is sometimes stressed:

> It is a fallacy to say that the relation is that of simple principal and agent. The person who is managing for himself as well as others . . . I think it is more nearly true to say that [directors] are in the position of managing partners, appointed to fill that post by a mutual arrangement between all the shareholders.[10]

5 *Foss v Harbottle* (1843) 2 Hare 461 at 493.

6 (1866) 2 Ch App 77 at 89; see also *Willmott v London Celluloid Co* (1886) 34 ChD 147 at 150, per Cotton LJ, virtually making board and company interchangeable.

7 See ch 2, below, especially pp. 23–24.

8 *Percival v Wright* [1902] 2 Ch 421. But see ch 6, pp. 110–111, below.

9 *Allen v Hyatt* (1914) 30 TLR 444.

10 *Automatic Self-Cleaning Filter Syndicate Co Ltd v Cunninghame* [1906] 2 Ch 34 at 45, per Cozens-Hardy LJ.

Certainly their position is peculiar because of the very great extent of their powers and the absence of superior control except, e g the sanction of being removed by the shareholders by ordinary resolution.[11] The authority of a managing partner to bind an unincorporated firm, however, will often surpass that of a director, who must observe any restrictions on his power which are contained in the memorandum and articles (of which third parties are deemed to have notice). 'Managing agent' is perhaps a better analogy,[12] the type of duties owed being the same in each case.

INTERNAL ARRANGEMENTS

Although section 176 of the Companies Act 1948 provides that every public company registered after 1929 must have at least two directors, and every private company must have at least one, section 455 in defining a director states that it 'includes any person occupying the position of director by whatever name called'. Thus the Act leaves the members to decide, in theory, who shall conduct the business, so long as there is someone, and articles may provide for 'managers' or a 'council of management' instead of the traditional board. As with directors designated as such, the management powers will depend upon the extent of delegation contained in the articles, and the fiduciary obligations assumed by the 'managers' will be similar. Where, however, managers are appointed below board level they are merely senior employees of the company,[13] not its organs, whose status internally is governed by the law of master and servant but externally by principal and agent. They will only be able to bind the company in contracts to the extent of any actual authority conferred on them by the directors, or by virtue of any apparent authority which they derive from their subordinate position. Even among directors, there is no individual authority, the power of the company prima facie being vested in the board as a whole.

2 Extent of powers

THE ARTICLES

The articles of association of a company will indicate the scope of the directors' powers.[14] In addition, the members in general meeting may ratify acts of the directors which otherwise would have

11 S. 184. A resolution requiring a simple majority of members present and voting.
12 *Re Faure Electric Accumulator Co* (1888) 40 ChD 141 at 151.
13 See further, pp. 17–20, below.
14 And also their limitations, e g Table A, art 80.

exceeded them.[15] It should not be supposed, however, that the shareholders stand in relation to the directors and their authority as a man might in relation to a dog with a bone, free to afford or withhold it at will. If the act of the directors is ultra vires the company, it cannot be ratified, although the memorandum might be alterable with regard to similar, future acts. The transaction is void and of no effect, except to the extent to which a third party may rely on it under section 9 (1) of the European Communities Act 1972.[16] Conversely, powers once ceded and validly exercised cannot be retrospectively withdrawn, so that if the articles permit the directors to exercise general control, the members cannot by ordinary resolution exercise it instead, or purport to overrule its exercise in any particular case. It is possible for powers to be exercised concurrently, although certain functions are regarded by the courts as being exclusive to the management, e g to sell the company's assets[17] or exercise borrowing powers. The filling of board vacancies is regarded as concurrent.[18]

The modern basis of delegation is article 80 of Table A:[19]

> The business of the company shall be managed by the directors who may not exercise all such powers of the company as are not, by the Act or by these regulations, required to be exercised by the company in general meeting subject, nevertheless to . . . such regulations . . . as may be prescribed by the company in general meeting . . .

The final words do not, in practice, offer the shareholders the opportunity to overturn decisions of the board unless they are inconsistent with the articles or contrary to some statutory provision. Their effect is, more likely, to recognise that the general meeting may pass a resolution changing the regulations to inhibit the directors' powers for the future. Because a special resolution would be necessary, it would technically be simpler to procure the removal of the board under section 184, although in such a case threatened directors can usually rely on proxy votes to secure their position.[20] Directors, exercising their powers bona fide under

15 *Bamford v Bamford* [1970] Ch 212, [1969] 1 All ER 969.

16 Such third party must have acted in good faith, in respect of a transaction decided on by the directors.

17 *Quin and Axtens Ltd v Salmon* [1909] AC 442; also *Mercantile Bank of India Ltd v Chartered Bank of India, Australia and China* [1937] 1 All ER 231. Pennington *Company Law* (4th edn) p. 524. For public listed companies there will be a Stock Exchange requirement to such shareholders' consent in the case of a material acquisition or deposit.

18 *Worcester Corsetry Ltd v Witting* [1936] Ch 640.

19 A model form of constitution set out in Sch 1 of the Companies Act 1948.

20 A special resolution requires a three-fourths majority of members present and voting at the meeting, of which at least twenty-one clear days' notice has been given: s. 141 (2).

delegated authority, have little to fear in the way of interference from the body of members, and no doubt efficient company administration dictates that this be so.

POWER TO BRING ACTIONS

The board's control is perceived in *John Shaw & Sons (Salford) Ltd v Shaw.*[2] The directors resolved to commence proceedings in the name of the company but the shareholders passed a resolution in general meeting censuring their action. The Court of Appeal held that this inhibiting step was of no effect. Greer LJ said:[3]

> If powers of management are vested in the directors, they and they alone can exercise these powers. The only way in which the general body of the shareholders can control the exercise of the powers vested by the articles in the directors is by altering their articles, or . . . by refusing to re-elect the directors of whose actions they disapprove. They cannot themselves usurp the powers which by the articles are vested in the directors any more than the directors can usurp the powers vested by the articles in the general body of shareholders.

When the shareholders choose to reserve their powers the exercise of them cannot be regarded as done on behalf of the company, even where they are specifically allotted to the general meeting.[4] On the other hand, the delegate board is always treated as a collective agent of the company responsible to its principal (and not to the shareholders) for the consequence of its acts.[5] It is precisely because the directors are not the members' agents in general that the latter are unable to exercise day-to-day control over them.

3 Abuse of powers

The room to manoeuvre given by article 80 or any similar regulation places directors in a highly privileged position which carries with it corresponding obligations. These obligations are commonly called fiduciary' and form the basis of the discussion in chapter 2. Overridingly, directors must exercise their powers in a regular manner and for the benefit of the company, and the court will intervene to restrain an excessive exercise amounting to abuse, or restore to the general meeting default powers where the directors

1 *Scott v Scott* [1943] 1 All ER 582.
2 [1935] 2 KB 113, CA.
3 At 134.
4 *Alexander Ward v Samyang Navigation Co Ltd* [1975] 2 All ER 424, [1975] 1 WLR 673.
5 *Northern Countries Securities v Jackson and Steeple* [1974] 2 All ER 625, [1974] 1 WLR 1133.

are guilty of non-feasance[6] or are otherwise incapable of discharging their functions.[7]

WHO IS THE COMPANY?

An initial difficulty is to determine exactly who or what constitutes the company whose welfare governs what the directors must or must not do. This was explored in the well-known Savoy Hotel Investigation Report[8] conducted by Mr (afterwards Sir Edward) Milner Holland QC, appointed by the Board of Trade to investigate the affairs of Savoy Hotel Limited under section 165 of the Companies Act 1948. The directors of the company had evolved a plan designed to frustrate the attempts of outsiders to gain control by acquiring stock in the open market. The reason for the plan was that it was apprehended that the outsiders would use the company's property other than for its traditional business. A new company was floated to purchase the property, which was then leased back to subsidiaries in the Savoy Group, subject to a covenant that it should only be used as a hotel. The new company's ordinary shares were allotted to trustees of a benevolent fund of Savoy staff. The result was to make it impossible for any new controlling shareholder to compel a change of use of the property from a hotel to offices, even though the latter would have yielded a higher return to Savoy shareholders as a whole.

The purpose of the investigation was to establish whether or not the directors were in breach of their duty. It was found that they acted throughout in good faith in what they considered to be the best interests of the company. However, the Inspector noted:[9]

> Powers conferred by the shareholders or directors for the purpose of managing the business of the Company cannot be used for the purpose of depriving those shareholders of such control as under the regulations of the Company they may well have over the Company's assets.

The plan was therefore an invalid use of the powers of management. The directors could not set up the company on a pedestal, isolated from the interests of the shareholders.[10] On the other hand, the Savoy case (which has no legal binding force) leaves open the question whether 'the company' as the focal point of the board's loyalty is constituted only by its present shareholders, or whether

6 See Gower *Modern Company Law* (4th edn, 1979) pp. 147–148.
7 For example, where there is deadlock or no quorum: *Barron v Potter* [1914] 1 Ch 895.
8 14 June 1954, Second Report (HMSO).
9 Para 17.
10 See also *Hogg v Cramphorn* [1967] Ch 254, [1966] 3 All ER 420.

the interests of future shareholders must be considered as well. If the latter approach is correct – and it has recently received judicial support[11] – it would render more difficult the claim of a shareholder that the directors had not exercised their powers for the company's benefit, since such directors have an unrivalled opportunity to assess the company's future position and how the interests of its then shareholders are likely to be best served.

In small concerns where directors are also the shareholders, distinctions such as these will seldom need to be made. In public companies, however, where the investor's only remedies are in the name of the company,[12] it becomes of crucial importance to be able to huddle under the umbrella of the designation 'company' so as to show that the directors owe fiduciary duties to him.

It is this relatively narrow concept that has, for example, until recently, exonerated directors from taking account of the interests of employees[13] as a matter of company law, although the practical position has long been that management ignores labour at its peril. Nor are the directors' duties limited to the company in an abstract sense, since it is clear that they must protect the interest of creditors, and prevent the company's funds from being needlessly depleted so that lawful debts cannot be discharged. A statutory example is section 332 of the Companies Act 1948. If in a winding-up it appears that any business of the company has been carried on with intent to defraud creditors or for any fraudulent purpose, the court may declare, inter alia, that any of the directors who were knowingly parties to the fraud shall be personally liable for all or any of the debts of the company. Where the directors carry on business when they know that the company has no reasonable chance of paying off the debts thus incurred, there is a proper inference of an intent to defraud under this provision.[14]

ABUSE IN PRACTICE

Many of the decisions on abuse of powers concern situations where a section of the company's membership is given a special advantage or subjected to undue disadvantage, or where the directors operate principally for their own benefit. The issue of new shares by the directors under exclusive powers conferred in the Articles, to themselves or their nominees, not for the purposes of raising further

11 *Gaiman v National Association for Mental Health* [1971] Ch 317 at 330. This, however, is a case about articles of association.
12 Subject to the exceptions discussed in ch 5, below.
13 *Parke v Daily News* [1962] Ch 927, [1962] 2 All ER 929. Now reversed by s. 74 of the Companies Act 1980.
14 *Re William C Leitch Bros Ltd* [1932] 2 Ch 71.

capital but merely to retain their voting control at shareholders' general meetings is unlawful.[15] At the other extreme, where they unquestioningly follow the instructions of a majority of members without realistically exercising their discretion, which might have been exercised for the benefit of the company as a whole, they are in breach of duty.[16] Moreover the exercise of power may be impartial, but capricious, and liable to be set aside on that ground. Where directors had power from the Articles to refuse to register a transfer of shares if 'in their opinion it is contrary to the interests of the company that the transferee should be a member thereof', the court held that registration could only be denied if there was some personal objection taken to the transferee. It was not enough if they simply thought that a particular transfer was a device by the transferor to increase his voting power at meetings.[17] This aspect of 'proper purpose', which can be regarded as distinct from the general duty to act bona fide in the interests of the company, was emphasised in a Government addition to the unenacted Companies Bill 1978, clause 44 (2):

> The directors of a company shall not perform any of their functions for a purpose not contemplated by the instrument or resolution conferring or imposing that function.

The reference to 'imposing a function' is arguably wrong usage, and indeed the test of 'contemplated purpose' is dubious since, especially in the case of Articles of Association which routinely adopt Table A, it is uncertain whose contemplation is relevant – why not, for example, the directors themselves? Nevertheless this provision, which has not found its way into the Companies Act 1980,[18] imperfectly expressed a true principle, namely that powers are conferred by shareholders or directors to achieve predicted ends, not to justify acts of autocracy.

Recently the court has intervened to prevent abuse in connection with the normally exclusive power to issue shares: *Howard Smith Ltd v Ampol Petroleum Ltd.*[19]

> Howard Smith and Ampol both bid for the shares in RWM Ltd but since Ampol together with an associated company already held 55 per cent, there was no possibility of the other bidder succeeding, despite having the support of RWM'S directors. The directors therefore issued new capital to Howard Smith, giving

15 *Piercy v S Mills & Co Ltd* [1920] 1 Ch 77.
16 *Scottish Co-operative Wholesale Society v Meyer* [1959] AC 324 at 363.
17 *Re Bede Steam Shipping Co Ltd* [1917] 1 Ch 123.
18 See ch 2, p. 38, below.
19 [1974] AC 821, [1974] 1 All ER 1126, PC.

them a majority position. Ampol sued to set the allotment of the shares aside.

The Privy Council found that while the directors were not motivated by any personal consideration of self-interest, this was not enough to establish that they had acted bona fide for the company. Their primary aim was not to satisfy RWM Ltd's admitted need for new capital but to denigrate the majority holding of Ampol. Lord Wilberforce pointed out that even though the issue of the shares was intra vires the directors and formally valid, the power to issue them was a fiduciary power. As such it had to be exercised for the purpose for which it was granted. This involved both ascertaining a 'primary' purpose and inquiring objectively into the factual circumstances which induced individuals to act in a particular way at a particular time. If their actions were not convincing in that context, this was evidence of abuse.

If a director disregards a limitation on his authority, the question will not be whether his purpose was lawful, but whether an outsider can treat the company as bound. This is discussed below.[20]

4 The board

The conferring by the Articles of managerial powers (subject to any particular limitations) on the directors operates in favour of the board as a whole, and not individual directors.[1] The powers can only be exercised, collectively, at properly constituted board meetings. This raises two questions, (1) the permissible methods of transacting business and (2) the consequences of not observing such formalities and limitations as are prescribed by regulation vis-à-vis persons dealing with the company.

PROCEEDINGS OF DIRECTORS

The only statutory requirements for companies registered under the Companies Acts is that minutes of proceedings shall be kept.[2] Whereas the procedure for convening, and transacting business at general meetings of members is elaborately governed so as to protect all classes of shareholders and to ensure that resolutions are properly notified, directors are free, subject to the articles, to decide their own routines. If the Articles of a company adopt articles 98–106 of Table A, the following principles apply:

20 See pp. 13–17, below.
1 Cf the Partnership Act 1890, s. 5.
2 Companies Act 1948, s. 145.

(1) *Discretion* Directors 'may meet together for the despatch of business, adjourn, and otherwise regulate their meetings, as they think fit' (article 98).

(2) *Notice* Every director is entitled to have reasonable notice of a meeting but such notice need not be given to a director who is absent from the United Kingdom (article 98).

(3) *Voting* Questions shall be decided by a simple majority vote and in the case of an equality of votes the chairman shall have the second or casting vote (article 98). Formal resolutions are usually put and minuted, but precise wording is unnecessary and voting is only required when the sense of the meeting demands it.

(4) *Quorum* The quorum necessary for the transaction of the business of the directors may be fixed by the directors, and unless so fixed shall be two (article 98). If and so long as the number of directors is reduced below the number constituting a quorum, the continuing directors or director may act for the purpose of increasing the number of directors to that number, or of summoning a general meeting of the company but for no other purpose (article 100).

(5) *Chairman* Directors may elect a chairman from their number to preside at board meetings (article 101). By itself, however, this confers no special executive function.

(6) *Resolutions in writing* A resolution in writing, signed by all the directors entitled to receive notice of a meeting of the directors, shall be valid as if it had been passed at a board meeting duly convened and held (article 106). There is no requirement that the signatures be contemporaneous, but no director need be concerned at signing before others have signed, since his own signature will not bind him unless it ultimately appears as one of a series.

The more important of these considerations to be borne in mind by the chairman and company secretary when organising meetings are adequacy of notice and the actual physical arrangements. Often board meetings need to be convened at short notice although decisions to be taken thereat are no less important than at routine gatherings. What is sufficient is a question of fact: three hours' notice was held inadequate where directors had other commitments to fulfil, even where these and the meeting place were all in the City of London;[3] whereas five minutes' notice may suffice where neither distance nor commitments prevent attendance.[4] The notice is really

3 *Re Homer District Consolidated Gold Mines Ltd, ex parte Smith* (1888) 39 ChD 546.

4 *Browne v La Trinidad* (1887) 37 ChD 1.

a summons, and hence there is no need to specify the business which it is intended to discuss.

As to the necessity of having a quorum physically present, opinion is divided. There is a Canadian authority[5] which has held that discussion over the telephone, where the directors were separated by a considerable mileage, was incapable of constituting a meeting. In an era of telex, Rapifax, and closed-circuit television, however, this is an outmoded approach and it is unlikely that legal objection would now be taken to a telephone conversation between, say, two directors sitting at the company's offices and a third at the offices of an overseas client, provided that all participants had access to similar information and papers.

CONSEQUENCES OF IRREGULARITY

The significance of these minimum arrangements is the effect of non-compliance. If a notice of meeting is not properly given, the proceedings are void, at least until the director concerned has had the opportunity to attend a freshly-convened meeting. However, an outsider is not affected by the irregularity if he was unaware of it.[6] In the absence of formal arrangements the remaining directors have no authority to reach decisions on their own: and it is immaterial that such directors constitute a majority in favour of a particular course of action, and that the absent directors would anyway have voted against.

5 Validity of acts

TYPES OF AUTHORITY

Proceedings of the board may be substantively as well as procedurally defective, i e the directors may have exceeded the powers which the regulations confer. In such a case it becomes important to establish how far, if at all, third parties may rely on the board's appearance of legitimacy. This invokes the so-called rule in *Royal British Bank v Turquand*.[7]

Very broadly, an agent who enters into a transaction on behalf of his principal will succeed in binding his principal if it can be shown that the agent was acting within the scope of the authority which

5 *Re Associated Color Laboratories* (1970) 12 DLR 388.
6 *County of Gloucester Bank v Rudry Merthyr Steam and House Coal Colliery Co* [1895] 1 Ch 629; *Re Fireproof Doors Ltd* [1916] 2 Ch 142.
7 (1856) 6 E & B 327.

the principal has conferred on him.[8] The authority is classified as (1) actual, (2) usual, or (3) apparent.

(1) *Actual* This is the express power vested in the agent and for companies will consist either of authorisation contained in the Memorandum or Articles of Association, e g in relation to borrowing powers, or bestowed by a resolution of the board or by the members in general meeting. Authority of this kind may be given retrospectively by ratification, provided the agent disclosed that he acted for an identifiable principal. Moreover, powers reasonably incidental to the carrying out of the agent's express authority may be implied from the circumstances:[9] and this is no less actual authority for not having been spelt out.

(2) *Usual* An agent occupying a particular position may be assumed to be possessed of certain capabilities in relation to his principal's business which are usual or normal for that position or business, e g a manager purchasing goods on credit.[10] The principal will be bound by the agent's acts unless his authority has been expressly restricted and such restriction communicated to the third party.

(3) *Apparent* This is not actual authority at all, but is based upon estoppel, the principle that a person who makes a representation which is relied on to another's detriment, cannot afterwards adopt a different position which is inconsistent with his statement. Thus a principal who holds out an agent as possessing powers which he does not, in fact, have will nonetheless be bound if the agent purports to act in exercise of those powers, if the third party bona fide assumed they were valid.

CONSTRUCTIVE NOTICE

The scope of the authority is normally to be ascertained from the company's regulations. However the general rules of apparent authority have been developed to embrace the situation where, apart from the Memorandum and Articles of Association of a company and such other documents as are required by law to be filed with the Registrar,[11] an outsider has no means of knowing whether or not the byelaws of 'internal management' have been complied with. These developments cover not only (1) a failure to

8 For a fuller account, see e g Lowe *Commercial Law* (5th edn, 1976) pp. 25–38.

9 *Wragg v Lovett* [1948] 2 All ER 968.

10 *Watteau v Fenwick* [1893] 1 QB 346.

11 E g special resolutions under s. 143 of the Companies Act 1948, and ordinary resolutions increasing capital (s. 63).

convene board meetings in accordance with agreed regulations, as discussed above, but also (2) a failure to convene any board meeting at all and (3) restrictions imposed which are not made known to the third party with whom the directors purport to deal on behalf of the company.

Conventionally, the Memorandum and Articles act as constructive notice of any limitation or prohibition on what otherwise would be the board's usual or apparent authority. For example, if directors are given authority only to borrow money or allot shares up to a certain amount,[12] an outsider will not be able to sue the company for any excess of that amount,[13] since they are deemed to have the public documents of the company in their pocket when negotiating with its representatives. Subject to that, however, the outsider is not concerned about the status or authority of the person with whom he deals, provided he *appears* to have the requisite power and there is nothing to put him on enquiry.[14] The justification for this rule is commercial convenience.

In *Mahoney v East Holyford Mining Co Ltd*[15] the shareholders of the company, who were entitled to appoint directors, acted as directors without any formal appointment by signing cheques. The Articles provided that cheques should be signed as the board might direct.

It was held that the company was liable on the cheques, as the drawee of the cheque had no independent means of ascertaining whether or not the board had exercised its powers over cheques. (In fact he made no enquiries.)

The absence of actual authority is no bar to a claim provided:

(1) the outsider can show that he entered into the contract on the basis of a representation made, expressly or impliedly, that the company's agent occupied a position giving him the necessary authority,[16]

(2) the representation was made by persons who did have actual authority to manage the company's business.

It follows that an outsider would not expect a junior clerk to be invested with the necessary power to, e g lease cars for the company, and should not negotiate with him. But if a person writes a letter on company headed paper as director or secretary or senior

12 See now s. 14 of the Companies Act 1980.

13 Unless the company in general meeting ratifies the transaction

14 *Royal British Bank v Turquand* (1855) 5 E & B 248.

15 (1875) LR 7 HL 869.

16 *Rama Corpn v Proved Tin and General Investments Ltd* [1952] 2 QB 147, [1952] 1 All ER 554.

manager, the outsider is entitled to assume that that person has the delegated authority of the board as a whole, either general or particular.[17] This is so even if the person had not been appointed at all.[18]

These exemptions do not apply if the outsider is relying on a document, purported to be executed by the company, which is in fact a forgery.[19] A company, like an individual, can never be bound by a forged instrument; or, it seems, by one which is not a forgery but is executed for a different purpose.[20] Also, the mere fact that a document is authenticated does not of itself entitle the outsider to assume that the transaction to which it relates is valid.[1]

STATUTORY PROTECTION WHERE RESTRICTIONS DISREGARDED

Section 9 (1) of the European Communities Act 1972 provides that if a company enters into a transaction which has been decided on by the directors but which is beyond the limits of its memorandum or articles, the outsider may treat the company as bound if he can show good faith. This exceeds the *Turquand* principle because it allows third parties to ignore express restrictions, and thus considerably weakens the 'constructive notice' rule which otherwise applies to the company's public documents.[2] It only applies however, to decisions of the board as a whole: the validity of any act of a delegate director or officer is unchanged.

Protection may also be available under the Companies Act 1948, section 180 and Table A, article 105. The latter provides:

> All acts done by any meeting of the directors or of a committee of directors or by any person acting as a director shall, notwithstanding that it be afterwards discovered that there was some defect in the appointment . . . or that they or any of them were disqualified, be as valid as if every such person had been duly appointed and was qualified to be a director.

A meeting irregularly convened, for example, so that an appointment is invalid, would be covered by this provision. But where there has been no appointment at all, the person claiming

17 See further, Gower *Modern Company Law* (4th edn, 1979) pp. 190–205.
18 *Duck v Tower Galvanising Co* [1901] 2 KB 314; cf *Morris v Kanssen* [1946] AC 459, [1946] 1 All ER 586.
19 *Ruben v Great Fingall Consolidated* [1906] AC 439; *South London Greyhound Racecourses Ltd v Wake* [1931] 1 Ch 496.
20 *Kreditbank Cassel GmbH v Schenkers Ltd* [1927] 1 KB 826.
1 *Dey v Pullinger Engineering Co* [1921] 1 KB 77.
2 The section appears to apply whether the transaction is ultra vires the company or merely beyond the powers of the directors.

against the company will fail if he himself was one of those purporting to act as director.[3] 'Insiders' are not protected by these provisions or by the rule in *Turquand's* case.

EXECUTIVE AND NON-EXECUTIVE DIRECTORS

The indivisibility of the functions of the board has, as a corollary, the equality of status of its members, unless particular powers have been delegated. It follows that there can be no distinction between the position of executive and non-executive directors, or those employed under service contracts and those not. If a breach of duty is to be attributed to a board on the basis that all of its members were present at a meeting which approved a wrongful act, then the liability of the directors is joint and several and no allowance is made for the fact that some are part-timers and may have acquiesced in a situation which they did not fully understand.[4] For these purposes directors are in the same position as trustees of a fund. This consideration is important when proposals are made for the creation of 'two-tier' boards which separate management and advisory, or audit functions.[5] On the other hand, as we shall see in chapter 3, professional directors appointed as such to a board may well owe higher duties of care and skill than the other members. Also, as discussed in chapter 5, certain reliefs and indemnities are available to directors who, by reason of their own intermittent involvement, come to rely on the acts and representations of the whole-time executives.

6 Delegation

GENERALLY

Because management powers are vested exclusively in the board as a whole, delegation to committees or subordinate officers requires express permission in the articles or by a general meeting.[6] To allow flexibility of management, arrangements are usually made for the powers of the board (and therefore, effectively, the company) to be exercised by a relatively small number of executive directors who may operate the day-to-day business of the enterprise without reference to the larger body. Even with large public companies power is invariably entrusted to a handful of full-time directors who

3 *Morris v Kanssen*, above.
4 *Re Lands Allotment Co* [1894] 1 Ch 616. See also p. 49, below.
5 Report of Committee on Industrial Democracy (Cmnd 6706 (1977)).
6 *Mercantile Bank of India Ltd v Chartered Bank of India, Australia and China* [1937] 1 All ER 231. See e g Table A, art 102.

report to the main board at fairly long intervals, e g monthly or quarterly. The presence on a board of non-executives makes this deployment essential.

Articles will enable persons, sometimes not even directors, to be appointed under a power of attorney to discharge, usually for a specified time or a particular transaction (e g handling a rights issue of shares or negotiating a take-over), the function of the board. Such powers are capable of being revoked by the appointing party[7] at any time.

When there has been delegation to a committee there should, if possible, be applied the same rules as regards notice of meetings and minuting of resolutions as apply to the main board, since the liability of the company (or the directors themselves) often depends upon the evidence of their decisions or deliberations. For example, under the Companies Act 1980, section 46, directors are 'to have regard' to the interests of employees. This provision gives rise to a number of problems[8] but it is thought that directors will be safe from attack provided they can be said to have formally considered the employees' position, even if thereafter they choose to disregard it in acting in what they take to be the best interests of the company. Thus, suppose the reorganisation of a company's undertaking is referred to a committee of directors, to avoid a continuing trading loss. Decisions will be required about disposal of assets or property, relocation, perhaps even redundancies. Minutes which show that the interests of the employees were considered when reaching such decisions may prevent later assertions that the board were disregarding their statutory powers and functions.[9]

Where functions are delegated they are removed from board control, just as members' powers in general meeting are removed by delegation in the articles to the directors. Until the authority to act is revoked, the appointing authority will be bound by the acts of the delegate and so will the company. It does not follow, however, that the directors will be personally liable for defaults of their subordinate officers, such as managers. They are only responsible for wrongful acts or omissions procured or acquiesced in by themselves; the rest are for the account of the company itself.

MANAGING DIRECTORS AND MANAGERS

The board will normally appoint a managing director under Table A, article 107 or its equivalent. Article 109 permits the delegation to

7 *Manton v Brighton Corpn* [1951] 2 KB 393, [1951] 2 All ER 101.
8 See pp. 38–39, below.
9 There will, of course, be consultation on other procedures to be followed under the Employment Protection (Consolidation) Act 1978, etc.

him of any of the powers which could otherwise be exercised by the board itself. This delegate position once again implies that it can be summarily revoked, unless the appointee is specifically invested with rights by the articles which ensure that his fellow directors may not interfere with the running of the company.[10] The position of the managing director vis-à-vis outsiders is the same as for any person transacting business on the company's behalf, i e it depends upon showing that he has actual or apparent authority from his principal. If there is no power to appoint a managing director in the articles, however, no special authority can be given or inferred.[11]

A director or managing director may be employed under a service contract, which may govern his remuneration, conditions of work, etc similar to any other employee, but does not affect his fiduciary position in relation to the company such as to diminish the duties of good faith, skill and care which he owes by virtue of his office. If a director is removed by ordinary resolution in general meeting, or a managing director has his powers revoked by the board, there may be a claim for damages for breach by the company of the contract of service, but the right of removal itself cannot be ousted.[12]

Because he is supposed to be a delegate of the functions of the whole board, a managing director enjoys an apparent authority not shared by any other director or officer of the company. The extent to which outsiders may rely on the trappings of power seemingly bestowed on a particular individual is demonstrated by the case of *Freeman and Lockyer v Buckhurst Park Properties (Mangal) Ltd*:[13]

> The company had appointed no managing director although under the Articles it was permitted to do so. Nonetheless, a director (with the company's approval) assumed the mantle of a managing director and entered into a contract on the company's behalf with a firm of architects. This transaction was within the ordinary authority of a managing director of a property company. It was held that the plaintiff architects were entitled to assume that the director possessed the necessary power by virtue of a formal appointment, so that the company was bound by his acts.

A director who has not been held out as a managing director will normally have no authority to bind the company, unless it has been especially conferred. The same will be true of a manager or other employee unless the transaction in question is a usual one having

10 *John Shaw & Sons (Salford) Ltd v Shaw* [1935] 2 KB 113.
11 *Boschoek Pty Co Ltd v Fuke* [1906] 1 Ch 148.
12 *Shindler v Northern Raincoat Co* [1960] 2 All ER 239.
13 [1964] 2 QB 480, [1964] 1 All ER 630, CA.

regard to the employee's position, or there is an express authorisation or a holding out upon which the third party can rely. In certain cases it has also been held that the chairman of the board has a greater executive authority than the other directors, corresponding to that of the managing director.[14] Unless such chairman has also been designated chief executive, however, it is unsafe to rely upon the doctrine of apparent authority. If the board desires to confer particular powers on individual members, they should do so by express minute. The same applies to a subordinate committee of directors. Too often this simple formality is omitted.

In normal circumstances the directors will in turn delegate functions to managers, who are invariably employed under contracts of service. In such cases the company remains liable, e g for their tortious acts under the principles of vicarious liability, and for commercial transactions upon the usual principles of agency. Employees owe duties to the company which are based upon master and servant concepts of fidelity and confidentiality, and their duties may overlap with those of directors. Nevertheless directors have the conduct of the company's business as a whole, and are trustees of its property, and so the position of a manager, while often highly responsible, will not inevitably carry the same liabilities as fall upon the board or a managing director or committee either under common law or by virtue of express provisions in the Companies Acts. The rules concerning conflicts of duty and interest can be regarded as more strict for directors, if only because directors are more often in a position to influence the company's affairs to their own advantage. Misuse of confidential information, however, such as insider dealing, applies both to directors and employees who happen to acquire it.[15]

AUTHORITY TO SEAL

Where the company's seal has to be affixed to documents, and the articles require the presence of certain officers, e g a director or secretary, an outsider receiving a duly sealed document is entitled to assume that the witnessing signatures are those of persons who have in fact been authorised to place them. It is probably also reliable evidence of a board resolution authorising the affixing of a seal.[16]

14 *British Thomson-Houston Co Ltd v Federated European Bank Ltd* [1932] 2 KB 176, CA.

15 See ch 9, below.

16 *Duck v Tower Galvanising Co* [1901] 2 KB 314.

7 Statutory reforms and proposals

The organic position occupied by a director by virtue of his agency function and the duties of skill and care which he owes as a manager of the company's affairs[17] are worked out exclusively from rules of common law and equity. There is nothing in the Companies Acts 1948–1976 which provides a formulation of these principles.[18] Increasing recognition, however, of directors as employers of labour as well as manipulators of capital resources, and the widespread belief that they should be accountable other than to occasional, stage-managed, meetings of shareholders have set the legislature along an interventionist path. As early as 1962 the Report of the Jenkins Committee[19] considered the question whether or not there should be a statutory statement of directors' duties. This was thought desirable provided it did not amount to a codification, as opposed to a mere consolidation, and hence become inflexible. In 1977 the Bullock Report recommended that if its proposals for worker directors and a two-tier board structure be accepted, some redefining of the standards to be expected of directors in discharging their functions was timely and necessary. It also proposed that the responsibility and power of the board to operate the company should be established by law, and not merely left to the Articles of Association.

Although the two-tier board has been tried successfully in Continental Europe, and in particular in Germany (since 1861), Bullock recommended that the board of a company with 2,000 or more employees should remain a single board, but that it should be constituted by a '2X + Y' formula, i e shareholders and employees should each elect an equal number of directors and they should then jointly co-opt a third group.[20] The rights of employee directors thus appointed were to be entrenched, i e they were not to be removed by ordinary resolution under section 184 of the Companies Act 1948. The Bullock proposals were not unanimous and a minority of the Committee rejected the revised board structure in favour of greater worker participation through Works Councils and other joint machinery. As a consequence the Conservative Government elected in 1979 has not adopted them as part of its industrial policy. Meanwhile some organisations have appointed worker directors, such as the Post Office and the British

17 See ch 3, below.

18 Although various provisions implicitly recognise that these duties exist, e g s. 205 (relief from liability) and s. 332 (misfeasance proceedings).

19 Cmnd 1749.

20 Report of the Committee of Inquiry on Industrial Democracy (Cmnd 6706 (1977)), chs 7 and 9.

Steel Corporation, although such experiments have not been wholly successful.[1] One basic problem that remains is whether the unity of board responsibility is to be split, i e the employee directors owing duties only to the work force and the 'shareholder' directors owing duties only to the present and future members.[2] Any such division would weaken the principle that a director, however appointed, owes a duty to act in the best interests of the company as a whole. If the draft EEC Fifth Directive is proceeded with,[3] a different framework for company boards may yet appear.

Hard on the heels of the Bullock Report was the Command Paper, 'The Conduct of Company Directors'.[4] This is a useful indication of legislative thinking for the 1980s, and is reproduced in full as Appendix 2, below. Much of what was proposed has since appeared as Parts IV and V of the Companies Act 1980. There was also proposed the codifying statutory statement of duties which the Jenkins Committee had rejected, and appropriate provisions were included in the Companies Bill 1978. Except for that relating to a director's duties to employees, these were not adopted into the Companies Act 1980.[5] Assuming a satisfactory formulation can be attained, however, directors are likely to find new legislation defined in the foreseeable future. Interest is still focused on the position of the non-executive director (considered in paragraph 20 of the Command Paper) and on 'Audit Committees' of persons owing fiduciary duties and having a review function in relation to the performance of the company as a whole. Whatever constraints are imposed, however, the company board (or at least its executive committee) is likely to consolidate its central position in modern business administration and alternative structures such as worker-committees would require a major change in both political and economic attitudes.

1 See P Biannen *Workers on the Board* (1976).

2 The artificiality of this division has been demonstrated by analogous proposals that local authorities should consist of two classes of members, elected respectively by the citizens and by the council's workforce.

3 In 1975 it met opposition and had to be revised. See Department of Trade *Timetable and Progress of Draft Directives and Other Proposals* (1981).

4 7037, November 1977.

5 For the reasons explained at pp. 37–38, below.

2 Fiduciary duties

1 Basically an agent

We have seen that a convenient way of describing a director's position is in terms of his agency function in relation to that artificial principal, the company, exercised collectively through the board. Reference to the duties of a commercial agent will almost always provide an answer to a director's question, 'Have I done the right thing?'. These duties may be summarised as follows:

(1) *Obedience* An agent acting under express or implied contract with his principal is bound to carry out his instructions, and not to depart from them unless given a discretion.[1] Where his authority or instructions are vague or open ended, however, he performs his duty by acting reasonably and in what he considers to be the interests of his principal.[2]

In a simple case, if a director is authorised by his board to enter into a contract at a fixed price, and he binds the company to a higher price (either carelessly or because, perhaps, he stood to earn commission from the other contracting party), he will be liable in damages for not conforming to his instructions even though the company will have to accept the contract as negotiated.

(2) *Care and skill* An agent must display such reasonable care as an ordinary prudent man might be expected to take in the same circumstances on his own behalf.[3] He is not, however, liable for errors of judgment. Where an appointee professes a particular calling, e g solicitor, accountant or surveyor, he must show the degree of skill appropriate thereto.[4]

(3) *Personal performance* A principal selects an agent because he reposes trust and confidence in him to carry out on his behalf a particular transaction or to act for him generally. The maxim

1 *Fraser v B N Furman (Productions) Ltd* [1967] 3 All ER 57, [1967] 1 WLR 898.
2 *Pariente v Lubbock* (1856) 8 De GM & G 5.
3 *Re Brazilian Rubber Plantations and Estates Ltd* [1911] 1 Ch 425 at 437.
4 *Hart and Hodge v Frame, Son & Co* (1839) 6 Cl & Fin 193.

delegatus non potest delegare therefore applies – an agent may not delegate his job, only the manner of performing it.

As a company board is directly appointed, shareholders are entitled to assume that directors will not hand over their responsibilities and discretions to others – unless the articles provide for delegation to a managing director or a committee. The ability of the board to delegate to officers and employees the executive tasks of conducting the business may, however, be inferred from the very discretion it has been given, or from the circumstances of the case including the size and location of the company's operations.[5]

What is not permissible is the abdication by the agent of his power over his principal's affairs in favour of a third party who has not been expressly authorised by the principal to intervene. Thus a firm of management consultants engaged by the board to advise upon particular problems must not be invited to take over the direction of the business or pass resolutions on behalf of the board which would have that effect. The corollary of this third rule is that an agent must give his personal attention to the work in hand: although except in the case of a full-time executive director of a company, this will not entail exclusive attention.[6]

(4) *Good faith* An agent is in a fiduciary position to his principal and as such he must act bona fide and must not allow his interest to conflict with his duty. This fiduciary obligation extends particularly to property belonging to the principal over which the agent has control. It also covers the making of a secret profit.

The rule applies fully to company directors[7] but is not peculiar to them. If an agent makes a profit for himself without having disclosed his dealing, he is liable to account to his principal for the money received. This is, of course, the non-statutory basis of a director's liability for insider dealing[8] in securities.

2 The director as trustee

The position of trust occupied by an agent, any agent, has long been established. As was argued as early as 1795:[9]

5 *De Bussche v Alt* (1878) 8 ChD 286.
6 *Re Forest of Dean Coal Mining Co* (1878) 10 ChD 450; see also p. 45, below. The fact is recognised by allowing for a quorum of directors below the 'establishment'.
7 *Cook v Deeks* [1916] 1 AC 554.
8 See ch 6, below.
9 *York Buildings Co v Mackenzie* (1795) 8 Bro Parl Cas 42 at 64. See also Sealy

> The office of a common agent has already been described in this case, and it is needless to enter into refinements or niceties as to the nature of trusts or the specific name of trusts. There is no magic in the term: He is a trustee (in technical style) who is vested with property in trust for others: but every man has a trust, to whom a business is committed by another, or the charge and care of any concern is confided or delegated.

Because this responsibility fell short of the full range of duties owed by a trustee of a settlement, it was regarded as a 'quasi trust', and ultimately as a 'fiduciary' obligation:

> What is a fiduciary relationship? It is one in respect of which if a wrong arises, the same remedy exists against the wrongdoer on behalf of the principal as would exist against a trustee on behalf of the [beneficiary].[10]

The emphasis is on the relationship of confidence which is created between principal and agent by virtue of the latter's appointment, and the right of the former to take proceedings if this confidence is abused or not used to the best advantage of the appointor.

THE HISTORICAL ANALOGY

Company law has developed the fiduciary nature of a director's job to a high degree. This has been misleadingly interpreted as making a director a trustee in the strict sense. As Professor Gower points out,[11] this confusion has an historical origin. Before 1884 most companies other than chartered or statutory corporations were not distinct legal entities as we now recognise them, but operated under Deeds of Settlement with property and powers actually vested in trustees. The managers or directors of the companies equated with the trustees and it was not until the adoption of limited liability with separate boards that the roles became distinct. A vestige of the old form is seen in the modern unit trust where the underlying deposited property is vested in trustees (who owe obligations as such to unit holders) but the funds are controlled by managers, who exercise much greater discretion but are still to be regarded as fiduciaries.[12]

'Fiduciary Relationships' [1962] CLJ 69. For a modern judicial restatement, see *Selangor United Rubber Estates Ltd v Cradock (No 3)* [1968] 1 WLR 1555 at 1575, per Ungoed-Thomas J.

10 Per Fry J in *The West of England and South Wales District Bank, ex parte Dale & Co* (1879) 11 ChD 772 at 778.

11 *Modern Company Law* (4th edn) pp. 571–572.

12 See Day and Harris *Unit Trusts, Law and Practice* p. 130.

Secondly, the rules of company law have been worked out in the courts of chancery which administered rules of equity as opposed to common law, and there has been a natural tendency for judges of those courts to emphasise the equitable aspects of a company director's position.[13] It is still the case that company disputes are heard in the Chancery Division of the High Court by a judiciary principally versed in trusts, land law, and mortgages.

DIFFERENCES

The notion of strict trusteeship is, however, quite inappropriate. Trustees are usually required to act unanimously, whereas a simple majority of the board of directors will suffice. Again, trustees must exercise a degree of restraint and conservatism in their investment judgments, and take absolutely no risks, whereas directors will often be expected to display entrepreneurial flair and accept commercial risks to satisfy shareholders that a sufficient return is being produced on capital. At this point the trustee analogy breaks down.[14] It is generally upon trust principles that directors are made accountable for their handling of the company's property and, like trust property, assets wrongfully disposed of may be traced into the hands of third parties. However, individual directors, unlike individual trustees, have no obligation to assume control over the company's property and to retain it in their hands. Powers delegated to the managing director permit him to deal with a company's assets on his own, and to engage in commercial transactions not only of a type expressly forbidden to trustees, but involving snap judgments which a committee of trustees is not structured to make. A further difference is that it is recognised that a dissenting director cannot be held responsible for the acts of others,[15] whereas a trustee in the strict sense may be guilty of wilful default under the Trustee Act 1925 if he fails to remain vigilant about the non-delegated activities of his fellow trustees or agents appointed by the trustees, or fails to take steps to put right any irregularities which such vigilance ought to have revealed.[16]

Most of the examples of the 'trustee test' occur with the early Deed of Settlement companies, and are not particularly helpful when it comes to advising a director how he should behave.[17] The

13 *Joint Stock Discount Co v Brown* (1869) LR 8 Eq 381.

14 See Sealy 'The Director as Trustee' [1967] CLJ 83 at 86–87.

15 *Land Credit Co of Ireland v Lord Fermoy* (1870) 5 Ch App 763.

16 *Re Lucking's Will Trust, Renwick v Lucking* [1967] 3 All ER 726.

17 *Re Gloucester, Aberystwith and South Wales Rly Co, Maitland's Case* (1853) 2 Eq Rep 53; *Re German Mining Co, Ball's Case, ex parte Chippendale* (1854) 2 Eq Rep 983.

true test would seem to be that directors are trustees in a loose sense of the company's property and of the powers vested in them, but that they owe different duties of care and skill which are less onerous.[18] The fiduciary duties are usually separated into two, i e the duty to act bona fide and the duty not to allow one's interest and responsibility to conflict. There is thus a group of cases where a director's liability has rested solely on his control over the company's property. These matters will now be considered in more detail.

3 Bona fides

COLLATERAL PURPOSES

A director is required to act bona fide in what he considers – not what a court may consider – is in the interests of the company, and not for any collateral purpose.[19] This is a subjective test, so that provided his motives were honest, and it can be shown that he was satisfied in his own mind that a course of action was beneficial or correct, a director is normally immune from proceedings that he should have acted in some different way or that, with hindsight, a better judgment was possible. Thus, in relation to the payment of dividends, the question whether there are profits available is left to the subjective judgment of the board based on bona fide appraisals of valuations, stock-takes, depreciation provisions, etc.[20] This is a very much lower threshold of liability than for a trustee. Liability attaches only if the director's purpose was divided. The most cogent evidence of this is when the director himself, or his immediate family stand to gain from the proposed transaction he procures the company to enter into. This is discussed below.[1] However, personal profit need not be the only motive involved:

> The articles of a company provided that no transfer of shares which were not paid up were to be approved. M, a jobber, offered to take up a large number of £10 shares at par, paying £2 per share at once, provided the directors paid a commission to the broker who introduced the shares to him. This was done. M transferred the shares to P with the directors' approval, and P became bankrupt and was unable to pay the balance of £8 per share. It was held that the directors were personally liable, not for

18 See ch 3, below.
19 *Re Smith and Fawcett Ltd* [1942] Ch 304 at 306.
20 *Re Mercantile Trading Co, Stringer's Case* (1869) 4 Ch App 475; *Re Kingston Cotton Mill (No 2)* [1896] 1 Ch 331; cf Companies Act 1980, s. 39.
1 Pp. 31–35.

this balance, since P was a person whom they genuinely thought was a suitable transferee, but for the amount of the commission, since the application of the company's money for this purpose was a breach of their duty and amounted to misfeasance.[2]

A company was under an obligation to comply with an option agreement to issue certain shares, and gave an undertaking to use its best endeavours to obtain a Stock Exchange listing for them. The company sent out notices convening a general meeting to approve the increase in capital, but accompanied by a circular from the directors which was clearly not calculated to induce the shareholders to vote in favour of the resolution in that it stated, on the advice of leading counsel, that the undertaking did not bind the shareholders who were free to act as they chose. It was held, inter alia, that the directors were under a duty to ensure compliance by the company of its legal obligations, which they had failed to do, and that a fresh circular endorsing the resolution would have to be sent out; but that they were not in breach of their duty to act bona fide simply because, as shareholders themselves, they had a motive for opposing the resolution and voting against it (which they were free to do).[3]

A company, C Ltd, had power to charge its property to secure the performance of any obligation, either of its own or any other company or person with which it was concerned or interested. The controlling director and shareholder caused the company to execute a charge to secure the indebtedness to the bank of the parent company, P Ltd. The director was motivated by the interests of the group as a whole and did not consider C Ltd's interests separately. A purchaser of the charged property, who found the title encumbered, claimed against the bank that the charge was ultra vires the Memorandum. On the question of the director's failure to regard C Ltd separately, it was held that since the exercise of the power to charge was intra vires the Memorandum of Association, the instrument was valid and the foreign purpose of the director at the time was not material.[4]

It has been objected by one commentator[5] that the test of 'best interests of the company' assumes a single legitimate motivating factor, from which the others must be separated: whereas in reality a board will have a variety of considerations to take account of. In

2 *Re Faure Electric Accumulator Co* (1888) 40 ChD 141.
3 *Northern Counties Securities Ltd v Jackson and Steeple Ltd* [1974] 2 All ER 625, [1974] 1 WLR 1133.
4 *Charterbridge Corpn Ltd v Lloyds Bank Ltd* [1970] Ch 62, [1969] 2 All ER 1185.
5 Sealy *Cases and Materials on Company Law* (2nd edn) p. 262.

such cases the court must, it is said, look for the dominant motive, which occasionally produces inconsistent results on similar facts. This, it is submitted, is inevitable given a subjective test of bona fides. As was said in the *Charterbridge* case considered above:

> The proper test . . . in the absence of actual separate consideration must be whether an intelligent and honest man in the position of a director of the company concerned could . . . have reasonably believed that the transactions were for the benefit of the company.[6]

MOTIVE AND PURPOSE

If the motives are mixed but the purpose is lawful, the bona fide test will be applied. However, even where the directors have acted in what they consider to be the company's interests, they will face liability if they have in fact acted beyond their own or the company's powers, or if they have applied the powers for a purpose which, as a matter of construction of the Memorandum and Articles, could not legitimately be contemplated. It has been pointed out[7] that by introducing an objective element it has been made more difficult for directors to comply with their duties, since the validity of their acts must be based upon subsequent rationalisations. While this has force, it is essential to an understanding of a director's position that 'motive' and 'purpose' be kept apart. The agency position of the board, considered in chapter 1, proceeds fundamentally upon a theory of division of powers, and a proper use of those powers by the persons to whom they are delegated. Insofar as this can be established only by construing the precise words contained in the Memorandum, Articles or other authority-giving document, an objective standard must be admitted. The fiduciary duty of good faith is really a gloss on this basic principle, i e it assumes that the powers are being properly applied and merely enquires into the director's motives for applying them in a particular manner. The more recent English authorities are quite clear on this:

> The directors of the defendant company allotted shares to the trustees of the staff benevolent and pension fund (as in the *Savoy Hotel* case), which carried special voting rights, in order to frustrate a take-over bid. The directors bona fide considered that such a take-over was not in the best interests of the company, in that it foreshadowed a change in the nature of the company's business which would be unsettling to the employees. It was held

6 [1970] Ch 62 at 74.
7 *Sealy* p. 269.

that, notwithstanding their motives, the use of the power to allot shares in these circumstances was improper; it was a manipulation of the voting position which was in breach of the fiduciary obligations to the shareholders. As such it could only be ratified by the shareholders.[8]

FAIRNESS

A further refinement is to apply a test of equality or fairness where it is clear that the directors have more than one interest to consider, e g different classes of shareholders. In an Australian case[9] a director who was also an ordinary shareholder procured a resolution of the board under which accumulated profits were distributed by way of fully paid bonus shares. This gave the ordinary shareholders enhanced voting powers as against the existing preference shareholders. It was not disputed that the majority directors had acted honestly in what they believed were the interests of the company. Nevertheless, questions were raised about the position of the director who stood to gain personally from the arrangement. The court pointed out that it was a fact of life that many directors were also shareholders and therefore their motives were mixed. Moreover,

> Where there are preference and ordinary shares a particular decision may be of such a character that it must necessarily affect adversely the interests of one class of shareholders and benefit the interests of another class. In such a case it is difficult to apply the test of acting in the interests of the company. The question which arises is sometimes not a question of the interests of the company at all, but a question of what is fair as between different classes of shareholders . . . A director who holds one or both classes of such shares is not, in my opinion, required by the law to live in an unreal region of detached altruism and to act in a vague mood of ideal abstraction from obvious facts which must be present to the mind of any honest and intelligent man when he exercises his powers as director.[10]

This pragmatic approach recognises the difficulties and conflicts by reducing the fiduciary test to a series of commonsense principles. We are a long way at this point from the law of trusts.

8 *Hogg v Cramphorn Ltd* [1967] Ch 254, [1966] 3 All ER 420. See also *Punt v Symons & Co Ltd* [1903] 2 Ch 506, and *Piercy v Mills & Co Ltd* [1920] 1 Ch 77.
9 *Mills v Mills* (1938) 60 CLR 150.
10 Per Latham CJ.

4 Conflict of duty and interest

THE GENERAL TEST

Because they are fiduciaries, directors must not allow themselves to get into a position where there is a conflict between what they ought to do for the company, and what they might do for themselves.[11] Although the principle is stated in broad terms, while many of the authorities turn upon particular aspects such as failure to account for secret profits or failure to disclose an interest in a contract, it is still a true test. Where a director, for example, takes up an engagement with a third party to do work on a private basis which could have been done by the company itself, this is a clear breach.[12] This does not, however, preclude a director from holding outside offices. Such a person may often be invited to join a company board because of his particular expertise – and as a consequence he may owe a higher duty of care and skill.[13] What is prohibited is a situation where a director has a pre-existing and continuing duty to the company which he then jeopardises by secret discussions with the outsider which will benefit him in a personal capacity. This is so even if the company itself is unlikely to secure the contract.

Where a director or employee of a parent company is appointed to the board of a subsidiary, such director is bound to consider the interests of the subsidiary as a distinct obligation and not sublimate them to the requirements of the group. It might be thought that such appointment is automatically the substance of conflict, but this has been held not to be so.[14] In the case of wholly-owned subsidiaries, the requirement of separation of interests may be less well-observed, since there is no other shareholder to sue for breach of duty – and a creditor is unlikely to do so, unless the company's assets have been wilfully depleted.[15]

DISCLOSURE OF INTERESTS

Where a conflict exists, the director becomes liable to disclose his interest to the company. The extent to which the Companies Acts have elaborated on this requirement is considered in chapter 4.

11 *Aberdeen Rly Co v Blaikie Bros* (1854) 1 Macq 461.
12 *Industrial Development Consultants v Cooley* [1972] 2 All ER 162.
13 See ch 3, pp. 50–51, below.
14 *Bell v Lever Bros Ltd* [1932] AC 161 at 195–196.
15 *Scottish Co-operative Wholesale Society Ltd v Meyer* [1959] AC 324.

SECRET PROFITS

A profit derived from a fiduciary office must be accounted for, unless previously disclosed and authorised: as between principal and agent, beneficiary and trustee, shareholders and director. No dishonesty need be involved, so that it is no defence for a director to say he was acting bona fide. Many instances, of course, occur when the offender merely 'keeps quiet'. Any accrued personal gain can be regarded as secret for the purpose of this rule, unless and until disclosure is made. The following are merely recurring examples:

(1) a director is in possession of confidential information about the company's state of affairs, e g its impending profits results or an approach by a take-over bidder, and makes a profit through buying or selling securities;[16]
(2) a director is authorised by his board to negotiate insurances for the company's property. He does so, and receives a secret commission from the insurer;[17]
(3) the business of a company is sold off, the buyer paying sums of money to the directors for procuring the consent of shareholders or otherwise negotiating the transaction;[18]
(4) a company promoter makes payments to a director, which are not afterwards disclosed, to induce him to act, or offers benefits in the form of shares which are not fully paid up.[19]

The profit may or may not involve 'trust' money. If a director receives a bribe, this is a windfall which the company may recover. If he actually uses company funds, e g for share speculation, or pockets the interest on deposit account balance, he becomes a trustee in a strict sense and the company may not only sue him but trace the profit into his private bank account.[20]

It has to be shown that the profit was derived by virtue of the office. In *Regal (Hastings) Ltd v Gulliver*, where share profits were made, it was said:

> The directors standing in a fiduciary relationship to [the plaintiff company] in regard to the exercise of their powers as directors and having obtained these shares by reason and only by reason of the fact

16 See ch 6, below.
17 The same would apply to any 'rake off' on a contract with the company: *Boston Deep Sea Fishing and Ice Co v Ansell* (1888) 39 ChD 339.
18 *General Exchange Bank v Horner* (1870) LR 9 Eq 480; *Gaskell v Chambers* (1858) 26 Beav 360.
19 *Re British Provident Life and Guarantee Association, De Ruvigne's Case* (1877) 5 ChD 306.
20 See ch 5, p. 93, below.

that they were directors . . . are accountable for the profits which they have made out of them.[1]

It would seem to follow that a benefit derived from information *exclusively* obtained from an external source, would be immune, but it would be very difficult for a director to negative the presumption that he acted as an insider. There are also a number of borderline situations involving use of other company property:

Illustration 1 A director travels abroad on the business of his company, fares and accommodation paid. He runs a small import-export agency of his own, not using any confidential information. He combines the business trips with following up his own agency contacts, letting it be known that he is a senior executive with a reputable company in the UK and is thus a person of good credit and standing.

Illustration 2 An engineering company generates a large regular amount of waste metal material. It is normally carted away in bulk by the local authority, without payment. A director makes arrangements with a local contractor for its removal, receiving a small money payment for each load of scrap, which he does not credit to the company.

In either case, is there an obligation to account? It has been suggested in *Industrial Development Consultants Ltd v Cooley*[2] that the use of company property to an insignificant extent may be ignored. However, in Illustration 1 there is no detriment to the company because the travel and accommodation costs are anyway being incurred legitimately on its business; but in Illustration 2, unless the payments are both small and irregular, the use of company property (the scrap) for personal gain may be thought to be an improper advantage. (It could perhaps be argued otherwise if (1) the company had abandoned 'property' in the scrap or (2) its removal was available to other employees besides the director.)

KNOW-HOW

The notion of the company's proprietary interest is also relevant where an individual makes use of confidential information. If the information is such that it is capable of being protected by legal proceedings, e g injunction to restrain publication of customers' lists or novel industrial processes, then it has the quality of 'belonging' to the company or other organisation. As such it may

1 Per Lord Russell of Killowen [1942] 1 All ER 378 at 389.
2 [1972] 2 All ER 162 at 169.

not be exploited by a director to his own gain without express permission. The position is analogous to that of any employee who owes an implied contractual duty to his employer not to divulge trade secrets. Any reward procured in breach of this obligation belongs to the company.[3]

What happens if the 'property' alleged to be misused is self-generated? In *Cranleigh Precision Engineering Ltd v Bryant* [1964] 3 All ER 289, [1965] 1 WLR 1293 an employee perfected a valuable technical process which was exclusive to his employer. It was held that he was liable to account for the benefits he received, since his obligation as an employee compelled him to hold the 'property' so created as an accretion to the employer's existing assets.[4]

It is not a defence that the plaintiff company itself would be unable, if contracting on its own, to obtain the benefit that the defendant director has derived:

> The plaintiffs provided major construction services mostly in the private sector and engaged the defendant architect as managing director to help expansion into the public sector. The defendant failed to secure a contract for the plaintiffs with the Gas Board because the latter thought the firm unsuitable, but the Gas Board wanted to procure his personal services so he resigned as director, ostensibly on the grounds of ill-health. He was subsequently offered employment by the Board to undertake substantially what the plaintiff company would have done, had it won the contract. It was held (1) that he was in breach of fiduciary duty to the plaintiffs for not disclosing to them while managing director the discussion pursued for his personal benefit with the Gas Board; and (2) that he was liable to account for all the benefits he had received or would receive under the new contract of employment.[5]

MISUSE OF POSITION TO MAKE PROFIT

Principles of trusteeship have been applied even where there is no clandestine element in the making of the profit, or where there appears to be formal ratification of the breach of duty:

> Two directors paid off a debt due from a company to themselves, and as the company was in a perilous financial state the payment

3 *Measures Bros Ltd v Measures* [1910] 2 Ch 248, CA.
4 See also *Burland v Earle* [1902] AC 83; *Heyting v Dupont* [1964] 2 All ER 273, [1964] 1 WLR 843, CA; but cf *Baker v Gibbons* [1972] 1 WLR 693 at 700.
5 *Industrial Development Consultants Ltd v Cooley* [1972] 2 All ER 162, [1972] 1 WLR 443. See also *Amalgamated Industrials Ltd v Johnson and Firth Brown* (1981) Times 15 April.

was challenged as being a fraudulent preference over the other creditors, contrary to section 320 of the Companies Act 1948.[6] It was held that they were liable to repay the debt, since their action in preferring themselves was an exploitation of their position, a misapplication of company funds and, hence, a breach of fiduciary obligation.[7]

Directors of a company who, between them, were also the majority shareholders took personal advantage of an opportunity to enter a lucrative business contract which, had it been negotiated for their company, would have been (1) capable of being performed by the company and (2) greatly to its benefit. This was undoubtedly a breach of duty which they purported to ratify by resolution in a general meeting of shareholders.

Held: the 'lost' benefit nonetheless belonged to the company and they were liable to account.[8]

Where a director sells property already owned by him to the company, it is a fiduciary transaction and voidable, but he is not automatically under a duty to account for profits, i e if it disclosed and approved. Similarly, where he acquires property or advantage from a third party he will not hold it for the company unless it is clear that he was acting as agent or was entrusted specifically to secure it for the company's sole benefit,[9] for only then does a conflict of interest and duty arise.

5 Trusts affecting property

CONTROL OF FUNDS

Many of the authorities hold a director liable simply because he is in control of the company's funds, and must not apply them except for its lawful purposes. Occasionally this obviates the need to demonstrate a secret profit or an improper motive.

Directors made payments of interest and dividend although the company had never made any profit. The payments were authorised under the Articles.

Held: the directors were in breach of trust in making the distributions, they were ultra vires.[10]

6 S. 320(1) states that any conveyance etc of property by a company within six months of its winding-up may be a fraudulent preference and invalid accordingly.

7 *Wallesteiner v Moir* [1974] 3 All ER 217, [1974] 1 WLR 991.

8 *Cook v Deeks* [1916] AC 554, PC.

9 See also *Parker v McKenna* (1874) 10 Ch App 96.

10 *Masonic and General Life Assurance Co v Sharpe* [1892] 1 Ch 154.

C bid for a majority shareholding in S Ltd, which he obtained in the following ways:

(1) procuring his nominees to serve on S Ltd's board, which
(2) authorised a substantial loan to W Ltd;
(3) W Ltd lent this sum to C;
(4) C paid most of it, through an agent, to the former shareholders of S Ltd as the purchase consideration for their shares. S Ltd afterwards went into compulsory liquidation.

The Board of Trade initiated proceedings in the company's name to recover the sum improperly paid away.

Held: the nominee directors (inter alia) were liable for breach of trust. All their property in their hands or under their control was theirs for the company, i e for the company's purposes in accordance with their duties, powers and functions. To apply it otherwise was a misapplication and a breach of fiduciary duty.[11]

A controlling shareholder wished to make provision for his widow. He entered into a service agreement with his company which provided for a pension to be paid to her, on his death.

Held: as the transaction was not made to benefit the company, the service arrangement was a misapplication of company assets and accordingly was liable to be set aside.[12]

It is a misapplication of company funds for a board to make a payment for compensation for loss of office without the consent of the company's members. It is probably a misapplication if directors issue shares at par when they could have been issued at a premium, for the company has lost the additional revenue. A payment to a contracting party under an improper agreement under which the benefit accrued to a third person, has been set aside.[13] And it has been held to be a breach of duty to sell the assets of a business at a gross undervalue.[14] However, if a director ratifies or confirms an improper payment which the other directors have already sanctioned, there is no breach, because the loss of property to the company would be the same, even if he had not given his consent.[15]

11 *Selangor United Rubber Estates Ltd v Cradock (No 3)* [1968] 2 All ER 1073, [1968] 1 WLR 1555; Ungoed-Thomas J's judgment is also illuminating on the liability of others (notably C) as constructive trustees, being fixed in the same way as the directors themselves with knowledge of the improper application of funds.

12 *Re W and M Roith Ltd* [1967] 1 All ER 427, [1967] 1 WLR 432.

13 *London Trust Co v Mackenzie* [1893] WN 9.

14 *Re New Traveller's Chambers Ltd* (1895) 12 TLR 529.

15 *Ramskill v Edwards* (1885) 31 ChD 100.

OPTION CONTRACTS

One specific aspect of the fiduciary standard is now contained in section 25 of the Companies Act 1967. Directors are prohibited from buying options to buy or sell shares or debentures of their companies, if such securities are listed on the Stock Exchange. This removes a source of speculative activity which is inconsistent with a director's task of not allowing his interest and duty to be at odds.

6 Statutory reforms and proposals

FIDUCIARY DUTIES

The Companies Bill 1978, clause 44, originally provided as follows:

> (1) A director of a company shall observe the utmost good faith towards the company in any transaction with it or on its behalf and owes a duty to the company to act honestly in the exercise of the powers and the discharge of the duties of his office.
>
> (2) A director of a company shall not do anything or omit to do anything if the doing of that thing or the omission to do it, as the case may be, gives rise to a conflict or might reasonably be expected to give rise to a conflict, between the duties of his office and his private interests or, without prejudice to the foregoing, between those duties and any duties he owes to any other person.

These provisions were foreshadowed in 'The Conduct of Company Directors' (1977), and follow wording suggested by the Jenkins Committee. They were, however, roundly attacked by the professional bodies,[16] principally on the basis that no précis of legislative drafting could hope to encompass the considerable variations of case law that had built up. In relation to clause 44(1), it was objected that the good faith that the director had to show was not directed at any particular end or purpose. As Lord Justice Bowen had said in *Hutton v West Cork Railway Co*:[17]

> Bona fides cannot be the sole test, otherwise you might have a lunatic conducting the affairs of the company, and paying away its money with both hands in a manner perfectly bona fide yet perfectly irrational. The test must be what is reasonably incidental to, and within the reasonable scope of carrying on, the business of the company.

It was also not clear whether the duty of good faith was owed by the board or by individual members of it.

16 See e g Memorandum by Law Society's Standing Committee, December 1978, pp. 42 ff.

17 (1883) 23 ChD 654.

Clause 44(2) was criticised because it stated a principle which did not exist, namely that a director acts illegally merely because he does, or omits, anything which puts him in a position where his own interests conflict with his office.[18] The true test, so it is said, is that he must avoid the consequences of such a conflict, e g by not profiting from a transaction in which he has a personal interest.

As a result of representations the Government accepted amendments to clause 44, which it is submitted were somewhat clumsy, so that it read as follows:

> (1) The directors of a company (whether performing their functions or acting individually) shall act honestly in relation to the company and observe the utmost good faith towards it and accordingly shall perform their functions in what they consider to be the best interests of the company as a whole.
>
> (2) The directors of a company shall not perform any of their functions for a purpose not contemplated by the instrument or resolution conferring or imposing that function.
>
> (3) A director of a company shall not
>
> (a) allow a conflict to arise between the duties of his office and his private interests or any duties he owes to any other person; or
>
> (b) do anything which, at the time it was done, could reasonably be expected to involve his contravening paragraph (a) above.[19]

Clause 44 fell with the Labour Government in May 1979. It may yet, however, be resurrected in different form, hopefully as a supplement to and not a substitute for existing provisions.

DUTIES TO EMPLOYEES

The sole provision relating to directors' general duties which survived the 1978 Bill is that relating to employees, which appears as section 46 of the 1980 Act. The first attempt at legislation was the Duties of Company Directors Bill 1977.[20] This declared that it should be the duty of every director of a company to further the interests of that company, having particular regard to its shareholders and employees. It cannot be said that this presaged any great changes in company law, although for the first time it did put the employee on the legislative map. The corresponding provision of the 1978 Bill was arguably stronger, it being suggested that employees would have the right, in certain circumstances, to ask the court to restrain a proposed exercise of the directors' powers if such

18 See per Diplock LJ in *Boulting v Association of Cinematograph, Television and Allied Technicians* [1963] 2 QB 606, [1963] 1 All ER 716.

19 For the remainder of clause 44, dealing with the use of corporate information and opportunity, see Gower *Modern Company Law* (4th edn) pp. 591–592.

20 A private member's bill, drafted for Adam Butler MP, by the present author.

exercise was thought to be detrimental to their interests.[1] The disadvantage, of course, of granting statutory rights to one particular class of person to whom directors, in exercising their functions for the benefit of the company, should have regard, was that it prejudiced the position of another class, i e the shareholders, who in most cases could only sue *through* the company. Section 46 of the 1980 Act avoids this difficulty:

> (1) The matters to which the directors of a company are to have regard in the performance of their function shall include the interests of the company's employees in general as well as the interests of its members.
>
> (2) Accordingly, the duty imposed by subsection (1) above on the directors of a company is owed by them to the company (and the company alone) and is enforceable in the same way as any other fiduciary duty owed to a company by its directors.

Because the section states that the duty is owed only to the company and is enforceable identically to any other fiduciary duty, the intention is to prevent class actions being brought, e g by trade unions, on behalf of groups of employees. The effect of the section is therefore merely cosmetic, its only practical utility being to remove any vestigial restriction on the directors providing employee benefit schemes.[2] It is submitted that it would be difficult to enhance legal duties owed to the workforce without creating a serious imbalance as regards the rights of others.

One specific limitation on powers has been checked. By section 74 of the 1980 Act a company is enabled to provide for employees on the cessational transfer of a company's business, notwithstanding that this course may not be adjudged 'in its best interest' according to the general law. This overturns the decision in *Parke v Daily News Ltd*[3] which held that it was ultra vires the company and its directors to make payments to employees on such a cessation. Previously, the directors were only allowed to see the company's property in terms of the shareholders and creditors. It is not thought that a relaxation of this principle will necessarily jeopardise those interests.

1 Memorandum by Law Society's Standing Committee, p. 53.
2 Hare 124 Sol Jo 602.
3 [1962] Ch 927, [1962] 2 All ER 929.

3 Skill, care and diligence

1 The general position

Judges have exhibited extreme reluctance to work out any kind of legal framework for directors broadly equivalent to the objective standard of performance of duties expected of professional men. The law of negligence as applied to directors therefore has a distinctly antique ring about it. The reasons commonly asserted for this are that:

(1) company law evolved at a time when businessmen were not expected to devote their services exclusively to the undertaking which they promoted or served, and hence were not to be assumed to be exercising that degree of care or diligence which might reasonably be expected of a full-time executive or managing director;[1]

(2) a company director is not, per se, an expert, either in the task of general management of the business in which the company is engaged, or with regard to particular aspects of administration, such as finance, personnel, or legal services, for which a professional might reasonably be recruited;[2]

(3) if the standard of care required of a director is too high, persons of entrepreneurial ability will be discouraged from taking office for fear that their experience and judgment will always be the subject of scrutiny with the benefit of hindsight; or that, in the case of persons of no special ability who nonetheless desire to set up business and achieve incorporation, more will be expected of them than, in their ordinary lives and personal affairs, they are able or willing to give;[3]

(4) while courts of law are well qualified, to consider liabilities of trustees, and to assess observance or breach of fiduciary duties of loyalty and good faith, they are not equipped to undertake

1 *Re Forest of Dean Coal Mining Co* (1878) 10 ChD 450 at 452.
2 *Re Brazilian Rubber Plantations and Estates Ltd* [1911] 1 Ch 425 at 437.
3 *Lagunas Nitrate Co v Lagunas Syndicate* [1899] 2 Ch 392 at 435.

the task of assessing managerial or business competence, since these do not admit of any objective criteria.[4]

If a director exercises powers over property by virtue of a fiduciary position, his abuse of those powers is as much a breach of duty if the property involved is small, as it is for property of great value. Suppose a director of a small concern (unless he is also the sole shareholder capable of ratifying his excesses) regularly uses equipment belonging to the company for his own purposes. He thereby gains a secret profit. This is just as much a breach of his obligation as a quasi-trustee as if a chief executive of a large public company was able to 'channel' its incoming cash through his personal bank account, so as to get the benefit of its interest or use.[5] The law has no difficulty in setting a strict and objective standard in relation to companies generally by virtue of the position of trust that the director occupies in relation to the property which he is enabled to manage and control. However, when it comes to consider the duty of care that a director is expected to show in the performance of his functions, an obvious dilemma presents itself. If a director of a small private company was expected to exhibit the skill normally exercised by the chief executive of a multinational corporation, the two persons would in theory be able to change places (and salaries!) without difficulty. Put another way, the small-company director, but for an accident of circumstance and opportunity, would himself have been on the board of the large concern exercising dominion over thousands of employees and tens of millions of pounds worth of assets. It is clear that such a juxtaposition is far-fetched, and that directors and senior executives of large public companies are invariably (although not always) men and women of exceptional resource and skill whose services are much in demand by rival concerns. It would represent a Utopian ideal if the law required every director, of every company,[6] to achieve the same level of professional competence. Accordingly, as pointed out in the Government's White Paper, 'The Conduct of Company Directors',[7] a director is only required to exercise that degree of skill which may reasonably be expected of a person of *his* knowledge and experience. The standard of skill is a subjective one which, in theory, exonerates the honest but incompetent person on the basis that he can do no better. When such a lowly test is criti-

4 *Howard Smith Ltd v Ampol Petroleum Ltd* [1974] AC 821 at 832, PC.

5 This would, perhaps, assume a very poor standard of financial control – but it has happened (Department of Trade Report, Peachey Property Corporation Limited (1978)).

6 There were in 1977 approximately 611,500 private companies registered and 15,600 public companies.

7 Cmnd 7037 (1977), reprinted at Appendix 2, below.

cised,[8] it is answered that the incompetent director is not likely to last long since his shareholders will be able to have him removed under section 184 of the Companies Act 1948 by ordinary resolution. Again, the larger the business he manages, the greater his knowledge and experience (and his suitability) will become. Unless a breach of trust is involved, however, the devastation he may inflict upon the company's affairs in the meantime will go unremedied.

The modern law does nevertheless draw a distinction between skill and care. For the standard of care, an objective test is set, namely that to be expected of a reasonable man. If a person drives a motor car, it matters not whether he is a professional driving instructor or an elderly and infirm weekend motorist, for the purpose of imposing a duty to be careful in relation to other road users. If it be said that the elderly and infirm driver is *unable* to achieve the requisite standard, the answer must be that he should not attempt the task. The corollary to this is that where a person professes to exercise some special skill, e g as an accountant or lawyer, then he must exhibit both the skill and care which a reasonably competent practitioner, judged objectively, could be expected to achieve.

Illustration A person with entrepreneurial flair for selling goods is appointed a director of a small private company. There is no finance director so the appointee undertakes some day-to-day book-keeping. He is averagely competent at figures, with an elementary knowledge of accounts, but no special skill. At the end of the financial year the auditors discover that the accounting records are inaccurate, and deficiencies have occurred. On the tests considered above, the director will be liable if he was careless in the preparation of the books and the checking of the figures; but he will not be liable if the application of the sort of skill which he would apply to his own personal affairs was insufficient to prevent the deficiencies occurring – provided he did not hold himself out as being specially qualified to undertake the accountancy work.

A consideration of the cases, therefore, will show that the courts are attempting to apply a dual test of liability, with the concept of the 'reasonable man' attaching only to the degree of carefulness which the director must show in and about the tasks which he is regarded as being competent to perform.

The question of diligence is related. This has already been mentioned as an aspect of fiduciary obligation.[9] It can also, however, be recognised in terms of the duty to take care. This aspect is now considered in more detail.

8 See below, pp. 54–55.
9 See p. 24, above.

2 Diligence

A director owes a duty to be diligent in relation to the company's affairs. The amount of attention which he is bound to give in terms of time spent will vary according to the organisation of the company's administration and the number of directors or executives who are participating.[10] In the days when businessmen acquired directorships like credit cards, the position of 'ordinary' directors was not at all onerous. They were required:

> to use reasonable diligence having regard to their position, though probably an ordinary director, who only attends at the board occasionally, cannot be expected to devote as much time and attention to the business as a sole managing partner of an ordinary partnership, but they are bound to use fair and reasonable diligence in the management of their company's affairs, and to act honestly.[11]

The consequence of this is that except where there are so few directors that there is a risk of sole control being exercised (and abused) by one person,[12] the requirement of attendance will be limited to such occasions as are necessary for the director concerned to maintain a reasonable understanding of the company's affairs and the performance of his fellow officers.

Assuming there is no breach of duty in this regard, a director may rely on the acts of others, and will not be liable for their sins or omissions if he has no knowledge of them, or if he has not acquiesced in them:

> In *Dovey v Cory*,[13] the manager and chairman of a bank caused substantial losses by reason of issuing false balance sheets and making improper loans. The House of Lords held that a co-director who was innocent of the frauds both as regards participation and actual or constructive knowledge, was not liable for carelessness or want of diligence in failing to discover them.
>
> Lord Davey said:[14] 'I think the respondent was bound to give his attention and exercise his judgment as a man of business on the matters which were brought before the board at the meetings which he attended, and it is not proved that he did not do so. But I think he was entitled to rely upon the judgment, information, and advice of the chairman and general manager, as to whose integrity, skill, and competence he had no reason for suspicion.'

10 *Re Cardiff Savings Banks, Marquis of Bute's Case* (1892) 2 Ch 100.
11 *Re Forest of Dean Coal Mining Co* (1878) 10 ChD 450 at 452, per Jessel MR.
12 *Re Denham & Co* (1883) 25 ChD 752.
13 [1901] AC 477.
14 At 492.

This principle cannot apply to persons who are appointed, usually under service contracts, to be full-time directors of the company. They will be subject to a combination of duties:

(1) that of an employee bound to give exclusive service to his employer;
(2) that of a trustee bound to administer the company's property; and
(3) in the case of specialist appointments, that of a 'professional' bound to give such attention and skill to the job for which he has been recruited.

3 Care and skill

RE CITY AND EQUITABLE FIRE INSURANCE CO

The cornerstone for over fifty years of the law on a director's liability to his company is the judgment of Romer J in *Re City Equitable Fire Insurance Co.*[15] Although only a decision of first instance, [16] the case has been cited with approval so often, and its underlying assumptions accepted so readily, that any account of the modern law must treat it in some detail.[17]

> The company was put into compulsory liquidation and an investigation revealed a deficiency of assets of £200,000 due principally to the deliberate fraud of the managing director. The question arose whether, in respect of the period during which such fraud was perpetrated, the other directors were to be held personally liable for negligence or breach of duty. The Articles of Association contained a clause exonerating the directors and other officers for the acts, neglects and defaults of the others unless resulting through their own wilful neglect or default.[18] It was held that in the circumstances, the other directors were not liable because as they had acted honestly and with due diligence (in the sense considered above), they could reasonably rely on their co-directors and officers to ensure that the affairs of the company were regularly conducted. In discharging their own duties they were bound to exercise care and skill but they were not liable for errors of judgment.

15 [1925] 1 Ch 407.
16 Affirmed in the CA on different grounds.
17 It is similarly relied on in the White Paper, Cmnd 7037.
18 This is a common relieving clause for trustees and others in a fiduciary position, see ch 5, pp. 95–96, below.

Diligence, care and skill are terms used almost interchangeably in Romer J's review of the older authorities, and 'negligence' arises in a very restricted agency context and not as an independent tort. There are three elements: (1) the extent of 'carefulness' or supervision required, (2) the difference between 'gross' and 'ordinary' negligence, and (3) the degree of skill required to be exercised.

SUPERVISION OF DAY-TO-DAY AFFAIRS

The court held that it was not the duty of a director of a big insurance company to supervise personally the safe custody of the securities of the company. It would have been impracticable, on every purchase of securities, for actual delivery thereon to be made to the directors or, on every sale, for the delivery to the brokers of the securities sold to await a meeting of the board or a committee of directors. The duty of seeing that securities were in safe custody must of necessity be left to officials of the company such as its managers or accountants.

> The position of a director of a company carrying on a small retail business is very different from that of a director of a railway company. The duties of a bank director may differ widely from those of an insurance director, and the duties of a director of one insurance company may differ from those of a director of another. In one company, for instance, matters may normally be attended to by the manager or other members of the staff that in another company are attended to by the directors themselves. The larger the business carried on by the company the more numerous, and the more important, the matters that must of necessity be left to the managers, the accountants and the rest of the staff.[19]

The question of supervision is thus not merely a matter of diligence: it is a matter of deciding, as an efficient businessman, how an organisation should be run. A director of a large public company who immerses himself in the details of day-to-day operations, would probably be incapable of taking more abstract and important decisions at board level. His diligence in this connection might even be evidence of a failure to discharge his duties of skill in the boardroom.[20]

The general principle to be deduced, therefore, is that where functions are properly delegated, and the director does not concern

19 *Re City Equitable Fire Insurance Co* [1925] 1 Ch 407 at 427, referring to *Dovey v Cory* [1901] AC 477 at 488.

20 A criticism often levelled at wartime Generals appointed above their 'ceiling' is that they continued to act as if they were regimental officers, engaged in the detail of a tactical battle.

himself with them, he is not liable if a loss results from the wrongful acts of the delegates or subordinates.[1]

The legal exoneration arises only where there is no trace of participation in the wrongful act by the director himself.[2]

GROSS NEGLIGENCE AND NEGLIGENCE

A distinction evolved on the earlier cases between 'culpable' or 'gross' negligence, and 'ordinary' negligence. [3] This was subject to further analysis in *Re City Equitable Fire Insurance Co.*[4]

> In discharging the duties of his position thus ascertained a director must, of course, act honestly; but he must also exercise some degree of both skill and diligence. To the question of what is the particular degree of skill and diligence required of him, the authorities do not, I think, give any very clear answer. It has been laid down that so long as a director acts honestly he cannot be made responsible in damages unless guilty of gross or culpable negligence in a business sense. But as pointed out by Neville J in *In Re Brazilian Rubber Plantations and Estates Ltd*, [5] one cannot say whether a man has been guilty of negligence, gross or otherwise, unless one can determine what is the extent of the duty which he is alleged to have neglected. For myself, I confess to feeling some difficulty in understanding the difference between negligence and gross negligence, except insofar as the expressions are used for the purpose of drawing a distinction between the duty that is owed in one case and the duty that is owed in another. If two men owe the same duty to a third person, and neglect to perform that duty, they are both guilty of negligence, and it is not altogether easy to understand how one can be guilty of gross negligence and the other of negligence only. But if it be said that of two men one is only liable to a third person for gross negligence, and the other is liable for mere negligence, this, I think, means no more than that the duties of the two men are different. The one owes a duty to take a greater degree of care than does the other . . . If, therefore, a director is only liable for gross or culpable negligence, this means that he does not owe a duty to his company, to take all possible care. It is some degree of care less than that. The care that he is bound to take has been described by Neville J in the case referred to above as 'reasonable care' to be measured by the care an ordinary man might be expected to take in the circumstances on his own behalf.

1 *Land Credit Co of Ireland v Lord Fermoy* (1870) 5 Ch App 763; *Department of Health and Social Security v Wayte* [1972] 1 All ER 255, [1972] 1 WLR 19; *Re New Mashonaland Exploration Co* [1892] 3 Ch 577.

2 *Selangor United Rubber Estates Ltd v Cradock (No 3)* [1968] 2 All ER 1073, [1968] 1 WLR 1555; *Re Lands Allotment Co* [1894] 1 Ch 616; and *Ramskill v Edwards* (1885) 31 ChD 100.

3 *Lagunas Nitrate Co v Lagunas Syndicate* [1899] 2 Ch 392.

4 [1925] 1 Ch at 427.

5 [1911] 1 Ch 425 at 437.

This, last, observation is fundamentally important. There is no concept of the 'reasonable director' as such. The test is whether the director has shown ordinary care and prudence, as he would have done if, being a reasonable man, he was conducting his own affairs. To the extent that this part of the duty of a director is objective, one is not allowed to assume that a person may be incompetent even in the standards of his personal life. A director may forget to pick up his pay cheque at the end of the month; but carelessness of this type would not be a defence if he was sued by his company for failing to take reasonable steps in raising invoices on company customer accounts, so that some of the debts became bad.[6]

In relation to cheques, a director who signs a cheque that appears to be drawn for a legitimate purpose is not responsible for seeing that the money is in fact required for that purpose, or that it is subsequently applied for that purpose, assuming that the cheque arrives for signature in a regular way.[7]

> In a company formed for the purchase of a business, where the power to make the purchase was distinctly conferred on the directors, though the character of the business turned out to be ruinous, it was held that the directors were not personally responsible unless the character was obviously apparent when the purchase was made.[8]

> A director of a company voted, without enquiry, for a payment for brokerage and commission, which was in fact for fraudulently raising the price of the company's shares in the market. The payment was included in a much larger item on the annual balance sheets and passed without objection. It was held that the director was liable to repay the amount on the grounds of misfeasance, and although the director's liability was not based on that of a trustee, he was bound to show reasonable care in the company's affairs.[9]

DEGREE OF SKILL REQUIRED

The standard of *care* is that of an ordinary man, the reasonable human being who is a central feature of the general tort of

6 Unless it is the best policy for the company not to press for payment: *Re Forest of Dean Coal Mining Co* (1878) 10 ChD 450.

7 See also, in relation to Customs and Excise offences, *Huckerby v Elliott* [1970] All ER 189.

8 *Overend and Gurney Co v Gibb* (1872) LR 5 HL 480.

9 *Re Railway and General Light Improvement Co, Marzetti's Case* (1880) 42 LT 206; *Re MacFadyen* [1908] 2 KB 817. *Prefontaine v Grenier* [1907] AC 101.

negligence.[10] The duty of *skill* is apparently a duty for the individual to do his best in particular circumstances. This was emphasised in *Re City Equitable Fire Insurance Co.* The director is to be judged by reference to his own knowledge and experience, such attributes to be deployed as skilfully as may be, but if they are not found to exist in large measure, the scope for identifying a breach of duty is remarkably small.[11]

> L Co was promoted and formed by the directors of L Syndicate for the purpose of purchasing part of the property of the Syndicate, consisting of nitrate works. Two years after the acquisition the shareholders of L Co, believing the property had been acquired at an over-value, appointed an independent board of directors who brought an action against the Syndicate. It was held that since the shareholders had notice from the company's Memorandum and Articles, and elsewhere, that the original directors were involved in the Syndicate, such involvement (in the absence of any misrepresentation or concealment) could not bring about rescission of the purchase contract. Also, the defendant directors had not been guilty of such negligence or breach of trust as to render them liable in damages for the loss occasioned to the company, or in equity to make good such loss.[12]

The Court of Appeal indicated that if the directors act within their powers, and honestly for the benefit of the company, then their want of knowledge or experience cannot render them liable even though more skilful directors might not have allowed the loss to arise. They could not be liable for mistakes or errors of judgment, even though such mistakes affect the relations of their company to another company of which they are also members, and even though the interests of the two companies may conflict. Similarly, Romer J said in *Re City Equitable Fire Insurance Co*[13] that 'a director of a life insurance company, for instance, does not guarantee that he has the skill of an actuary or of a physician'.

The limitations of this test, at least on the older authorities, is made plain by a dictum in *Re Brazilian Rubber Plantations and Estates Ltd*:[14]

10 *Blyth v Birmingham Waterworks Co* (1856) 11 Ex 781. See further, Winfield and Jolowicz *Law of Tort* (11th edn, 1979) at pp. 87 ff.

11 'If we pay in peanuts, we must expect to get monkeys': *The Observer* 18 December 1966.

12 *Lagunas Nitrate Co v Lagunas Syndicate* [1899] 2 Ch 392.

13 [1925] 1 Ch 407.

14 [1911] 1 Ch 425 at 437.

[A director] is, I think, not bound to bring any special qualification to his office. He may undertake the management of a rubber company in complete ignorance of everything connected with rubber, without incurring responsibility for the mistakes which may result from such ignorance; while if he is acquainted with the rubber business he must give the company the advantage of his knowledge when transacting the company's business.

The shortcomings of the director's skill are bound to increase his reliance upon outside expert advice, if he has the sense to take it, in which case the standards considered above apply.[15] As with trustees, directors cannot rely on the advice to the extent of abrogating their discretion. But to the extent that they exercise their judgment bona fide, it seems that a court will not be prepared to interfere.[16]

4 A higher duty owed

UNDER SERVICE CONTRACTS

The modern board of directors commonly consists of a handful of 'non-executives' the presence of whom may add status or prestige to the company, attract customers, be useful for lobbying purposes, or merely look impressive on the company's notepaper; and a lesser number of full-time operatives, mainly employed under contracts of service, who will be concerned with the administration of the business on a level of continuous participation. As we have seen, full-time directors are expected to show a high degree of diligence. A corresponding enhancement of their duties of care cannot be inferred from any principle of law dealing with the position of a director as such. Such inference must be drawn, if at all, from rules of agency,[17] or where the traditional master and servant relationship and any express or implied contractual terms applicable thereto, can be invoked. This could be held to mean that a director operating under a service contract and working full-time in the business, owed higher duties than a director who did not operate under such a contract, but derived his authority (and the payment of his fees and expenses) from the Articles of Association.

In the case of ordinary employees, the courts have readily inferred an implied term of the contract of employment, requiring the exercise of reasonable skill in the performance of the duties of

15 *Re Faure Electric Accumulator Co* (1888) 40 ChD 141.

16 *Howard Smith Ltd v Ampol Petroleum Ltd* [1974] AC 821 at 832, even as regards managing directors: *Holdsworth & Co (Wakefield) Ltd v Caddies* [1955] 1 WLR 352 at 356.

17 Which particularly apply in the case of professional agents, see section 5, below.

the job.[18] There is no reason why the same test should not be applied to an employed director, and certainly an employed managing director: the assumption of a greater liability is a *quid pro quo* for the greater security afforded by a service contract in terms of statutory protection and redundancy and pension rights. Thus a director who is engaged under a contract of employment and is dismissed by ordinary resolution of the company, may sustain an action in damages for wrongful dismissal (he may even be reinstated). A non-employed director is not in this position.

THE EXPERT DIRECTOR

Two types of experts could be appointed to a board. First, persons having specific knowledge of the business in question, who would be bound to use such knowledge for the furtherance of the company's interests.[19] Second, there are those who are engaged because they are specialists in a certain part of the company's administration, e g as chartered surveyors or accountants. The law is well settled that, for the latter type, there must be shown such a degree of skill as a reasonably competent practitioner would show. The test is objective. The director is trusted with a specific task because, by virtue of his professional qualifications and experience, he is regarded as capable of fulfilling it. This does not imply a possession of skill to the highest degree, but it is obviously well above that of the ordinary man in the street. The standard to be achieved by the professional is to be judged by his peers:

> The point, therefore, to be determined is, not whether the defendant arrived at a correct conclusion upon reading the letter, but whether upon the occasion in question, he did or did not exercise a reasonable and proper care, skill and judgment. This is a question of fact, the decision of which appears to us to rest upon this further enquiry, viz, whether other persons exercising the same professional calling, and being men of experience and skill therein, would or would not have come to the same conclusion as the defendant.[20]

Liability also arises where a person holds himself out as being suitable or competent to do a particular job or perform it with a parti-

18 *Lister v Romford Ice and Cold Storage Co Ltd* [1957] AC 555, [1957] 1 All ER 125, HL.

19 *Re Brazilian Rubber Plantations and Estates Ltd* [1911] 1 Ch 425 at 437.

20 *Chapman v Walton* (1833) 10 Bing 57. See generally *Charlesworth on Negligence* (6th edn, 1977) paras 925, 927, where, however, the learned editor mistakenly assumes that company directors are automatically in the category of persons professing special skill.

cular degree of skill. Evidence of failure on either count sounds in damages.[1]

COMPARISONS WITH OTHER PROFESSIONS

A study of the decisions relating to negligence by certain professional men is not necessarily helpful in determining a specialist director's liability for breach of duties to his company, since it may be that such a director would be held liable not so much for failing to exercise professional skill, but for failing to apply it by analogy to a general management problem within the company.

Illustration A solicitor is qualified by his law studies and his period in articles to exercise a critical, detached judgment and to rely on the results of his own enquiries rather than the assertions of others. Suppose a director of a company, who also happens to be a solicitor, is sought to be rendered liable for defalcations by subordinate officers because he failed to make certain enquiries which would not have occurred to a non-specialist director to make. It is suggested that he could be liable under such circumstances, because the judgment of his professional peers would impute to him a course of conduct which, while not based on any legal learning, could be said to be usual or prudent for a man of his general professional background.[2]

Accepting that possibility, some specific examples of professional negligence ought to be considered:

(1) *Accountants* Where an accountant's duty includes the checking of books of account, he has been held to be negligent in not obtaining a bank certificate to verify the cash, but relying instead on a cash book which had been falsely prepared by a dishonest clerk.[3] Where an accountant has been employed to advise upon the sale of business albeit on an informal basis, a liability for negligence arose where the advice given was misleading.[4] On the other hand, where an accountant was engaged to investigate the books of a company but failed to find out that the stock was overvalued, he was held not liable because in the absence of suspicious circumstances he was entitled to rely on the accuracy of the stock sheets.[5]

1 *Esso Petroleum Co Ltd v Mardon* [1976] QB 801, [1976] 2 All ER 5.
2 See also Report of the Law Society of Scotland on the Companies Bill 1978.
3 *Fox & Son v Morrish Grant & Co* (1918) 35 TLR 126.
4 *Bradford v Wright Stephens and Lloyd* (1962) Guardian 27 February.
5 *Henry Squire Cash Chemists Ltd v Ball, Baker & Co* (1911) 27 TLR 269.

(2) *Surveyors and engineers* The professional liability of a surveyor or engineer who is also a director will only be apparent if the business of the company includes property transactions or engineering works, and the director is involved as an expert with these matters. We have already seen that the director can be liable, in a fiduciary capacity, where he does not act in the best interests of the company, but this has nothing to do with his professional skill.[6] It has been held that structural engineers were liable for not designing a building fit for the purpose for which they knew it would be required.[7] It would follow that a surveyor-director of a property company who was shown plans which turned out to be negligently prepared by a contractor, but yet accepted them and caused the company loss, would be liable independently of any claim the company might bring against such contractor. Similarly, it has been held that an architect and surveyor employed to give a general report but not a detailed survey on a property were negligent in failing to discover woodworm and dry rot.[8] So a specialist director deputed by his board to inspect new head offices which the company might acquire, could be similarly liable. An architect has been held liable for issuing interim certificates to a builder when the work had not been carried out.[9] Persons in the position of architects, surveyors and engineers will be deemed to have a knowledge of law and practice which is appropriate to their calling.[10]

(3) *Solicitors* Solicitors appointed to the board may be asked to give advice in a number of capacities. They may be consulted on contracts with third parties, liabilities of the board itself, company procedure, and the rights and duties of employees. It is clear that they are under a duty to be careful when giving advice in all these situations. As Lord Denning MR has said:

> Nowadays . . . it is clear that a professional man who gives guidance to others owes a duty of care, not only to the client who employs him, but also to another who he knows is relying on his skill to save him from harm. It is certain that a banker or accountant is under such a duty. And I can see no reason why a solicitor is not likewise.[11]

6 *Industrial Development Consultants Ltd v Cooley* [1972] 2 All ER 162, [1972] 1 WLR 443.

7 *Greaves & Co (Contractors) Ltd v Baynham Meikle & Partners* [1975] 3 All ER 99, [1975] 1 WLR 1095.

8 *Sincock v Bangs (Reading)* [1952] CPL 562; see also *Philips v Ward* [1956] 1 All ER 874.

9 *Sutcliffe v Thackrah* [1974] AC 727, [1974] 1 All ER 859.

10 *Jenkins v Betham* (1855) 15 CB 168.

11 *Dutton v Bognor Regis UDC* [1972] 1 QB 373 at 395.

A solicitor has been held liable for not explaining the true effect and purpose of documents which the client is being asked to execute.[12] He is liable when acting for a client who is advancing money to a third party, for not ensuring that the security documents are properly executed or legally effective.[13] A solicitor, like an accountant, will be liable for not taking reasonable care of documents entrusted to him or else for disclosing confidential information which has been communicated to him.[14] A solicitor's role in business matters may be more restricted unless he is specifically engaged to undertake them:

> A plaintiff wished to get her life story published and retained literary agents, and also a solicitor to advise her generally. The agents prepared a contract which was sent to the solicitor to advise on. He had gone abroad but his articled clerk, for whom he accepted responsibility, approved the agreement. This involved the plaintiff in a considerable tax liability. She claimed damages against him for failing to advise as to such liability, or for not referring the matter to an expert tax consultant. It was held that the defendant was not liable, because a reasonably competent solicitor could not be expected to perform as an expert in non-legal (tax) matters. The proper scope of his contractual retainer was limited.[15]

It would presumably be otherwise if the solicitor, as a 'man of affairs', with experience of business or tax matters, undertook to advise a client generally or to navigate him through the pitfalls and hurdles of a complex transaction. It is also suggested that the solicitor would be negligent if, knowing that a problem which he could not himself answer existed, and which was relevant to the client's affairs, did not draw his client's attention to the need to take advice involving an even higher degree of skill.

(4) *Company secretaries* A company secretary is invariably employed under a contract of service, and will owe a duty under that contract to perform that office competently. However, a company secretary is often appointed a director, especially in smaller concerns, and in many cases will assume a role within the management and administration of the company which exceeds the statutory duties of the secretary as such.[16] For a number of years the secretary has been recognised as an important officer of the

12 *Stannard v Ullithorne* (1834) 10 Bing 491.
13 *Whiteman v Hawkins* (1878) 4 CPD 13.
14 *Weld-Blundell v Stephens* [1920] AC 956.
15 *Duchess of Argyll v Beuselinck* [1972] 2 Lloyd's Rep 172.
16 He could be held liable as a quasi director under s. 455, Companies Act 1948.

company,[17] and under section 79 of the Companies Act 1980 it is the duty of the directors of a public company to take all reasonable steps to secure that the secretary is a person who appears to them to have the requisite knowledge and experience to do the job.[18] The elevated status of the secretary may carry increased liabilities with it, especially in the case of a secretary who is required to be qualified. An appointee to a major public company, especially if he achieves a seat on the board, will be required to exhibit a knowledge of law, business affairs, management, tax, and employee rights which collectively exceeds anything any other specialist board member can hope to offer. Such a position would be quite unenviable, and it is submitted that in the context of his potential liabilities the secretary would be better off to remain a servant of the board, and do without the glamour of a seat on it.

5 Should the general standard be raised?

Although it was intended to operate in substitution for the existing law, clause 45 of the Companies Bill 1978 did not attempt to reform it. It provided:

> In the exercise of the powers and the discharge of the duties of his office, in circumstances of any description, a director of a company owes a duty to the company to exercise such care and diligence as could reasonably be expected of a reasonably prudent person in circumstances of that description and to exercise such skill as may reasonably be expected of a person of his knowledge and experience.

Diligence and care continue to be distinguished from skill where the test remains largely subjective. The Conservative Opposition in Parliament attempted, however, to introduce at the Committee stage an amendment which would have had the revolutionary effect of putting directors on a par with other professionals by making them liable for failing to comply with an objective standard of competence. The amendment was defeated,[19] but raises a most interesting question for company law reform in the near future.

Essentially, a shift of emphasis away from the subjective abilities of the director himself, towards the requirement of what is reasonable to do *for the company* in the particular circumstances, introduces a 'relative' standard of skill which is shared by many professional groups. It is not suggested that the director of a small firm

17 *Panorama Developments (Guildford) Ltd v Fidelis Furnishing Fabrics* [1971] 3 WLR 440, CA.

18 This is actually a highly subjective requirement. S. 79 has had a somewhat chequered history in Parliament.

19 By two votes. It was also heavily opposed by the CBI.

should exhibit the skill displayed by the senior management of major companies. It is inherent in *Duchess of Argyll v Beuselinck*,[20] for example, that persons exercising skill within the same profession may do so to different degrees, according to their eminence or speciality. Again, a general practitioner is not expected to exhibit the operating skill of a consultant surgeon. An objective test as applied to company law would do no more than require of a director that he shows the acumen appropriate to the class of business in which he is engaged, and the size of enterprise over which he has control. For smaller concerns this is unlikely to produce any great change. However, for large companies with thousands of shareholders on whom public attention focuses, a higher level of legal responsibility might well be thought desirable to maintain (or restore) public confidence in the workings of the higher echelons of industry.

How is the director's skill to be judged? There is no profession of director as such, and although it has been noted that many professional men and women serve on company boards and contribute their specialist expertise, the law has not identified a class of skill which is peculiar to the office of director. In the Department of Trade Inspector's Report on the affairs of Lohnro Ltd[1] the Inspector states that:

> the duty of a board of directors is to impart a sense of purpose and direction to a Group's affairs, to formulate wise policies and to monitor the carrying out of these policies by the executives.

That may well be true of the boards of the largest companies. It is less true of smaller companies where individual directors are concerned with day-to-day management, and it does not deal with the position of the individual and his relation to the board as a whole. Probably the nearest job description is 'higher management', and there is no doubt that managerial skills and training are distinct from those of the other professions. Nevertheless, the problem has to be faced that if the essence of an objective professional standard is the judgment of a man by his specialist peers, then such judgment must be based upon commonly accepted management or executive skills appropriately applied to the level of business in which the director is operating. The test would be, not 'Has this director done the right thing?', but 'Is this the judgment of a reasonably competent and experienced director of the size of company in question?'.

20 [1972] 2 Lloyd's Rep 172.
1 1976, para 10.1.

The arguments against any uprating of the existing standard have already been mentioned.[2]

A principal effect of a change in the law would be to lessen the dependence upon the inadequate requirement of bona fides. For example, in the *Savoy* case discussed in chapter 1,[3] it was suggested by counsel that the directors could properly embark upon their scheme if 'they were bona fide of the opinion that it would be in the better interests of the company that the new state of affairs so produced should be brought into existence'. However, on any rational and objective view there was a crucial objection to the scheme, namely that it would have deprived the company of the power of redeploying its assets, whether by changing the use of its property or selling it to a purchaser for a price reflecting a more remunerative user.[4]

2 See pp. 40–41, above.

3 P. 8, above.

4 I am obliged for this example to Dr R B L Prior's paper on Directors' Duties, published in 1977, on behalf of the Society of Conservative Lawyers.

4 Disclosure

1 Contracts with the company

GENERAL POSITION OF FIDUCIARY

Just as a director is liable to the company upon a contract with a third party if it results in a secret profit, so he is in a special position as regards contracts made with the company itself, in which he has a personal interest. He is under a duty to disclose the nature of the interest so that the company has an opportunity to ratify or repudiate it.[1] Non-disclosure renders the contract liable to be avoided by the company, both against the interested director and any other person who is aware of the breach of duty by him. It is not absolutely void, but is subject to the usual equitable rules allowing rescission only where it is possible to restore the parties to their original position.

> R acted as managing director of B Ltd. He agreed with the plaintiff, who was financing his own company P Ltd and had become a director of B Ltd, that B Ltd should, inter alia, indemnify the plaintiff in respect of his personal liability for loans to P Ltd. The matter was not reported to the Board of B Ltd, whose Articles required the same disclosure of directors' interests that is demanded under the Companies Acts. The plaintiff became liable on the loans, and sued B Ltd on the indemnity. It was held that the company was obliged to make the payments, since although the contract was voidable at its instance, it could not now be rescinded because it was completed and restitution *in integrum* was impossible.[2]

It might be suggested that if the interested director in circumstances such as above is sufficiently quick off the mark, he can bind the company irrevocably to a transaction without its approval. On the other hand, to make the contract void *ab initio* is to put third

1 *Aberdeen Rly Co v Blaikie Bros* (1854) 1 Macq 461.
2 *Hely-Hutchinson v Brayhead Ltd* [1968] 1 QB 549, CA; *Transvaal Lands Co v New Belgium (Transvaal) Land and Development Co* [1914] 2 Ch 488.

parties in a disadvantageous position, where they have relied upon the necessary internal formalities of the company being complied with. Moreover, the contract is not ultra vires the company, and a person with even the appearance of authority to enter into it can bind his principal.

Disclosure must be to the company itself, i e to shareholders in general meeting, and not merely to the board of directors. Although the board is bound to act in the interests of the company as a whole, it is obviously more difficult for individual directors to exercise a balanced and unbiased judgment about the merits of the case of one of their number. Nor must the consent of the company be taken for granted when disclosure is made: a resolution approving or ratifying a transaction is necessary, but if the director concerned is also a shareholder he may vote on such resolution provided this does not constitute a fraud on the minority.[3] Profits made out of a contract which is not so approved, must be accounted for in the usual way, even where the company would not otherwise have made them.

INDIRECT INTERESTS

The general principle extends to situations where the director receives no direct or obvious benefit such as a commission or share of profit. Where a director of a company has an interest as shareholder in another company, or is in a fiduciary position towards and owes a duty to another company, which is proposing to enter into engagements with the company of which he is a director, he is within the rule. He has a personal interest or else owes a duty which conflicts with his duty to the company of which he is a director. It is immaterial whether this conflicting interest belongs to him beneficially or as trustee for others. He is bound to do as well for his beneficiaries as he would do for himself. The validity or invalidity of the transaction cannot depend upon the extent of the adverse interest of the fiduciary agent any more than upon how far, in any particular case, the terms of the contract have been the best obtainable for the interest of the beneficiary concerned.[4]

On the other hand, a certain amount of common sense needs to be applied. The rule is directed to a state of affairs which discloses a real conflict of duty and interest and not to some theoretical or rhetorical interest. It is quite unnecessary to invoke it in the case of a director who takes too long a holiday or stays at too expensive an

3 *North-West Transportation Co Ltd v Beatty* (1887) 12 App Cas 589.
4 *Transvaal Lands Co v New Belgium (Transvaal) Land and Development Co* [1914] 2 Ch 488 at 503.

hotel; that is just a plain breach of his duty to serve the company faithfully. So also in the case of a director who negotiates too high a salary, because the Articles will normally permit the appointment of a managing director at a salary. The company will be said to have relaxed the rule and be prepared to let the director negotiate a salary and possibly even to vote on the amount in the boardroom.[5] Often the interpretation of the word 'interest' varies according to the Article of Association of the company which gives a qualified relaxation of the rule.[6]

2 Statutory requirement to disclose interest

SECTION 199, COMPANIES ACT 1948

The relative severity of the general law prompted many companies to incorporate in their Articles provisions which either permitted a director, without more ado, to be interested in contracts, or merely required disclosure to the Board. The effect of such Articles is considered in the next section. To some extent the legislature has recognised the need for a lesser requirement. Section 199 provides:

(1) Subject to the provisions of this section, it shall be the duty of a director of a company who is in any way, whether directly or indirectly, interested in a contract or proposed contract with the company to declare the nature of his interest at a meeting of the directors of the company.

(2) In the case of a proposed contract the declaration required by this section to be made by a director shall be made at the meeting of the directors at which the question of entering into the contract is first taken into consideration, or if the director was not at the date of that meeting interested in the proposed contract, at the next meeting of directors held after he became so interested, and in a case where the director becomes interested in a contract after it is made, the said declaration shall be made at the first meeting of the directors held after the director becomes so interested.

(3) [See p. 60, below.]

(4) Any director who fails to comply with the provisions of this section shall be liable to a fine not exceeding £100.[7]

5 *Boulting v Association of Cinematograph, Television and Allied Technicians* [1963] 2 QB 606 at 637–638.

6 *Todd v Robinson* (1884) 14 QBD 739, CA; *Imperial Mercantile Credit Association v Coleman* (1873) LR 6 HL 189; *Albion Steel and Wire Co v Martin* (1875) 1 ChD 580.

7 To be increased under the Companies Act 1980, to a fine on indictment unlimited in amount, and on summary conviction to the statutory maximum (presently £1,000).

(5) Nothing in this section shall be taken to prejudice the operation of any rule of law restricting directors of a company from having any interest in contracts with the company.

The section is concerned with a 'declaration' of interest, whether direct or indirect. It must be made in circumstances where the other directors can take into account the interest in deciding whether or not to go ahead with the transaction. If the interested party absents himself, accidentally or on purpose, from the board meeting at which the contract is first taken into consideration, then he must make a disclosure at the next meeting (and not merely at the next meeting which he himself attends). A director cannot assume, simply by disclosing, that his interest will be confirmed, less still where he has personally negotiated the contract in question. On the other hand, where there is a board minute which evidences the declaration followed or preceded by a recommendation that the contract be entered into, this can be taken as a permission for the director to remain interested or retain any pecuniary advantage. The disclosure must be sufficiently full and frank to enable the board to make a considered judgment.[8]

A common occurrence is for a person to be accepted on to a company board by virtue of his professional expertise exercised through a firm which already nets for it. In such a case a general declaration under section 199(3)[9] must be made at the time of his joining. It will be a matter of judgment for the chairman of the board, or the company secretary, whether to remind the board of the director's interest when a relevant contract is discussed. Much will depend upon the frequency of the occurrence. Section 199(3) now reads:

(3) For the purposes of this section, general notice given to the directors of a company by a director to the effect that
(a) he is a member of a specified company or firm and is to be regarded as interested in any contract which may, after the date of the notice, be made with that company or firm; or
(b) he is to be regarded as interested in any contract which may after the date of the notice be made with a specified person who is connected with him (within the meaning of section 64 of the Companies Act 1980):

shall be deemed to be a sufficient declaration of interest in relation to any such contract;
provided that no such notice shall be of effect unless either it is given at a meeting of the directors or the director takes reasonable steps to secure that it is brought up and read at the next meeting of the directors after it is given.[10]

8 Gower *Modern Company Law* (4th edn) p. 585.
9 As substituted by Sch 3 of the Companies Act 1980.
10 The proviso remains from the 1948 Act.

Section 199 is extended by section 60 of the Companies Act 1980, so as to require disclosure of any transaction or arrangement (whether or not constituting a 'contract') in which a director is directly or indirectly interested, made on or after the appointed day. Any transaction or arrangement of a kind described in section 49 of the new Act (loans etc) is treated as one in which the director is interested:[11] whether or not the transaction is made unlawful by that section.[12]

Illustration On the authority of the managing director, a public company guarantees to a finance house the instalment payments to be made by X, a director, in respect of the hire purchase by him of a motor car, which is to be partially used for business purposes. The guarantee relates to a 'credit transaction' under section 49(2)(b) and, unless validated by section 50(3) or (4), may be illegal. In either event, X must disclose at the next available board meeting under section 199(1) that he has an interest in the guarantee that has been given.

Section 199 is also made to apply to a newly identified category of 'shadow director'. A 'shadow director' is a person in accordance with whose directions and instructions the directors of a company are accustomed to act.[13] This could include a controlling shareholder who is not formally appointed to the board. A person who acts in the office of managing director so as to bind the company vis-à-vis third parties, but who similarly lacks formal authority, is likely to fall within the definition: since, as we have seen,[14] an apparent authority is based upon a holding out by the company itself (acting by the remainder of its board), which presupposes that the board has acquiesced in the dominant position of the person in question. Directors will not be held to be accustomed to act on the directions or instructions of a third party where such instructions and directions consist of professional advice. This will prevent the company's solicitor or accountant per se from becoming a shadow director.

The Companies Act 1980, section 63(3) makes section 199 apply to a shadow director in a different way from an ordinary director, in that a shadow director must declare his interest, not at a meeting of the directors, but by a notice in writing to the directors which is either (a) a specific notice given before the date of the meeting at which, if he had been a director, a declaration would be required by

11 S. 60(2).
12 See Prentice *Companies Act 1980* para 281. And pp. 69–72, below on the kind of transactions embraced by s. 49.
13 S. 63 (1).
14 See p. 19, below.

section 199(2) to be made; or (b) a notice which under section 199(3) falls to be treated as a sufficient declaration of that interest or would fall to be so treated apart from the proviso it contains.

RELATION OF SECTION 199 TO GENERAL LAW

It is important to note that section 199 does not abrogate the requirement that a director should, as a matter of general law, seek approval of the company in general meeting by ordinary resolution, of the transaction in which he has an interest. It is thought that sections 63 and 64 cannot be extended by analogy so as to require the categories of shadow directors or connected persons to be disclosed as well. The Companies Act 1948, section 199, however, was not drafted in a vacuum but assumed the existence in most companies' Articles of clauses which would either waive the rules regarding conflicts of interest or else require disclosure only to be made to the board and to be legitimised thereby. Indeed such Articles appear in Table A and it is to these that we now turn.

3 Waiver clauses

DISQUALIFICATION

It was formerly the practice for companies to incorporate a provision in their constitutions whereby a director who was interested in any contract (except merely as a shareholder of another company) should be disqualified and vacate office.[15] Disqualification was and is a principle well-known to local government but it has less relevance to commercial enterprises, and as such Table A in the Companies Act 1948 does not include it. Quite the contrary, article 84(3) expressly states that directors are not disqualified by contracting with the company. It was always open to companies to modify or exclude this disqualifying clause, since it is not an entrenched equitable principle.

TABLE A, ARTICLE 84

Companies incorporated under the 1948 Act, and those which have modified their Articles to take account of changing conditions, commonly adopt article 84:

> (1) A director who is in any way, whether directly or indirectly, interested in a contract or proposed contract with the company shall

15 As in, e g, art 47, Table B, Joint Stock Companies Act 1856; ss. 85–87, Companies Clauses Consolidation Act 1845.

declare the nature of his interest at a meeting of the directors in accordance with section 199 of the Act.

(2) A director shall not vote in respect of any contract or arrangement in which he is interested, and if he shall do so his vote shall not be counted, nor shall he be counted in the quorum present at the meeting, but neither of these prohibitions shall apply to—

(a) any arrangement for giving any director any security or indemnity in respect of money lent by him to or obligations undertaken by him for the benefit of the company; or

(b) any arrangement for the giving by the company of any security to a third party in respect of a debt or obligation of the company for which the director himself has assumed responsibility in whole or in part under a guarantee or indemnity or by the deposit of a security; or

(c) any contract by a director to subscribe for or underwrite shares or debentures of the company; or

(d) any contract or arrangement with any other company in which he is interested only as an officer of the company or as holder of shares or other securities;

and these prohibitions may at any time be suspended or relaxed to any extent, and either generally or in respect of any particular contract, arrangement or transaction, by the company in general meeting.

(3) A director may hold any other office or place of profit under the company (other than the office of auditor) in conjunction with his office of director for such period and on such terms (as to remuneration and otherwise) as the directors may determine and no director or intending director shall be disqualified by his office from contracting with the company either with regard to his tenure of any such other office or place of profit or as vendor, purchaser or otherwise, nor shall any such contract, or any contract or arrangement entered into by or on behalf of the company in which any director is in any way interested, be liable to be avoided, nor shall any director so contracting or being so interested be liable to account to the company for any profit realised by any such contract or arrangement by reason of such director holding that office or of the fiduciary relation thereby established.

(4) A director, notwithstanding his interest, may be counted in the quorum present at any meeting whereat he or any other director is appointed to hold any such office or place of profit under the company or whereat the terms of such appointment are arranged, and he may vote on any such appointment or arrangement other than his own appointment or the arrangement of the terms thereof.

(5) Any director may act by himself or his firm in a professional capacity for the company, and he or his firm shall be entitled to remuneration for professional services as if he were not a director; provided that nothing herein contained shall authorise a director of his firm to act as auditor to the company.

This article recognises that it may be more advantageous to have dirctors who can advance the interests of the company by their connection, and, by allowing them a commission, to make it worth their while to introduce business to the company, than to have the benefit of their advice in every proposed transaction.[16] Paragraph (2) of the article precludes a director from voting 'in respect of any contract or arrangement' except in the specific cases set out. It is clear that 'arrangement' is intended to be distinct from 'contract', and the word occurs again in the Companies Act 1980, Part IV.[17] It would appear to include transactions which are not legally enforceable but are made upon condition, or are made parallel to some other transaction or agreement and by reference to it. The words 'in respect of' confine the prohibition to a vote on the contract itself or perhaps a renewal of it. A subsequent decision required by the board in the ordinary course, which incidentally affects the benefit which the contract confers would it is submitted be too remote an event to require the director's abstention: unless as a matter of general fiduciary duty he acknowledged (or could be persuaded) that a conflict of interest still subsisted.

Because the Articles are a contract between shareholders the permissions contained in article 84, e g as to providing professional services, can be taken as a standing consent given to a director so that, provided there is statutory disclosure (which cannot be negatived), no further authorisation is necessary.[18] As waiver clauses in Articles amount to a kind of shield for a director, it follows that non-compliance with their strict terms will have the effect of substituting the general equitable principle, with its consequences of voidability and accounting for profits.[19]

One difficulty that sometimes arises on the construction of article 84, para (4) is the quorum at board meetings. Generally, in reckoning a quorum directors who are not entitled to vote, because they are interested in the contract under discussion, must not be counted.[20] Suppose that the quorum is two and three directors are present, A, B and C, of whom two, B and C, are interested in a transaction. On principle, it ought not to be possible to evade the quorum requirement by proceeding as follows:

(a) the proposed resolution is split into two, each resolution making reference to one only of the interested directors;

16 *Buckley on the Companies Acts* (13th edn) p. 878.
17 Expecially ss. 48 – 54; see also *Manning v Eastern Counties Rly Co* (1844) 13 LJ Ex 265 at 273.
18 As to companies listed on the Stock Exchange, see Requirements for Admission to the Official List, Sch VII, Pt A, para D2.
19 *Imperial Mercantile Credit Association v Coleman* (1873) LR 6 HL 189.
20 *Re Cleadon Trust Ltd* [1939] Ch 286, CA.

(b) A, the independent director, votes with B to pass the resolution giving an interest to C;
(c) A and C pass a resolution giving an interest to B.[1]

However, under the present article, if the quorum were two, and B and C were the only directors present, they could constitute a quorum, and B could vote C into an office of profit and C could vote B into an office of profit. The resolutions would be binding in the absence of fraud.

If the Articles are not in the form of article 84 but contain some wider exemption which is inconsistent with either the equitable principle or section 199, it will be no defence to rely upon such an article where an action is brought by the company, e g for restitution of profits. Nor does a provision in the Articles relieving a director from disqualification when contracting with the company, in any way diminish the criterion of 'interest' if such Articles go on to require disclosure.[2]

LIMITS ON DISCLOSURE

Article 84, like section 199, only requires disclosure of personal interests in contracts and arrangements. It does not extend to disclosure of other matters affecting a director's fiduciary position. As we shall see, [3] there are severe limitations on the ability of a company by its Articles to exempt a director from liability for breach of duty such as negligence. Such a provision would thus merely compromise the director's position without affording him any protection.[4] In consequence, there is no general rule that a director must disclose conduct which is not concerned with an interest in contracts:

> A plaintiff brought an action to recover damages for wrongful dismissal and commission and arrears of salary. He had committed acts of misconduct but his dismissal was not based on them, although it was regular and justified. The defendant contended that the salary should not be paid since the plaintiff had misled them by not revealing his misdoings. It was held that an employee was not under a duty to confess or disclose his misdoings and so there was no breach of contract by him which justified withholding salary.[5]

1 *Re North Eastern Insurance Co* [1919] 1 Ch 198.
2 *Victors Ltd v Linguard* [1927] 1 Ch 323.
3 See pp. 95–96, below.
4 Moreover, the law of disclosure has not achieved the status of a Catholic confession.
5 *Healey v Société Anonyme Française Rubastic* [1917] 1 KB 946; approved in *Bell v Lever Bros* [1932] AC 161, HL.

Under the analogy of trusteeship, however, the director may be liable to disclose the deficiencies of his fellow directors once he becomes aware of them, in the sense that a failure to do so may permit them to treat him as a co-defaulter and seek a contribution for losses caused to the company's property.

4 Disclosure in directors' report

The directors' report means the report by the directors of the company which, by section 157 of the Companies Act 1948, is required to be attached to every balance sheeet of the company prepared under section 150 and the Companies Act 1976, section 1.[6] By section 16 of the Companies Act 1967 certain additional matters of a general nature are required to be dealt with in the report, the obligation for which falls on the directors as a body. Thus a failure by the company to comply with section 157 renders every person who was a director immediately before the end of the relevant period liable to fine.[7] The only defences are for a director to prove that he took all reasonable steps for securing compliance with the statutory requirements, or that he reasonably believed that a reliable and competent person had been charged with securing compliance. Since some of the additional matters in section 16 concern a director's personal interest in contracts, it follows that a failure by an *individual* director to disclose his interest so that the requisite particulars are not included in the report, is inter alia *his* failure. The duty must therefore be regarded as a personal one.

Section 16(1)(c) required that where during a financial year a director had a 'material interest' in any contract (other than his contract of service),[8] which in the directors' opinion is significant in relation to the company's business, then the directors' report must have contained certain particulars about the contract. Under section 16(1)(d) where arrangements exist to which the company is a party and under which directors of the company are enabled to acquire benefits by means of the acquisition of shares or debentures in the company, particulars of such arrangements are also required.

Section 16(1)(c) has been repealed by the Companies Act 1980 and merged into a more elaborate set of provisions which require disclosure in the *accounts* of the company of details of a range of

6 Companies Act 1967, s. 15.
7 Ibid, s. 23, substituted by Companies Act 1976, Sch 2.
8 Although members of the company have a right of inspection of that under Companies Act 1967, s. 26. See also Companies Act 1980, s. 4.

transactions made with directors, shadow directors and connected persons. Section 16(1)(d) is unrepealed and remains an item for the directors' report.

5 Disclosure in accounts – the 1980 Act

SCOPE OF SECTION 54

The disclosure requirements of section 54 are one aspect only of the regulatory code contained in Part IV of the Companies Act 1980 which deals with specific situations where a director's duties and personal interests are at odds. Certain loans, quasi-loans and credit transactions (whether or not prohibited by section 49), together with transactions that would have fallen with section 16(1)(c), and some others, are to form notes to the accounts and fall under the scrutiny of the auditors as well as the shareholders. These provisions replace the disclosure requirement of section 197 of the Companies Act 1948, which were often circumvented because it imposed only aggregate disclosure.

Under section 54(1) a holding company is required to disclose in the group accounts, in respect of any financial year ending on or after the appointed day for the coming into force of the section,[9] the particulars mentioned in section 55 of:

(a) any transaction or arrangement[10] of a kind described in section 49 entered into by the company or by a subsidiary of the company for a person who was at any time during the financial year in respect of which the accounts were prepared a director of the company or connected with such director;

(b) any agreement by the company or by a subsidiary of the company to enter into any such transaction or arrangement for a person who was at any time during the financial year in respect of which the accounts were prepared a director of the company or connected with such director;

(c) any other transaction or arrangement with the company or with a subsidiary of the company in which a person, who was at any time during the financial year in respect of which the accounts were prepared a director of the company, had, directly or indirectly, a material interest.[11]

A similar requirement is imposed in relation to companies other than holding companies, those that produce accounts of their

9 22 December 1980.

10 A 'transaction' must be understood as a deal, not necessarily a formal contract, between two parties. An 'arrangement' is a wider term, covering a series of events possibly involving third parties, which brings a 'transaction' or contract about.

11 For the exact text, see p. 194, below.

own.[12] The reference in (a) above to section 49 is a reference to loans, quasi-loans and credit transactions, considered below, and (b), in referring to 'any such transaction or arrangement' is also a reference to section 49. Only section 54(1)(c) stands on its own and is concerned, as was its predecessor, with the concept of 'materiality' of interest.

CONNECTED PERSONS

It has been seen that shadow directors are treated as directors for the purposes of disclosure under the Companies Act 1948, section 199 as amended; so also are they treated for the purposes of the provisions[13] now under discussion.[14] In addition, section 54(1) refers to persons connected with a director and requires such persons to be placed on the same footing for disclosure purposes as the director himself. It should however be noted that the requirements[15] upon a director in such circumstances to secure compliance with the provisions of the Act in respect of any financial statements that are laid before the company in general meeting, or are filed, remains intact: he cannot say that it was up to the 'connected person' to make the necessary disclosure directly.

Under section 64(1), a person is connected with a director of the company if either

(a) he is (or she is) the director's spouse, child or stepchild; or
(b) he is (it is) a body corporate with which the director is associated; or
(c) he is a person acting as trustee of a trust, except in the case of an employees' share scheme or pension scheme; or
(d) he is a person acting in his capacity as a partner of the director concerned or of any person who is 'connected' under the rules above.

A person can be within one or more of the above categories, but not be connected, if he happens also to be a director of the company.[16]

Illustration X is controlling shareholder and managing director of the family firm X Co Ltd. X proposes that the company should obtain goods under a supply contract with X's son, S. S is a connected person (a fact which should be obvious from the name!) and so X must disclose the interest to the board. If S is

12 S. 54(2).
13 Except s. 54(1)(c) and (2)(c).
14 Companies Act 1980, s. 63(1).
15 Under the Companies Act 1948, ss. 149 and 150.
16 S. 64(1).

also a director, however, X will not be required to disclose, and that obligation will fall upon S himself. Also, if X is not a director but he 'controls' the board, he will be treated as a shadow director under section 63 and required to disclose under that heading.

It is necessary to give some further attention to defining the four categories. Thus (a) includes a separated spouse but not a former spouse. Category (b) includes any body corporate with which the director is 'associated'. The test of association is either by reference to an interest in shares or the exercise of control. If a director and the persons connected with him under section 64(1)(a), (c) and (d) above have an interest[17] in shares comprised in the equity share capital of a nominal value equal to at least one-fifth of that share capital, they are deemed to be associated. Also, if they are entitled to exercise or control the exercise of more than one-fifth of the voting power at any general meeting of the body corporate there is an association. As to category (c), trustees of fixed trusts the beneficiaries of which include the director himself, his spouse, or his children or an associated body corporate are included, as are trustees of discretionary trusts where they may appoint funds or interests in favour of any such persons.

LOANS AND SIMILAR TRANSACTIONS

Although the present chapter is concerned only with disclosure, some reference must be made to the categories of prohibited transactions under section 49[18] since section 54(1)(a) and (b) are made to apply to any transaction or arrangement 'of a kind' described in the earlier section. Restrictions concerning loans by a company to its directors and officers were previously contained in section 190 of the Companies Act 1948. These are entirely replaced by section 49.

A company, whether public or private, is prohibited by the section from making a loan to a person who is a director of the company or a director of its holding company. It is also prohibited from entering into a guarantee or providing any security in connection with a loan made by any person (e g a bank) to a director of the company or a director of its holding company.

Additionally, a 'relevant company', which broadly is a company within a group containing a public company,[19] is prohibited from making a 'quasi-loan' to a director or a connected person, or from

17 As defined in s. 28 of the Companies Act 1967.
18 For a full account, see Joffe *The Companies Act 1980* ch 9. See also Companies (No 2) Bill 1981, cl 100.
19 S. 65(1).

entering into any guarantee or providing any security concerning a loan or quasi-loan made to him.

By virtue of section 65(2)(a), a quasi-loan is a transaction under which one party ('the creditor') agrees to pay or pays otherwise than in pursuance of an agreement a sum for another, or agrees to reimburse the expenditure incurred by another and in either case:

(a) on terms that the borrower or a person on his behalf will reimburse the creditor; or
(b) in circumstances giving rise to a liability on the borrower to reimburse the creditor.

The main feature of this new unattractively styled concept is thus a 'bypass' arrangement whereby the company makes a payment to a third party on account of the liability incurred by the director, for which it expects repayment or in respect of which a deduction will subsequently be made if the expenditure is otherwise than for business purposes. If it did not expect repayment, it would of course be a gift or a 'float' for expenses. It is clear that the use by a director of a corporate credit card for personal purposes with deferred repayment arrangements, is a quasi-loan. Such an arrangement was not covered by section 190 of the Companies Act 1948. There are various anti-avoidance provisions.[20]

Similar to a quasi-loan is a credit transaction, defined by section 65(3) to include a transaction where the creditor supplies goods under a hire-purchase agreement or for periodical payments, or otherwise where payment is deferred. An example would be where a director is allowed to buy the company's own goods at a discount but does not have to pay for them until the end of the financial year.

A number of exceptions exist to these requirements, set out in section 50. These will be lawful transactions and arrangements which nonetheless fall to be disclosed under section 54.[21] These are:

(a) low value transactions;
(b) transactions between companies in the same group;
(c) transactions to enable directors to perform their duties;
(d) loans by money-lending companies; and
(e) certain credit transactions.

They apply in different ways to relevant and non-relevant companies.

OTHER TRANSACTIONS AND ARRANGEMENTS

Subject to certain exceptions, section 54(1)(c) and (2)(c) require disclosure in the group accounts or accounts prepared by any

20 See s. 49(3), (4).
21 Note that a transaction prohibited under s. 49 is still liable to be disclosed under s. 54(1) and (2): s. 54(7)(c).

company in respect of any relevant period or particulars of any transaction or arrangement with a company (or a subsidiary) *other than* a contract, arrangement or agreement relating to a loan or other transaction described in section 49. Here, the director concerned (or a director of a holding company) must be shown to have, directly or indirectly, a material interest. The rule also applies to connected persons.

By section 54(4)(b) an interest is deemed not to be material if the majority of the directors, other than the directors concerned, of the company preparing the accounts are of the opinion that the interest is not material. It will be recalled that, for disclosure in the directors' report under the Companies Act 1967, section 16(1)(c), materiality was considered alongside the significance of the contract in relation to the company's business. Such significance was a matter of subjective opinion but it did at least provide a yard-stick. Now the task appears more difficult. The Act refers not to a material contract, but to a material interest therein. It would thus appear that if the interest of a director is 100 per cent it must be a material interest even though the value of the contract is immaterial in relation to the affairs of the company. This may produce vexatious results:

> **Illustration** Director A loans his private car to a company for a fee, and the company allows him the use of it without charge as a perquisite. It is a contract in which the director has a material interest, *either* (a) because it is his car, or (b) because he is the only person to receive a fee for the hire, or (c) because he is the only person who will be allowed to drive it. The arrangement is subject to review by the board for the purposes of disclosure, and the test of materiality should not be affected by the amount of the fee and the length of the hire. Disclosure will be required whether the company is a multinational, with a turnover of £100 million per year, or a small private concern with £100,000. There will, however, be an exception from disclosure under the 'low value' provisions of section 58(3).

Those advising a board of directors may be uncertain if they should draw to the board's attention, as a formal item of business, transactions which appear to be small-scale. The directors cannot discharge their function under section 54 if they do not reach an opinion on materiality in good faith and in full knowledge of the circumstances of each individual transaction. However, two courses may be suggested:

(1) That transactions be referred, not immediately they occur, but at set intervals, the last referral being shortly before the

consideration of the report and accounts. This will enable relevant matters to be considered together.

(2) That details of all transactions be elicited from directors (for the purposes of the Companies Act 1948, section 199 as well as this section) and then subjected by the company secretary or other company officer to guidelines of materiality laid down by the board in advance. Any matter clearly within the guidelines, or on the border, can then be referred for express confirmation (or otherwise) that reference in the accounts will be required. In difficult cases the auditors should be consulted.

Transactions containing a personal element may be infrequent in many companies, and there should be no reason why all of these should not receive the consideration of their boards. Other companies, particularly those with a small number of controlling shareholders who may also be directors, may be prone to interest-contracts and it is essential that a proper system of 'vetting' be established.

PARTICULARS REQUIRED

Under section 55(1), the accounts for the relevant period must disclose the principal terms of the transaction, arrangement or agreement, and in particular contain:

(a) a statement that the transaction exists or existed during the financial year in question,[22] and
(b) the name of the person for whom it was made and, where this person is connected with a director, the name of such director;[1]

Thereafter disclosure depends upon the *type* of transaction:

(c) in the case of a director's material interest in a contract, the name of the director and the nature of the interest;[2]
(d) in the case of a loan or an agreement for a loan, or an arrangement within either section 49(3) or (4),[3]
    (i) the amount of the company's liability thereunder at the beginning and end of the relevant period;
    (ii) the maximum amount for which the company could be liable;
    (iii) the amount of any unpaid interest; and

22 S. 55(1)(a).
1 S. 55(1)(b).
2 S. 55(1)(c).
3 I e an assignment or back-to-back transaction.

(iv) the amount of any provision that the company has made in anticipation that the borrower will not discharge his liability.[4]

(e) in the case of any guarantee or security, the particulars set out in (i) and (ii) above and also a statement of any amount paid, and any liability incurred by the company in fulfilling the guarantee or discharging the security;[5]

(f) in the case of any other transaction, the *value* thereof must be expressed.[6]

The method of valuation can be complex. It is important not only in connection with disclosure but also for the purposes of ascertaining 'the aggregate of the relevant amounts' under the various loan exemptions contained in section 50, to see whether the permitted limits have been exceeded. Value is defined in section 65(4) and (5), in relation to the various types of transactions involved. Broadly, it is the principal amount of any loan, or the amount to be reimbursed of a quasi-loan, the amount of principal and interest guaranteed or secured; or, for any other transaction, the price that it is reasonable to expect could have been obtained for the goods, land or services if supplied elsewhere in the ordinary course of business. Where it is not possible to express the value of a transaction or arrangement in terms of a specific sum, that value is deemed to exceed £50,000.

All these details must be disclosed whether or not

(a) the transaction either is prohibited by section 49, or falls within one of the exceptions in section 50;

(b) the person for whom it was made either was a director, or was connected with a director at the time the transaction was made;

(c) a company was a subsidiary of the company at the time the transaction was made.[7]

Illustration X Limited becomes the guarantor of a lease of a flat to Y, an employee who is responsible for the rent. In the same financial year, Y becomes a director of either X Limited or X Limited's holding company. This is a credit transaction under section 65(3)(b), as the creditor (lessor) 'leases or hires any land or goods in return for periodic payments'. The giving of a guarantee by a company in respect of a credit transaction is one to which section 49 applies. Quite apart from its legality (which depends on the amount of the guarantee and whether or not X

4 S. 55(1)(d).
5 S. 55(1)(e).
6 S. 55(1)(f).
7 S. 54(7).

Limited is a 'relevant company'),[8] the transaction is liable to be disclosed under section 54, since Y is a director during some part of the relevant financial period. The particulars which must appear in the accounts are those prescribed by section 55(1)(a) (see above).

EXEMPTIONS FROM DISCLOSURE

The requirements of section 54(1) and (2) do not apply to certain transactions.

(1) *Intra-group trading* A transaction, arrangement, or agreement between one company and another, where a director of the first company (or the subsidiary or holding company) is interested merely by virtue of the fact that he is a director of the second company also, is not covered.[9]

(2) *Contract of service* Under section 26 of the Companies Act 1967, details of directors' service contracts are required to be open to inspection by shareholders. This requirement is extended[10] to include contracts with subsidiary companies and certain particulars of contract that require directors to work wholly or mainly overseas. This is felt to be sufficient disclosure and no reference in the accounts themselves need appear.[11] It may in future be considered desirable to include specific provision in directors' service agreements dealing with loans and other perquisites, so as to avoid the necessity for statutory publication. Similarly, when existing directors have no service agreements, but are simply governed by, and draw remuneration by virtue of, the Articles of Association, a company may consider the benefit of formalising the position.

(3) *Out-of-time transactions* An exemption applies to a transaction arrangement or agreement that was not entered into during the period and did not subsist at any time during the period. It should be pointed out that section 54(b)(c) uses the words '*or* did not subsist', but if the disjunctive approach is taken literally it would seriously undermine the presumed intention of the legislature. Thus a quasi-loan entered into before the commencement of a company's financial year in which the statutory appointed day fell, but which continued in existence throughout the relevant

8 See s. 49(2)(b) and s. 50(3).
9 S. 54(6)(a).
10 By s. 61(1) and (2).
11 S. 54(6)(b).

period, would not have to be disclosed because it satisfied the first extention of the sub-paragraph, although not the second. A better reading is to take the criterion as conjunctive, or as 'neither . . . nor'.[12]

Further, a transaction arrangement or agreement that was made before the appointed day, and did not subsist on or after the appointed day, is exempt.[13]

(4) *Aggregate transactions under £5,000* A financial threshold will prevent company accounts becoming clogged with details of small-scale commonplace transactions. The classes of these transactions are: credit transactions, or guarantees and securities associated therewith; and assignments and back-to-back arrangements concerning credit transactions.[14] The aggregate of the values of each transaction, arrangement or agreement made for the director or any person connected with him, less the amount (if any) by which the liabilities of the person for whom the transaction or arrangement was made had been reduced, must not at any time during the relevant period exceed £5,000.[15]

Illustration A company's financial year runs from 1 April to 31 March following. On 2 April, X, a director, is posted to the company's factory abroad and takes his company car with him. The company immediately agrees to hire for his wife, who also works for the company at its UK office, another car to facilitate her travel arrangements, a monthly deduction to be made from salary. This is a credit transaction and falls to be considered because X's wife is a 'connected person'. The value of the transaction, it is suggested, is the total amount of the hire charge (whether or not this is the scale of the monthly repayment) in the year. Suppose further, that after X's return he incurs car repair bills on his personal mileage which the company finances in the short term. This is again a credit transaction;[16] the value of which must be aggregated to see whether the limit of £5,000 is exceeded and hence disclosure required.

(5) *Interest contracts of limited value* Any transaction arrangement or agreement made by a company (or a subsidiary) for a person who, at any time during the financial year in respect of which the accounts were prepared, was a director and had a

12 See now Companies (No 2) Bill 1981, Sch 3, para 49(d).
13 S. 54(6)(d).
14 S. 58(2).
15 S. 58(1).
16 Example given in Parliamentary Debates, Standing Committee A, Eighth Sitting, 29 November 1979, cols 447–448.

material interest is exempted for the requirement of disclosure imposed by section 54(1)(c) and (2)(c) if the aggregate value of such transactions etc did not exceed £5,000 or 1 per cent of the value of the company's net assets at the end of the relevant period, whichever is the lower figure.[17] There is a threshold of £1,000, so that no transaction or series of transactions having a value below this sum fall to be disclosed.

OTHER MATTERS

In passing it should be noted that the above disclosure requirements are varied in the case of companies which are recognised banks.[18] Further, there is provision[19] for aggregate disclosure of transactions involving persons who are officers, but not directors, of a company.[20]

17 S. 58(3).
18 S. 57.
19 S. 56.
20 Note that certain further amendments to Part IV of the Companies Act 1980 are proposed in cl 100 and Sch 3 of the Companies (No 2) Bill 1981.

5 Remedies and reliefs

1 Extent of liabilities

A director who is in breach of statutory, common law, or equitable duties considered in chapters 2 and 3 becomes liable to civil process by the party to whom the particular duty is owed and who alleges that the relevant act or omission has caused him loss. If it is alleged that the whole board is to blame, then every director can be made a defendant. The type of legal remedy available depends both on the basis of the duty and the factual situation that has arisen. For example, if a director is proceeded against by the company on the grounds of his incompetence, the action is negligence-based and the normal remedy is damages, calculated according to the principles of remoteness and causation applicable in the general law of tort. In exceptional cases, where the damage is continuing or threatened the director concerned may be restrained by injunction as well. On the other hand, where a fiduciary duty is broken, such as the misappropriation of corporate property, the director becomes liable to pay compensation (the equitable equivalent of damages) but may have orders made against him for account of profits or for restoration of property if the property is traceable. Money payments may not be sufficient in such cases, since the commercial value of the property taken may be greater in the company's hands than a third party's e g document describing a secret industrial process. Also, the director may have disappeared or become insolvent, and the return of property in specie under principles of the law of trusts may be the only useful remedy.

The remedies will not always be available. A plaintiff company suing a managing director for damages for a serious breach of his contract of service, may fail because it has not mitigated the loss he has caused. An action for injunction to restrict a board from acting beyond its powers may be barred by lapse of time or knowledge of the circumstances, leaving only a claim for compensation. Restoration of property or rescission of a contract is impossible if the property has become physically mixed with other property or the contract in question has been postponed. These are failures of process. A second limitation on liability is provided by the conduct of the director himself, who may demonstrate that he has acted honestly and reasonably so as to come within the statutory protection of e g section 448 of the Companies Act 1948, or an indemnity in the Articles of Association e g article 136 of Table A. He may also be able to claim contribution from fellow misfeasors.

2 Remedies of company

IN CONTRACT

Directors as such have an agency relationship with the company. Although bound by the articles, they are not deemed to be parties to the contract that arises out of the articles between the shareholders.[1] This is thought to be so even if the directors are also shareholders. Quite often, particularly in smaller concerns certain of the terms upon which one or more directors, or specific office-holders such as the managing director, are appointed are set out in the articles.

These, however only amount to a direction to the company to comply with them, and are not necessary evidence of a separate contract of engagement.[2] Whether such a contract can be implied in the absence of express agreement, by both parties acting consistently with the terms (e g as to payment of remuneration or reasonable attendance at the company's premises) is unlikely unless there are also present certain common incidents of the normal employer-employee relationship.[3]

A director or office-holder may hold a service agreement with the company, in which case he is an ordinary employee. He has a right to be furnished with written particulars of his employment not later than thirteen weeks from commencing employment[4] and he will have the benefit of the employment protection legislation as regards unfair dismissal and redundancy. A material breach of the express terms of the agreement or of the fiduciary or other duties of office which may be said to underpin it, will entitle the company to terminate either summarily or on notice.

The effect of removal of a director by ordinary resolution of the company in general meeting under section 184 of the Companies

1 As to which see s. 20, Companies Act 1948.
2 *Boston Deep Sea Fishing and Ice Co v Ansell* (1888) 39 ChD 339 at 360.
3 As to which, see e g 16 Halsburys' Laws of England (4th edn) 501 – 502. As to inference of contract, see *Browning v Great Central Mining Co of Devon* (1860) 5 H & N 856.
4 S. 1, Employment Protection (Consolidation) Act 1978.

Act 1948 has been considered in chapter 1, section 6.[5] When the contract is for a fixed term, the question whether compensation is payable to the director for premature determination is decided in the same way as any other employment contract. Thus, if the employers' dismissal is justified no claim will lie at common law for compensation other than accrued remuneration.

In *Boston Deep Sea Fishing and Ice Company v Ansell*[6] the defendant was employed as managing director of a newly-formed company for five years at a yearly salary. The defendant, on behalf of the company, contracted for the construction of certain fishing smacks, but, unbeknown to the company, took personal commission from the shipbuilders.

Held: as the receipt of the commission was a good ground for dismissal, the defendant was not merely obliged to account to the company for the monies received, but was entitled to no compensation.

The contractual relationship between employer and employee gives rise to certain implied obligations, again no different for a director than for other persons, and indeed similar to the duties of an agent already noted.[7] Thus the employee must act in a reasonable manner and he must give personal service in the performance of his office. He is bound to obey reasonable instructions that are within the scope of his employment, and he must exercise good faith. There is also an obligation not to be careless. This is understood either to mean that a person possessing a particular skill fails to show it (i e the sense considered in chapter 3), or that a person possesses the necessary skill – or at least competence – but departs from it on one or more occasions, usually so as to damage the employer's property or interests.[8] Whether dismissal is justified on the second interpretation will always be a question of fact and degree.

The common law employment contract is much affected by statute. If a director holding a service agreement is dismissed, the company will have to show that the dismissal was 'fair' within the Employment Protection (Consolidation) Act 1978, otherwise there will be a claim for unfair dismissal. The mode of dismissal can be important. A person dismissed without notice, or without the opportunity to answer or remedy the complaints made against him, may have a cause of action even if there were good grounds for disposing of his services. Thus if the articles of a company[9] provide

5 P. 19, above.
6 Above.
7 Ch 2, pp. 23–24.
8 *Baster v London and County Printing Works* [1899] QB 901.
9 But not Table A, art 88.

for the vacation of office of a director if all his fellow directors so resolve, and this power is exercised, then not only may damages be payable for breach of a fixed term contract, but a claim for unfair dismissal may arise under the Act. Whether or not the dismissal is 'fair' is a large question to which the reader must stand referred to the works on employment law.[10]

Redundancy, in the statutory sense that the employer has ceased or intends to cease to carry on the business, or the need for employees to do a particular type of work has diminished or is expected to diminish, is prima facie a valid ground for dismissal. In such a case the director will become entitled to a redundancy payment, and this is not treated as 'compensation for loss of office' which is restricted under section 191 – 194 of the Companies Act 1948. A director *as such* has no right to these protections:[11] they are only available by virtue of the employment relationship which the company has chosen to expressly create or impliedly recognise.

IN NEGLIGENCE

A breach of the duty to exercise reasonable care, diligence and skill is actionable in damages by the company at common law. The measure of damages is either the loss sustained by the company or the profit which the director has made. Where a claim is based on misrepresentation, the measure of damages is normally the difference between the value of an asset or securities stated by the director concerned, and its real value.[12]

Reported instances of negligence by itself are relatively few, perhaps because of the lack of a completely objective test of skill;[13] more actions involved a breach of some fiduciary obligation where liability is easier to establish. Indeed there may be advantages in not pursuing a common law claim alone since the quantum of damages may be greater where the equitable obligation of a fiduciary to restore assets is shown.[14]

Honesty on the part of the directors will not relieve them of liability for negligence where they know an act is ultra vires the company:

> The directors entered into an agreement with a contractor who was to carry out certain works in return for shares and

10 E g Rideout *Principles of Labour Law* (3rd edn) pp. 89 – 119.
11 *Parsons v Albert J Parsons & Sons Ltd* [1979] IRLR 117.
12 *Exploring Land and Minerals Co Ltd v Kolckmann* (1905) 94 LT 234.
13 Cf *Hedley Byrne & Co v Heller* [1964] AC 465.
14 *Bartlett v Barclays Bank Trust Co Ltd (Nos 1 and 2)* [1980] 2 WLR 430 at 451.

debentures, some of which were under separate agreements to be issued to third parties without consideration.

Held: it was beyond the scope of a company to make over securities without consideration, and the directors were liable in negligence for failing reasonably to exercise their legal powers and avoid the mistake.[15]

But where honesty is coupled with the exercise of reasonable care having regard to the director's knowledge and experience, it will be sufficient to avoid liability.[16]

Negligent omission carries the same liability:

A company was formed to develop landed estates. Reports and balance sheets were issued and dividends and bonuses paid on alleged profits, although in fact these were payments out of capital. The directors did not go into the accounts (which omitted some significant liabilities), but relied on the secretary who had produced them. Auditors and accountants had been employed, but no proper valuations of the assets were made or ordered.

Held: the directors were personally liable for the dividends and bonuses together with interest, since they had not procured the giving of accurate financial information to the shareholders and the payments could not be justified.[17]

It may, however, be perfectly reasonable to rely on subordinates to perform specific tasks.[18]

BREACH OF FIDUCIARY DUTY

(1) *Personal advantage*

A director cannot enter into a contract for his own advantage.[19] Where he has an interest, any profit belongs to the company in the absence of disclosure and consent. Thus a director was held accountable for a profit made by selling his own goods to the company, even though the company was aware of his interest and the goods were such that the company would anyway have required them.[20] A director who agreed to place the shares of a company with customers of his own company was held accountable for the

15 *London Trust Co Ltd v MacKenzie* (1893) 62 LJ Ch 870 (statutory misfeasance).

16 *Overend & Gurney Co v Gibb* (1872) LR 5 HL 480; *Lagunas Nitrate Co v Lagunas Syndicate* [1899] 2 Ch 392; *Re National Bank of Wales Ltd* [1899] 2 Ch 629; *Ammonia Soda Co v Chamberlain* [1918] 1 Ch 266; *Re City Equitable Fire Insurance Co* [1925] 1 Ch 407.

17 *Municipal Freehold Land Co Ltd v Pollington* (1890) 59 LJ Ch 734; also *Rance's Case* (1870) 6 Ch App 104.

18 *Huckerby v Elliott* [1970] 1 All ER 189.

19 *Flanagan v Great Western Rly Co* (1868) LR 7 Eq 116.

20 *Albion Steel Wire Co v Martin* (1875) 1 ChD 580.

commission he received.[21] Where a director subscribes for shares himself at par, when their real value is above par, he is liable for the difference.[1] Where promoters have given him money, so that his ability to negotiate sales of property by such promoters is compromised, it belongs to the company.[2]

Further examples of profits resulting from arrangements of this kind are considered in chapter 2, section 4.

Not all profits will be liable to be surrendered. Where directors exercise their powers for the benefit of the company, at the same time securing a personal advantage, this is not evidence of abuse. The obtaining of a valuation of the company's assets which had the effect of uplifting the value of its shares, so enabling the directors to sell their own holdings at a profit, was held not to be a breach of trust and therefore not to give rise to a liability to account for the monies received.[3] Similarly where directors, within borrowing powers, issued debentures at 7½ per cent discount and some were taken up by one of their number, it was held that the issue was not illegal, and no account was required of the difference between 92½ per cent and par.[4] On the same principle, directors would not be liable if, on a rights issue of shares made to the general body of shareholders, they were able themselves to take up the rights at a price less than the market value.

Questions may arise where it is sought to make the director accountable after he has resigned office. A fiduciary obligation owed to the company ceases when the relationship from which it derives is terminated. Thus a director who acquires special skill or knowledge while in office, and is prohibited at that time from using it on his own account (because of the exclusivity of the relationship), is not bound to pay over to the company earnings or profits which he enjoys as a result of an activity carried on later.[5] Any restriction on such activity would have to be imposed as a result of an express covenant contained in the contract of service. However, where a director acts improperly, or in abuse of his power, while in office, and realises on a profit after ceasing to hold the office in such a manner that he would be accountable if he was still a director, then he will be accountable notwithstanding his resignation.

In *Cranleigh Precision Engineering Ltd v Bryant*,[6] a director developed a piece of equipment and resigned from his company

21 *Imperial Mercantile Credit Association v Coleman* (1873) LR 6 HL 189.
1 *Shaw v Holland* [1900] 2 Ch 305.
2 *Nant-y-Glo and Blaina Ironworks Co v Grave* (1878) 12 ChD 738.
3 *Hirsche v Sims* [1894] AC 654.
4 *Re Compagnie Generale de Bellegarde, Cambell's Case* (1876) 4 ChD 470.
5 *Nordisk Insulinlaboratorium v C L Bencard (1934) Ltd* [1953] 1 All ER 986.
6 [1964] 3 All ER 289, [1965] 1 WLR 1293.

to exploit it commercially by taking (through his own company) an exclusive licence from the original patentor. He argued that since no licence was in existence while he was a director, there could be no objection to him appropriating the development of the equipment to his own advantage.

Held: he was accountable, even after resignation, and that he had been in breach of his fiduciary duty to the company from the outset by not revealing the discovery of the patent and using his best endeavours to obtain a licence under it. Consequently, he continued to be liable as a constructive trustee for benefit subsequently received.

The consent of the company, either through the articles or the general meeting, may be sufficient to allow a director to retain profits made in these circumstances, provided full disclosure of the material facts is made known.[7]

(2) *Other default*

A director may be liable even if no personal advantage accrues from his breach of duty. The appropriate remedy is not an account of profits, but compensation corresponding to the amount of loss sustained by the company as a result of the breach of trust. In some cases, of course, the advantage secured is one that may be attributed to the director anyway, e g because the 'beneficiary' is a member of his family.[8] But a company may seek to impose liability as a result of breaches of duty by co-directors or subordinate officers, or because the board as a whole has permitted some outsider to gain in circumstances where the proper exercise of trusteeship would have protected the company's property. This is a clear indication that a director is not merely required to prevent conflict between his interest and his duty, but to act at all times bona fide in the interest of the company as well.

A special resolution of an insurance company was passed that 50 per cent of the premiums paid on life policies should be invested in gilts with trustees. Trustees were appointed and a prospectus issued stating that premiums would be applied in this way.

Held: that the directors were liable to account (i e provide compensation) in the winding up to the extent of the funds not invested, and invested but applied for the general purposes of the company, and such liability was for a 'misfeasance or breach of trust in relation to the company'.[9]

7 *Kaye v Croydon Tramways Co* [1898] 1 Ch 358.

8 *Re Crenver and Wheal Abraham United Mining Co, ex parte Wilson* (1872) 8 Ch App 45 (shares allotted to infant son).

9 *Re British Guardian Life Assurance Co* (1880) 14 ChD 335.

Shortly before the incorporation of the company the directors agreed that S, the promoter, should be made £3,500 for preliminary expenses. No vouchers were produced for such expenses and no further enquiries made, but S used part of the money to pay the calls on the directors' qualification shares. The company was later wound up.

Held: the directors were jointly and severally liable to repay the expenses, on the grounds that the money was paid to provide the directors' qualifications, and in the circumstances they had not exercised sufficient care and caution in examining the propriety of paying. The expenses were therefore a misapplication of the company's assets.[10]

The loss caused to the company may be too remote to recover, or it may be impossible to attribute it to a particular director:

In successive balance sheets the value of a company's stock-in-trade was greatly overstated, due to false certificates provided by one of the directors who was also the manager of the company's business. Dividends were paid on the footing that the balance sheets were correct. Even despite the overstatements, the company was not insolvent until the last year of its operation. In the subsequent winding up it was sought to make the directors liable for the dividends, and for damages alleged to have resulted on the footing that the accounts were correct.

Held: the directors (except the manager) were not liable for the dividend; and the additional damages claim was too remote, and they were not recoverable.[11]

Since such a claim amounts to a breach of trust, no limitation period applies.[12]

STATUTE

In a winding up a director is liable to proceedings under section 333 of the Companies Act 1948 for misfeasance, a composite term to cover all actionable breaches of duty involving misapplication of assets. The liquidator may apply to have the director examined on questions of fact and law and the court may make an order for restoration of property or repayment of money, or for compensation to increase the company's assets available in the liquidation. The remedy is not available where the cause of action is negligence

10 *Re Englefield Colliery Co* (1878) 8 ChD 338.
11 *Re Kingston Cotton Mill Co (No 2)* [1896] 1 Ch 331.
12 *Re Exchange Banking Co, Flitcroft's Case* (1882) 21 ChD 519.

alone i e it is not an appropriate forum to assess common law damages.[13] Nor does it create any new statutory rights, either as regards to the kind of liability which may attach to a director, or the persons who have a right to sue. Unlike a common law claim, however, the court has a discretion: in one case the court refused relief where the only persons having a pecuniary interest were the shareholders and it was demonstrated that the majority of these were prepared to waive the claim.[14] The amount of compensation required to be paid may also be reduced.[15] It is no defence that the alleged misfeasance was committed after the defendant had ceased to be a director, if he himself was a party to it.[16]

Under section 37 of the Companies Act 1967, the Department of Trade may institute proceedings in the name of a company against a director, following the report of an inspector or an inspection of the company's books and papers.

Section 332 of the Companies Act 1948[17] provides that if, in the course of the winding up of a company, it appears that any business has been carried on with intent to defraud creditors or for any fraudulent purposes, the court may on the application of the Official Receiver, the liquidator, a creditor or member, declare that any persons who were knowingly parties to the fraud shall be personally responsible, without any limitation of liability, for all or any of the debts or other liabilities of the company. Like section 333, this provision is not restricted to directors, but they are the commonest defendants in practice. While all successful claims will involve showing a serious breach of fiduciary duty, it is clear that not every breach is within the scope of the section, since it is necessary to show 'actual dishonesty involving, according to current notions of fair trading among commercial men, real moral blame'.[18] Monies recovered will be held for the general body of creditors, and so section 332 is not of advantage to a particular claimant. It is , nevertheless, a useful statutory procedure in circumstances where a general claim for negligence or breach of trust might be thought difficult to establish.[19]

13 *Re B Johnson (Builders) Ltd* [1955] Ch 634, [1955] 2 All ER 775.
14 *Re Sunlight Incandescent Gas Lamp Co Ltd* [1900] 2 Ch 728.
15 *Re Alexandra Palace Co* (1882) 21 ChD 149.
16 *Curtis's Furnishing Stores Ltd v Freedman* [1966] 2 All ER 955, [1966] 1 WLR 1219.
17 As amended by cl 88 of the Companies Bill 1981.
18 *Re William C Leitch Bros Ltd* [1932] 2 Ch 71 at 79.
19 See Gower *Modern Company Law* (4th edn) p. 115, where it is explained how it was intended to widen the scope of the provision in 1973.

3 Remedies by others

IN CONTRACT

A director may contract with a third party so as to make himself, rather than his company, liable. This can occur in two ways. First, the director can deliberately agree to accept liability simply because the third party will not accept the standing of the company itself. He may personally guarantee the company's overdraft or accept goods for use in the company's business in his own name, making personal payments to the supplier and hoping to recover this in due course from the profits of the company. This situation is common with small enterprises with a low credit rating.

Secondly, a contract may have been made with a third party and it is unclear who is liable, the directors, the company, or both. Thus if a director makes a contract in his own name, without disclosing that he is acting for the company, then applying the rule of the undisclosed principal from the law of agency, he becomes personally liable. If he contracts in his own name, but making it clear he is acting as agent, the company is liable. Where the words used are such that it is not clear to the third party that only the company is to be bound, then the director himself may sue and be sued. It is thus most important for directors wishing to restrict their exposure to ensure that the terms of any agreement are such that their representative capacity is established expressly or by necessary implication. A contract signed by 'X, a director of YZ Co Ltd' but not on paper headed with the company's name, is nevertheless an indication that the director is not the principal. However, where a director says 'I, being a director of AB Co Ltd, hereby agree . . .' there is the opposite presumption, since the description of his office is not inconsistent with the acceptance of personal liability.

In certain circumstances the liability will arise even if the director has expressly contracted as agent.[20] Section 108(4) of the Companies Act 1948 provides where directors have signed or authorised the signature on behalf of a company of any bill of exchange, promissory note, cheque or order for goods or money, and the name of the company is not mentioned thereon in legible characters, they shall be personally liable to the holder unless it is paid by the company.[21] Liability has been established where the word 'Limited' has been omitted, or the company identified by a wrong name.[22]

20 For pre-incorporation contracts, see *Gore-Browne on Companies* (43rd edn) para 8–7.
21 *British Airways Board v Parish* [1979] Ll L Rep 361.
22 See e g *Durham Fancy Goods Ltd v Michael Jackson (Fancy Goods) Ltd* [1968] 2 QB 839, [1968] 2 All ER 987.

MISREPRESENTATION

(1) *Generally*

A director cannot shelter under the umbrella of his company if he commits a wrongful act in the course of his duties. Thus, if he is guilty of fraud or misrepresentation or other tort, he will be personally liable, although the company may be liable as well. A frequently occurring instance of a director's liability for fraud or misrepresentation is in relation to the contents of a company's prospectus. This is considered in detail below. However, statements made by a board, whether oral or in writing, can induce an outsider to act in a variety of ways towards the company, not merely to purchase shares, and if loss results the outsider has a claim against those responsible. Thus where directors represented to the shareholders that it was necessary to secure the consent of the majority of the shareholders in order to effect an amalgamation, and induced the plaintiffs to grant them options to purchase their shares so that thereafter they could exercise the same and make a profit for themselves, it was held that they were trustees of the profit for the plaintiffs' benefit (not the company's).[2]

In all cases where misrepresentation is alleged it is necessary to show that reliance has been placed by the plaintiff on a false statement of fact made fraudulently, negligently or innocently by the defendant and that loss and damage has been occasioned thereby. The remedy available will depend upon the type of misrepresentation that has occurred.[3]

(2) *In prospectus*

If an invitation to subscribe for shares or debentures which contains false statements is made by a company or any other person, both civil and criminal proceedings may be taken against all those who are responsible for them. We are here concerned only with the civil remedies available by outsiders and shareholders against the director. If a shareholder wishes to rescind a contract of allotment to take securities, he will of course proceed against the company, since the directors do not make allotments on their own behalf. Remedies in damages for consequential loss, as an alternative to rescission, lie against the directors, though they may also lie against the company under the principle of vicarious liability.

Actionable misrepresentation consists of a false statement of fact, addressed to the plaintiff by the company or the person who offers the shares or debentures, whereby the plaintiff is induced to subscribe (i e enter into a contract) for the securities concerned. The

1 *Cullen v Thomson's Trustees* (1862) 4 Macq 424.
2 *Allen v Hyatt* (1914) 30 TLR 444, PC.
3 See Cheshire and Fifoot *Law of Contract* (9th edn) pp. 256–262.

shareholder may maintain an action for the tort of deceit (i e fraud) against the directors for bringing about this result. The liability is established where a purchaser, relying on the misrepresentation, can show that the directors intended to deceive and that the offending statements were wilful and fraudulent.[4] In an action for deceit it is necessary to prove actual fraud. Where a managing director, without any fraudulent intention, made a statement which was not true as to the receipt of information affecting the prospects of the company, whereby a shareholder was induced to sell at a lower price, it was held that an action against the director to recover the difference between the actual price received and the market value, could not be maintained.[5]

Misrepresentation may be aimed at securing a Stock Exchange quotation. Where the chairman of a mining company secured a quotation by falsely representing that two-thirds of the shares had been taken up, the plaintiff, a purchaser relying on this assumption, was held to have a right of action against the chairman for damages.[6]

The general test as to whether an individual shareholder can sue a director for misconduct is, if the transaction is such that the body of the shareholders could not have sanctioned it.[7] This would be the case, where false reports or accounts are produced, which are intended to be sent to individual shareholders and invest them with a misleading impression of the state of affairs of the company.

In *Davidson v Tulloch*[8] D and other directors of a bank systematically published false and fraudulent reports and made dividends purporting to be out of profits, while in reality the bank was insolvent.

Held: an action lay against D, at the suit of a shareholder, to recover damages for loss sustained in purchasing shares on the faith of such reports, and also to recover damages in respect of D's misconduct in misapplying the funds while shareholders continued to hold the shares.

The fact that a subscriber cannot rescind the allotment of the shares or debentures will not prevent him suing for damages for deceit,[9] except where he has actually subscribed for shares and is suing the company.[10]

4 *Eaglesfield v Marquis of Londonderry* (1876) 4 ChD 693 at 708.
5 *Tackey v McBain* [1912] AC 186.
6 *Bagshaw v Seymour* (1858) 32 LTOS 81.
7 See also *Prudential Assurance Co Ltd v Newman Industries Ltd* (1981) Times 30 July, CA (suing the company).
8 (1860) 2 LT 97.
9 *Peek v Gurney* (1873) LR 6 HL 377.
10 *Houldsworth v City of Glasgow Bank and Liquidators* (1880) 5 App Cas 317.

The amount of money which the plaintiff can recover is calculated as the difference between the price actually paid for the securities the subject of the misstatement, and their real value at the time of acquisition.[11] No remedy is available for prospective profits, i e increases in the value of the securities either determinate or indeterminate predicted by the prospectus or to be inferred from the favourable information which it contains.

NEGLIGENCE

As a result of the House of Lords' judgment in *Derry v Peek*,[12] the legal onus on a plaintiff became dependent on alleging fraud, which expression includes recklessness of intention. As a matter of evidence it is always difficult to convince a court of this level of culpability. The modern law of negligence has, however, developed in two ways to offer the chance of remedy where a less culpable intention on the part of the directors (or others responsible) can be shown. The first of these is the Misrepresentation Act 1967. Under section 2(1), if a person enters into a contract after a misrepresentation has been made to him by another party thereto, such that the misrepresentor would have been liable in damages had the misrepresentation been made fraudulently, he shall be liable notwithstanding that it is *not* made fraudulently. This 'fiction of fraud' operates unless the defendant can show that he believed, on reasonable grounds, that the facts that he represented were true. Even if the misrepresentation falls within the latter category, i e it is non-negligent, a plaintiff can still ask for damages in lieu of rescission under section 2(2) of the Act.

The effect of these provisions may be illustrated as follows. If a company issues a prospectus on a new issue of shares, complying with Schedule 4 of the Companies Act 1948 as to the matters to be included and any relevant Stock Exchange requirements, it will need to state, inter alia, particulars of 'material contracts' entered into by the company. Suppose the directors suppress information about a contract under which the company may or has incurred substantial liabilities, so as to reduce the net asset position of the business and the attractiveness of the new shares on offer. This is sheer fraud, and the tort of deceit will apply. Suppose, however, the particulars are left off because the board have carelessly omitted to check the final proof of the circular. The shareholder will now be able to claim damages against *the company*, on the fiction of fraud, for any loss suffered. It in turn may have remedies against solicitors, bankers and accountants who shared responsibility for

11 *McConnel v Wright* [1903] 1 Ch 546.
12 (1889) 14 App Cas 337.

producing the circular. It is difficult to see how such a misrepresentation or omission could be wholly innocent for the purposes of section 2(2) of the Act.

The other development is the recent acceptance by the courts that a common law liability for negligence can arise wherever statements are made by company officers to outsiders in situations of reliance.[13] The remedies under the Misrepresentation Act 1967 only apply where a contract has been entered into, and also against 'the other party thereto', which appears to rule out directors, who are deemed to be acting only as agents for the company. If it is desired to sue directors for negligent misstatement, therefore, it must be on common law basis. The extent of this liability, while not fully worked out, is founded on a special relationship between a person who asks for information and advice and the person who gives it, in circumstances where it is reasonable to rely on what is said.[14] It thus goes beyond contractual positions to cover information presented 'unsolicited' in a prospectus. It is this sanction which nowadays demands that directors, whether acting as a board or individually, exercise the greatest caution in offering statements to shareholders and others which (since the directors are insiders) are likely to be taken as sound and accurate, causing the addressees to change their legal position in reliance on the information given.

BREACH OF FIDUCIARY DUTY

As mentioned below[15] outsiders and members of a company may occasionally be able to show that duties are owed to them directly, and that their rights to sue the board are not merely derivative. The creation of this special relationship, analogous to that in the law of negligence, depends upon the assumption by the directors of a fiduciary responsibility in connection with a particular transaction, e g where they agree to act as agents for the shareholders in negotiating a take-over bid. It will not be necessary for the plaintiffs to sue in the names of the company. The position may be contrasted with that obtaining in the United States, where judicial interpretation of provisions of the Securities Exchange Act 1934 has given rise to a general duty owed by directors to all those with whom they have dealings in their company's securities. Meanwhile, it might be possible in the Articles of Association of a UK company to insert an express provision whereby the directors are constituted trustees

13 *Hedley Byrne & Co Ltd v Heller & Partners Ltd* [1964] AC 465, [1963] 2 All ER 575. For negligence other than misstatement, see *Fairline Shipping Corpn v Adamson* [1975] 2 QB 180.

14 For a recent application of the test see *J E B Fasteners* [1981] Com LR 116 (auditors).

15 See ch 6, pp. 110–111, above.

of the individual shareholders, as well as the company's assets. Although the articles do not bind the directors contractually such a provision might give rise to an obligation similar to that of a constructive trustee.

STATUTE

(1) *Prospectus*

In addition to the remedies discussed above, a person who is induced to subscribe for securities by means of false statements in a prospectus has the option of a claim for compensation under section 43 of the Companies Act 1948. The remedy is limited to direct subscription from the company, and does not cover transfer of shares already in issue which are nonetheless induced by circulars. There is, however, deemed to be a direct subscription where the shares are offered for sale through an issuing house or placed through a broker.

The claim lies against any person who allowed his name to be associated with the prospectus, and against every director of the company holding office when the prospectus was issued, whether he was expressly associated with it or not; also any promoter of the company and every person who has authorised the issue of the document.[16] No claim lies against the company itself, the object of the Act being to attribute blame where it lies rather than create an umbrella under which individual wrongdoers could shelter. Where it is sought to render an expert, e g solicitor or auditor, liable on the basis that he authorised the issue of the document, the liability will be limited to the matters contained in the experts report. This is not the case for a director or promoter.

A plaintiff jumps several of the same hoops as he would if the action were for deceit. It is necessary to show (1) an actual subscription, (2) a false statement, (3) reliance, and (4) consequential loss. He is not immediately concerned with the state of mind or intention of the defendant. The measure of damages is the same. In other respects, however, the claim is more akin to a Misrepresentation Act negligence suit, on account of the statutory defences which are available. Most of section 43 is concerned with these, which broadly differentiate between experts and others.

An expert (defined in section 40 as including an engineer, valuer, accountant and any other person whose profession gives authority to a statement made by him) may show:

(a) that having given his consent to the issue of prospectus, he withdrew it in writing before delivery of a copy of the document for registration; or

16 S. 43(1)(a)–(d).

(b) that after delivery but before allotment of shares, he withdrew his consent having become aware of the untrue statement and gave reasonable notice of such withdrawal; or

(c) that he was competent to make the statement or report complained of, and believed it to be true on reasonable grounds up to the time the plaintiff's shares or debentures were allotted.

The non-expert may show:

(a) that the untrue statement was contained in the expert's report which had not been withdrawn, and the defendant reasonably believed that the expert was competent to make the particular statement; or

(b) that the statement was one made by an official person or was an extract from a public official document; or

(c) the defendant believed the statement to be true on reasonable grounds up to the time when the plaintiff's shares or debentures were allotted; or

(d) having consented to become a director of the company, he withdrew his consent to act before the prospectus was issued, and did not authorise its issue; or

(e) that, being a director or promoter, he did not consent to the issue of the prospectus, and as soon as possible after becoming aware of its issue, he gave notice of his lack of consent; or

(f) that he became aware of the falsity of a statement after issue of the prospectus, but before any share or debentures were allotted he withdrew his consent and gave reasonable public notice.

'Reasonable public notice' is nowhere defined in the Act, but a director would have to issue a newspaper advertisement or cause a circular letter to be sent to the known addressees of the prospectus.

(2) *Section 38*

Section 38 of the 1948 Act provides for the particulars to be included in a prospectus relating to securities which are not similar to those already issued and listed on the Stock Exchange. A director or other responsible person can be made liable for non-compliance with the requirements unless, as with section 43, he can show certain defences.[17] The matters to be stated are those set out in Schedule 4 of the Act. The defences are (1) that the director was not aware of any matters omitted, or (2) that the non-compliance or contravention arose from an honest mistake.

17 See *Re South of England Natural Gas and Petroleum Co Ltd* [1911] 1 Ch 573.

(3) *Miscellaneous provisions*
The Companies Act 1948 provides the directors who are in default shall be personally liable to outsiders in the following cases:

(1) on an irregular allotment, to an allottee if loss or damage can be shown.[18]
(2) in the case of failure to repay application money for shares if the minimum subscription has not been subscribed.[19]
(3) in the case of failure to repay application money for shares if permission for the shares to be dealt with on the Stock Exchange is not given.[20]

4 Types of remedies available

DAMAGES AND COMPENSATION

These have already been considered.

ACCOUNT

This has already been considered at pp. 32–36, above.

There is a strict liability to pay over profits actually received as a result of abuse of a fiduciary position. The liability may arise either because of a director's interest in a contract with the company, or because he has used his position to effect a profitable arrangement with a third party. The company's right to an account will be lost if it does not exercise the right to rescind the contract or is otherwise debarred by lapse of time or acquiescence.[21] Because the director is being treated as a trustee and therefore the advantage he has obtained notionally belongs to the trust, it will be unnecessary for the plaintiff company to show that it has suffered actual loss, and this is the distinguishing feature from a claim for compensation or damages.

TRACING ASSETS

As a director is in control of the company's property, it may be possible on a misapplication of assets to sue for recovery of the property in its existing state:

> The plaintiff company entrusted £80,000 to T, its auditor, which he paid into his personal overdrawn bank account. T subsequently diverted part of the sum for unauthorised

18 S. 49(2).
19 S. 47.
20 S. 51.
21 *Hely-Hutchinson v Brayhead Ltd* [1968] 1 QB 549, [1967] 3 All ER 98, CA.

purchases. The plaintiff obtained a personal judgment against T, who was later also found guilty of fraudulent conversion. The defendant of the present claim was a company of which T was a director, and to whom some of the misappropriated money was paid. It was alleged that the company had knowledge of the fraud of T and became a trustee for the plaintiffs of the cash. Consequently it was recoverable in rem under the equitable remedy of tracing.

Held: that although the fact that T was a director was not itself sufficient to impute to the defendant company notice of the irregular payment, the company was liable to account to the plaintiffs, since they had failed to show that they were innocent volunteers having acted in good faith.[1]

The extent to which money or other property can be recovered in this fashion is entirely governed by the equitable rules relating to trustees.[2] Tracing is possible even if the original property has been disposed of, since if shares are sold and the proceeds used to buy a house, the house is clearly identifiable. On the other hand, if the monies are used up in living expenses by the director, they cannot be traced. More difficult questions arise when trust money is mixed with other monies in a bank account or other blended fund. In these circumstances it is for the person in a fiduciary position to prove what is trust property and what is his own; and if he cannot distinguish them the whole will be treated as trust property.[3] Because the remedy is founded on equitable principles the company will be unable to recover the property where it would be unjust to do so, so that the right to trace cannot be exercised against a bona fide purchaser for value without notice of the equity.[4]

Where the property clearly belongs to the company, there is no difficulty in recovering it, subject to the above. On the other hand, where what is alleged is a misuse of confidential information by the director in his fiduciary capacity, it is harder to show that there is any right to recover in rem at all, since if the information never 'belonged' to the company in any real sense, there is nothing to repossess. The personal remedy of account circumvents this difficulty. But there may be occasions where it is more valuable, particularly if the director is not worth suing, to attach a claim to the intangible property which has been exploited. In one case[5] it has

1 *G L Baker Ltd v Medway Building and Supplies Ltd* [1958] 3 All ER 540, [1958] 1 WLR 1216.
2 As to which, see Snell *Principles of Equity* (27th edn) pp. 284–292.
3 *Re Tilley's Wills Trust* [1967] 2 Ch 1179, [1967] 2 All ER 303.
4 *Re Diplock, Diplock v Wintle* [1948] Ch 465, [1948] 2 All ER 318.
5 *Boardman v Phipps* [1967] 2 AC 46 at 128.

been said that corporate information is not property in any normal sense but that equity will restrain its transmission to another if there has been a breach of some confidential relationship. This point is particularly relevant when considering a director's duty not to make use of inside information in relation to shares or other securities held by him, an aspect considered in the next chapter. Some authorities, on the other hand, have gone as far as saying that information confidential to the company, without being registered as a copyright or patent, is a species of asset and therefore capable of protection and recovery.[6]

INJUNCTION

An injunction is an equitable remedy compelling the defendant to do some act or to refrain from acting or continuing to act. Where damages are an adequate remedy, an injunction will not be granted. Thus if a plaintiff is suing for breach of fiduciary duty and alleges that he has suffered monetary loss, there is no point in seeking an injunction unless the breach complained of is continuing and likely to lead to further losses. Injunctions are useful where some abuse of power or unlawful act is threatened by the board, e g a proposal to commit the company beyond its powers. It will be no defence for the board to show that, under section 9 of the European Communities Act 1972, their conduct will bind the company in the hands of a third party since a shareholder may have an interest in preventing the company from incurring unnecessary liabilities. An injunction may also fulfil the same role as a restoration of property order, since if a director misappropriates confidential documents of value he can be specifically required to surrender them.[7]

5 Relief from liability

BY THE COMPANY

The effect of waiver clauses in articles has already been considered in relation to disclosure.[8] Compliance with the terms of a particular article can be regarded as a permission by the company to do or refrain from doing what otherwise would have been irregular. However, no provision in a company's articles or in a director's contract of employment may exempt him from the fiduciary duties and duty of care imposed on him by the general law.[9] Nor may any

6 *Bell Houses v City Wall Properties* [1966] 2 QB 656, [1966] 2 All ER 674, CA.
7 *Measures Bros Ltd v Measures* [1910] 2 Ch 248, CA.
8 See ch 4, pp. 62–66, above.
9 Companies Act 1948, s. 205.

indemnity be given which would achieve the same result. It can be seen that modern waiver clauses and the statute are apparently in conflict. Thus a director is under a general duty to prevent his personal interest conflicting with his position as an officer of the company. As such, one would have expected any clause which allowed him to be interested in contracts with the company, and to retain any profit made therefrom, to be completely nugatory. However, this is not the case. One argument would be that a relieving clause neutralises the fiduciary duties but cannot affect the obligation to show skill and care. It is submitted that this is too narrow a view of section 205. The better view[10] is that where articles correspond with provisions contained in Table A, they could be regarded as statutory exception to section 205, but otherwise the laws applies in full. The position is, however, unsatisfactory and was not improved in the 1978 Companies Bill.[11]

STATUTORY RELIEF

Section 61 of the Trustee Act 1925 ameliorated the strict duty position of the fiduciary in relation to trust funds by giving the court a discretion to grant relief where the trustee had acted honestly and reasonably. That provision is repeated almost word for word in section 448 of the Companies Act 1948, and is a further reminder of how the duties of trustees and directors are construed together. Section 448 provides:

> (1) If in any proceedings for negligence, default, breach of duty or breach of trust against an officer of the company or a person employed by a company as auditors (whether he is or is not an officer of the company) it appears to the court hearing the case that that officer or person is or may be liable in respect of the negligence, default, breach of duty or breach of trust, but that he has acted honestly and reasonably, and that, having regard to all the circumstances of the case, including those connected with his appointment, he ought fairly to be excused for the negligence, default, breach of duty or breach of trust, that court may relieve him, either wholly or partly, from his liability on such terms as the court may think fit.

A director who apprehends that he is about to be sued may himself apply to the court for the relief which he could claim as a defendant.

A company had two classes of capital, the voting shares being held by the directors. Two directors E and H had drawn on the

10 Expounded in Birds 'The Permissible Scope of Articles Excluding the Duties of Company Directors' (1976) 39 MLR 394.

11 Cl 44(6); see Gower *Modern Company Law* (4th edn) p. 602.

company from time to time for their personal needs during the financial year ending 1963. H left the company and transferred his shares to E. During the following year, E drew on the company as before. In October 1964 the company went into voluntary liquidation, and the liquidator reclaimed the payments made to E.

Held: (1) that the payments made in the year up to 1963 were not unlawful, since at the time of considering the accounts the voting directors could have constituted themselves into a general meeting and voted the payments as directors' remuneration; and (2) for the year 1964, on the question whether E was entitled to relief under section 448, it was right for the court to enquire into the practice of previous years and the fact that the advances in 1964, when the company was in financial difficulties, were not as great. In all the circumstances E had not acted unreasonably and he was excused from repayment.

The test to be applied in such cases is whether the director was acting in a way in which a man of affairs dealing with his own affairs with reasonable care and circumspection could reasonably be expected to act.

The touchstones of honesty, reasonableness, and fairness are considered in many cases on section 61.[12] However, no rules can be laid down as to the circumstances in which the court can grant relief, as these will vary with the particular facts.[13] A court is unlikely to apply the benefit of hindsight in assessing what a director ought to have done to avoid the breach or loss, and to that extent, in relation at least to negligence, there is a subjective assessment. In regard to breach of fiduciary duty involving a misapplication of the company's property however, a higher standard can be expected and therefore relief from liability more difficult to achieve.[14] Relief will not be given to a director who, although not guilty of personal dishonesty, has acted at the behest of a controlling shareholder in a nominee capacity without paying due regard to the propriety of the decisions he was required to make; for this amounts to an abrogation of his fiduciary responsibility to the company, and not merely a technical breach of it.[15]

12 See Snell *Principles of Equity* (27th edn) pp. 278–283.

13 *Re Kay, Mosley v Kay* [1897] 2 Ch 518 at 524.

14 *National Trustees Co of Australasia Ltd v General Finance Co of Australasia Ltd* [1905] AC 373.

15 *Selangor United Rubber Estates Ltd v Cradock (No 3)* [1968] 2 All ER 1073, particularly at 1155.

6 Indemnity and contribution

INDEMNITY

We have already seen that an indemnity cannot cover an act which is declared unlawful by section 205. Accordingly clauses in articles protecting the directors and auditors from liability for losses except in the case of their 'wilful default', or actual dishonesty, while held to be effective at the time, are probably no longer so.[16] More limited indemnities, like more limited waivers, will still be effective. Indeed, proviso (b) to section 205 expressly states that directors are entitled to be indemnified against any liability incurred by them in defending any proceedings, whether civil or criminal, in which judgment is given in their favour or in which they are acquitted or in connection with any application under section 448 in which relief is actually granted to them. It might be thought that this is a superfluous indemnity, since if a director is exonerated from liability in any proceedings, he suffers no loss. However, there may be occasions when the court does not award him costs, or else costs are taxed down, so that but for the promise of repayment by the company he would actually be out of pocket. Well-drawn articles of every company should include such a provision. In addition, where permitting the company to embark on a course of action which may have an adverse effect on its property, or is otherwise risky, the directors are well advised to obtain indemnities from third parties to cover the result.

CONTRIBUTION

Since the liability of directors is joint and several, the person entitled to damages may claim the whole amount from one or more of the directors who seem to him to have the most assets to satisfy any judgment. It is then up to the individual defendant to seek to obtain contribution from those fellow directors or officers who are thought to be in a similar degree of culpability.

If the claim is founded on negligence, the right to contribution arises under the Law Reform (Married Women and Tortfeasors) Act 1935, and a director will be entitled to serve notices under RSC 1965, Order 16, which bring in those responsible as co-defendants. Where the claim is for breach of fiduciary duty, the principles of contribution are those which apply to trustees. Again there is joint and several liability. If all are sued, the judgment may be executed against any one of them. However, the equitable

16 *Re Brazilian Rubber Plantations and Estates Ltd* [1911] 1 Ch 425; *Re City Equitable Fire Insurance Co* [1925] 1 Ch 407.

principle is that trustees who are liable must bear the burden equally, so that if one actually pays more than his share he can claim contribution, although it is unlikely this extends to costs. The former rule that there was no contribution between trustees who were guilty of fraud, has been abolished, and since the notion of fraud has been extended e g by the Misrepresentation Act in recent years, one or more directors who are sued for negligent misstatement in a prospectus may bring in the remainder of the board who were responsible for issuing it.

There may also be a right to recover from shareholders or creditors any property of the company which has been wrongly paid to them. This right will only arise if the recipient of the property had full knowledge of the facts, and can therefore be regarded as a constructive trustee. In one case, where the shareholder knew that there were no profits available for payments of dividends, he was liable to indemnify the directors in respect of the liability which they incurred as a result of paying them.[17]

Contribution can be claimed against the personal representatives of a deceased director.

If a company brings proceedings against directors to account for improper profits, each director is only liable to account for what he has actually received, although they are jointly and severally liable for costs.[18] A director who has resigned from office will be liable along with those who remain if he was a member of the board at the time when the breach of duty occurred, even if the loss resulting from it arose after his resignation. There is a general limitation of liability under the Limitation Act, which bars any rights for proceeding in negligence or other breach of duty more than six years after the alleged wrongful act or omission. If the cause of action is based on fraud or breach of trust, however, the time period does not begin to run against the claimant until the wrongful act has been discovered.

17 *Moxham v Grant* [1900] 1 QB 88; *Re National Funds Assurance Co* (1878) 10 ChD 118.
18 *Parker v McKenna* (1874) 10 Ch App 96.

Part two

Insider dealing

6 Insiders at common law

1 Insiders and outsiders

A limited company generates information merely by its existence. Particulars of directors, the address of the registered office, lists of members, details of share capital authorised and issued, and of charges secured on the company's property, the trading position as evidenced by the accounts, etc are among the matters which may be of interest to persons having dealings with the company. The importance of this information to trade creditor, member or employee alike is such that the Companies Acts require its disclosure by means of filing or registration with the Registrar of Companies. As with the Memorandum and Articles of Association, the information thereby acquires a 'public' character and persons affected are deemed as a general principle to have notice of it. The search facilities using microfilm and other modern techniques available at Companies Registration Office (industrial disputes permitting) are such that no member of the public can complain that basic facts about the corporate structure are denied to him. The tendency of recent legislation, culminating in the elaborate disclosure provisions of Part IV of the Companies Act 1980 and considered in chapter 4, is to require even more detailed information to be highlighted in this way: although the legislation is as much to prevent internal abuse as to enlighten and inform the interested spectator.

There is a further category of information which is neither 'public' in the above-described sense, nor yet confidential. A diligent observer of a company's affairs could easily discover by a physical inspection of its premises whether the work force was sizable or small, the factory or offices substantial or meagre, in each case a rough guide to the level of trading activity. By reading the financial pages of daily newspapers or the specialist business periodicals he could in time acquire knowledge of the performance of many companies, particularly those listed on the Stock Exchange where publication of additional information is a requirement of the Listing Agreement. Such companies will also be the subject of analysis and comment by experts of all kinds and a proportion of this material will be published and pass into the public domain. It is of course an open question at what point publication ceases to be an effective method of distributing knowledge. The *London Gazette*, which is the formal Government vehicle for advertising legal claims and petitions, is treated for notice purposes as if copies occur on every coffee table, yet is read by a very small number of persons. A financial newsletter, circulated to a body of subscribers, may contain investment analysis and advice drawn from widely available statistics, but where the conclusions are directed at a comparatively narrow audience. The Extel Information Service falls within this general category. As a principle, all such information and opinion is to be regarded as 'public', and therefore not of a character which requires its possessors to keep it confidential or to be subject to penalty if they do not (except, in appropriate cases, for breach of copyright).

A third category is information generated by the company which is confidential. Persons in possession of it are generally termed 'insiders'; those who are not, 'outsiders'. These terms have no statutory or legal base but express a concept that is readily understood. The word 'confidential' in this context has come to be treated as co-extensive with 'unpublished', although it is obvious that certain information which is not generally known or published is nevertheless not intended to be the subject of any confidence or privilege, e g the number of brooms used to sweep the factory floor. Equally, information which a company may choose to keep confidential, e g minutes of board meetings, or personnel records, may not of itself be of a quality that would affect the judgment of an outsider in his dealings with the company. The fact that an employee has a conviction for dangerous driving may well be a confidential matter, in the sense that no other employee, if he has access to the records, is to disclose it without cause or authority; but it is unlikely to be of any interest to a shareholder, or to a supplier deciding whether to offer the company credit for his goods. Not all information possessed or used by an 'insider' (and which he may be under a contractual duty not to reveal) is of relevance in assessing whether the general body of 'outsiders' has been tricked or disadvantaged. As we shall see[1] the test adopted for the statutory regulation of insider dealing is that the information must not only be unpublished but have a *price-sensitive* character, in other words be capable of affecting, up or down, the price at which the shares of the company change hands. Such a yardstick is naturally inadequate where there is no ready market for the company's securities: and in this case the law must

1 Ch 9, p. 156, below.

protect confidential information and its misuse, by some other means.

DIRECTORS AS INSIDERS

A director is an insider par excellence. Having control of the company's property through the authority of the board[2] he is in a position to acquire, accumulate and exploit facts about the company's operations which are secret outside the boardroom. No other individual, with the possible exception of a general manager, will have access to an equivalent range of detailed information. While almost every company employee is a repository of *some* confidential facts, e g list of customers or details of accounts, the departmental role will normally prevent them having an overview of the company's affairs. It is the director's privileged position which makes him a target for legal sanction against insider operations, particularly in relation to the securities of the company, rather than the existence of evidence that directors as individuals are prone to commit abuse of this kind. Indeed, the move towards legal sanctions in recent years has been occasioned by a handful of spectacular misdealings rather than any systematic misapplication of company assets.[3] The need to legislate to some extent indicates the failure of the previous philosophy, namely that the opportunity for abuse and the suspicions that it may arouse is greatly reduced by a full disclosure of interests in shares.[4] The disclosure requirements are considered in chapter 7.

Directors are invariably responsible for take-over negotiations affecting their company and because such negotiations are often of a highly secret character, the possession of information relating to the imminence or otherwise of a bid is a most valuable commodity. In unscrupulous hands, it is capable of being exploited by anticipatory purchases or sales of shares in either the offeror or target company. It is this kind of activity, taking place in a climate where amalgamations and mergers are the order of the day (as in the mid 1950s), that causes embarrassment in the securities industry and leads to demands for effective self-regulation. The City Panel on Takeovers and Mergers, consisting of nine persons nominated from various city bodies, and the more recently constituted Council for the Securities Industry, are the vehicles generated by the financial institutions themselves to ward off criticism from outside. Self-regulation is considered in chapter 8. There is also a market

2 See ch 1, section 6, above.
3 If the Takeover Panel are to be believed: Report for 1972/73.
4 Cohen Committee Report (Cmd 6659), para 87.

surveillance system consisting of monitoring the Stock Exchange's Market Price Display System, which shows some 720 of the 6,000 listed securities. The Stock Exchange imposes in its Listing Agreement a variety of requirements, and in 1977 published a Model Code for Securities Transactions by Directors of Listed Companies (see Appendix 3, below). The Stock Exchange also carries out its own investigations. None of these methods proved sufficiently effective to prevent pressure on Parliament to pass Part V of the Companies Act 1980, which makes insider dealing a criminal offence.

OTHER INSIDERS

It is clear that as well as directors, other officers of a company can be in possession of confidential information and that their position as officers or employees will enjoin them from disclosing it, or make them liable to sanction if they do. A modern listed company also relies heavily on outside professional advisers, such as auditors, accountants, brokers, solicitors, and investment advisers such as merchant banks, all of whom at some stage in the company's operation and particularly in a take-over period will acquire information which, if it were in the hands of the directors, would be non-disclosable. In certain cases, the advisers may be better placed to assess the future value of a company's securities than are the directors themselves, since (subject to any question of conflict of interest) they may have various clients yielding information which, when taken in the aggregate, has a price-sensitive quality in relation to the securities of one company. Rival bids is an obvious example. While the common law position of these advisers has never been fully developed, since the fiduciary duties which they owe are not clearly defined, the 1980 Act puts them squarely in the category of insiders who must not deal in the company's securities on their own behalf, or counsel or procure anyone else to deal, at times of price sensitivity.

SHAREHOLDERS

Shareholders of a company who do not at the same time wear one of the hats discussed above, in particular do not have a right to appoint a director, may nevertheless often be in a position where they can obtain confidential information. The larger the shareholder, the more likely the board is, necessarily informally, to make available material upon request. Occasionally the shareholder may be in such a dominant position that the board would not undertake a sale of the company's assets, or contemplate a takeover bid, without a prior indication of consent from him: on the basis that if the Stock Exchange require a Class 1 circular and a general meeting to approve the arrangements, it is highly desirable to know in advance what the likely outcome is. This is by no means a general rule, and many boards of directors keep shareholders in the dark about the business of the company (save what has to be disclosed in the Director's Report and Accounts), until compelled to make a disclosure. Whatever the circumstances, a shareholder who has acquired secondhand, i e through directors or the company's professional advisers, information which is price sensitive ought to be in the same position as anyone else regarding dealing. This is recognised in the Companies Act 1967 which introduced provisions similar to those applying to directors in regard to disclosure. These provisions are extended by the Companies Act 1976 and the Companies (No 2) Bill 1981. The requirement to disclose is not, of course, merely aimed at deterring insider dealing by shareholders, but also to discourage irregular movements of shares in the market, by means of so called 'dawn raids' or 'concert parties'.

2 Misuse of corporate property

EXTENT OF REMEDY

The Companies Act of 1980 imposes criminal liability for insider dealings. It offers no remedy to the company, or to an outsider, for damages as a result of loss sustained. This is not as anomalous as it may seem. If a director sells some shares prior to the announcement of a company's half-yearly results (which disclose a loss), so that he obtains a higher price than the market would bear after the announcement, then there is no loss, as such, occasioned to the company as there would have been, for example, on a misapplication of physical assets. Equally, if the director buys early and makes a profit, the shares are his own property, and if he is made liable to account to the company for the benefit received, it is for the company in the nature of a 'windfall'. Unless the unpublished half-yearly results can be regarded as information in which the company not merely has an interest, but a property, it is not immediately obvious why it should be entitled to claim compensation for the loss, or the windfall profit. After all, the company does not *own* the shares concerned even though it may have a substantial interest (in the sense of concern) in the price at which the securities are marketed, or whether they can be marketed at all.

Similarly, what legitimate claim has the shareholder who buys or sells at the 'wrong' price? In no real sense is he the victim of a misrepresentation about the value of the shares, because the value is that which obtains in the market at the time that he effects a purchase or sale. He has not been induced to transact at that price, unless it be said that the director had come under a duty to disclose to him, as a material fact, that the condition of the company was such that the market price of the securities would shortly change to his disadvantage. There is clearly no duty to disclose this, save to all the shareholders at the time by means of the circular or other document which the Stock Exchange may require to be issued – at which point the price changes anyway. No valid analogy with misrepresentation exists, and once again it is not immediately clear what right the shareholder has against the insider to claim the profit or compensation for the loss. The position is further complicated, in practice if not in law, by the difficulty of matching a buyer and seller of shares on the Stock Exchange given the currency of the 'Talisman' system of recording transactions.[5]

The common law has therefore developed on different lines. Instead of attaching importance to the proprietary aspects of corporate information, or the contractual rights of outsiders, it has focused attention on the fiduciary nature of the director's office and the requirement not to exploit his position by any means to make a profit for himself, or to avoid a loss. The use of the information for other than a valid corporate purpose constitutes a breach of trust, giving rise to the equitable remedies of compensation and account found to be effective in the context of the rule that a director must not allow his duty and his interest to conflict.[6]

> The rule of equity which insists on those, who by use of a fiduciary position make a profit, being able to account for that profit, in no way depends upon fraud or absence of bona fide, or upon such questions . . . as whether the profit would or should otherwise have gone to the plaintiff, or whether the profiteer was under a duty to obtain the source of the profit for the plaintiff, or whether he took a risk, or acted as he did for the benefit of the plaintiff, or whether the plaintiff has in fact been damaged or benefited by his action. The liability arises from the mere fact of the profit having been made . . . The profiteer, however honest and well intentioned, cannot escape the risk of being called to account.[7]

The extent to which confidential information is corporate property has been touched on in the previous chapter. In *Phipps v Boardman*,[8] a trust case, the judgments of the House of Lords are at variance:

5 As to which, see C Abrams 'The Legal Aspects of Talisman' (1980) The Company Lawyer (No 1) 17–23.
6 *Regal (Hastings) Ltd v Gulliver* [1967] 2 AC 134, [1942] 1 All ER 378.
7 [1942] 1 All ER 373 at 386, per Lord Russell.
8 [1967] AC 46.

> The Phipps Trust owned shares in L & H Limited. The beneficiaries were dissatisfied with the management and appointed one of their number, P, and B, a solicitor to enquire into various matters as a result of which P and B acquired inside information about the company. They discovered undervalued assets, and later took control of the company by subscribing personal shareholdings, and sold the assets at a profit in which the Trust as the other shareholder took a part. There was full disclosure and bona fides throughout. Nevertheless a beneficiary under the Trust sued B for an account of the personal profits he had made.
>
> Held (by the House of Lords, 3 to 2): the claim succeeded, on the basis that the defendant had obtained the information from the company on behalf of the Trust, and obtained it solely by virtue of his privileged position. It was not therefore available for him to turn to his personal advantage.

Lord Upjohn and Viscount Dilhorne, the dissenting minority in the court, criticised the notion that there had been an exploitation of trust property; information in itself could not be dignified as 'property'. The true test was to determine in what circumstances the information had been acquired – only if it was protected by confidence would equity intervene. To accept a general rule that information learned by a trustee during the course of his duties was a trust asset and could not be used by him would impose an intolerable burden on trustees generally.

While the issue of whether or not the 'inside information' about the company was corporate property, was crucial to the decision in *Boardman v Phipps*, it would not necessarily affect the basic liability of a director with regard to information obtained in the course of his office. Even on the narrower view, the information may not be used,

(1) in circumstances which, regardless of his position as director, would make it a breach of confidence for him to communicate to anyone, for it has been given to him expressly or impliedly as confidential, or
(2) in a fiduciary capacity, and its use would place him in a position where his duty and his interest might possibly conflict.

Information about a possible takeover bid is of the highest confidentiality and its use to buy or sell shares at an advantageous price would clearly be in breach of trust. However, if the minority in *Boardman v Phipps* were right it would be permissible, for example, for a director who had information about the inadequacy of sources of supply of material to the company, to go out and form another company in which he was personally interested and take over the role of supplier. Subject to full disclosure, any profit made could be retained.

3 No duty to shareholders

Although it is reasonably well established that where a director or officer has made use for his own purposes of price-sensitive information he will be in breach of his fiduciary duty to the company, there is no parallel duty owed to individual shareholders. In the much quoted case of *Percival v Wright*,[9] the facts were as follows:

> An action was commenced by former shareholders against directors claiming rescission of the contracts for sale of their shares on the grounds that they should have been informed that negotiations were in progress for the sale of the company's business. Had the information been known the shares would have achieved a higher valuation.
>
> Held: that matters arising in the ordinary course of management, such as negotiations of this sort, could not provide the basis of a duty of disclosure, and consequently there was no breach in failing to make the facts known.

The court's view was that a contrary result would place directors in an invidious position, as they could never buy and sell shares without disclosing negotiations, a premature disclosure of which might well be against the best interests of the company. Such an argument, it is respectfully submitted, would have carried more weight if the directors had not been beneficially involved with the shares, and the transfer had taken place between two shareholders both equally in a state of blissful ignorance. Nevertheless there was no finding of unfair dealing in the case, which might have produced a different result.

Despite its unfortunate overtones *Percival v Wright* is not a general licence to directors to use inside information for their own investment purposes.[10] The fact that the directors were not in a fiduciary position towards the plaintiff shareholders does not mean that they are not fiduciaries at all; and the *Boardman v Phipps* principle is unaffected.[11] Moreover, in a Privy Council case more recent than *Percival v Wright*,[12] it has been accepted that if a director in a

9 [1902] 2 Ch 421.
10 See the discussion in Rider and Ffrench *The Regulation of Insider Trading* p. 147.
11 A more recent example is *Industrial Development Consultants Ltd v Cooley* [1972] 2 All ER 162, [1972] 1 WLR 443.
12 *Allen v Hyatt* (1914) 30 TLR 444.

particular transaction expressly or impliedly becomes an agent of one or more shareholders the fiduciary duties arising out of the agency relationship may prevent him from realising a profit on the acquisition of securities to his own advantage. On the other hand, the civil remedies generally developed by the court in this area can be regarded as inadequate in two major respects:

(1) in the limited cases where a director-shareholder duty is found to exist it is dependent upon proving a definite agency with appropriate authority having been vested by the principal; and
(2) where duties are owed to the company, the company may choose not to exercise its rights of action against the delinquent director because his fellow directors do not wish to pursue the matter (they may be making separate profits themselves).

The likelihood of reluctance under (2) above is less in the case of public companies with independent board members, who themselves may be called to account if it is subsequently discovered that they failed to take any steps to safeguard the company's interests. There are many companies, however, which have a Stock Exchange listing, which are converted from private companies and remain controlled by a small number of family directors who may be tempted to close ranks.

DIFFERENCE IN REMEDIES

It has been noted (p. 93) that the equitable remedy of tracing or restoration of property is available to the company if it can be shown that there has been an actual misapplication of assets. Clearly, if corporate information is regarded as an asset, then the remedy in rem will apply here too. If not, the company is left with the sanction of requiring the director to account as a fiduciary, on a personal basis. Restoration of the property is inescapably tied in with the notion of a constructive trust over the wrongly appropriated asset: and the liability of a constructive trustee is more extensive from the plaintiff company's point of view. It will continue to be important to argue, therefore, especially where the director is financially unable to account, that the majority opinion in *Boardman v Phipps* supports a constructive trusteeship.

4 Corporate information or corporate opportunity?

In those cases where the question of whether mere information can be regarded as property has not been canvassed, the courts have fixed the fiduciary liability of the directors by reference to the *opportunity* they have acquired to make a profit for themselves such as to put themselves in a position of conflict with the company.

> A company owned a cinema and the directors decided to acquire two others on lease so as to sell all three as a going concern. The lessor of the cinemas demanded that the capital of the subsidiary company formed for the purpose be a certain figure, which could not be raised. Accordingly the holding company subscribed for some only of the necessary shares, and the directors took the rest. Instead of the business being sold, the shares of the company were disposed of at a profit. The new controller of the company then sued the former directors to recover such profit.
>
> Held: the directors were liable to account since what was done was an exploitation of a management opportunity, which should have been applied for the company's benefit.[13]

It appeared to make no difference that the company could not itself have exploited the opportunity to acquire the shares of its intended subsidiary since it did not have the necessary cash asset. Moreover the directors concerned, as controlling shareholders, could easily have passed a resolution in general meeting which would have ratified the transaction and legitimated the personal element of gain. The fact the directors were required to account operated as the merest windfall to the company's new controller.

Applying the principle, liability to account is found to be based on the obtaining of an opportunity while acting as director or officer of the company, in circumstances where it was reasonable to expect such director or officer to disclose the opportunity and where the same has arisen solely by virtue of the privileged position which he occupied.[14] The Companies Bill 1978, attempted to draw together the varying threads of the equitable rules as follows:

> **44.** (3) Without prejudice to subsections (1) and (2) above, a director of a company or a person who has been a director of a company shall not, for the purpose of gaining, whether directly or indirectly, an advantage for himself—
>
> (a) make use of any money or other property of the company; or
>
> (b) make use of any relevant information or of a relevant opportunity—
>
> (i) if he does so while a director of the company in circumstances which give rise or might reasonably be expected to give rise to such a conflict; or

13 For a strident criticism of this case, see Gower *Modern Company Law* (4th edn) pp. 593–594.

14 *Industrial Development Consultants Ltd v Cooley*, above, can be regarded as an 'opportunity' case although Roskill J based liability on secret profits.

(ii) if while a director of the company he had that use in contemplation in circumstances which gave rise to such a conflict.

(4) In this section—

'relevant information', in relation to a director of a company, means any information which he obtained while a director or other officer of the company and which it was reasonable to expect him to disclose to the company or not to disclose to persons unconnected with the company;

'relevant opportunity', in relation to a director of a company, means an opportunity which he had while a director or other officer of the company and which he had—

(a) by virtue of his position as a director or other officer of the company; or

(b) in circumstances in which it was reasonable to expect him to disclose the fact that he had that opportunity to the company.

It is noticeable that the provision draws a distinction between the misuse of physical assets on the one hand and the use of information or property on the other. Although it is right to present them as separate categories, there would inevitably be a degree of overlap. A further importance of the distinction is that, in the case of misuse of information or property giving rise to a liability to account, the company could ratify the action. In the case of breach of duty giving rise to a constructive trust, it is not within the power of the company so to do.[15]

Clause 44(3) adopts as a basis for liability, whether in relation to property, information or opportunity, misuse 'for the purpose of gaining, whether directly or indirectly, an advantage for [the director] himself'. A director's motive in procuring a breach of trust has not been developed in any of the cases considered above, and is a statutory rationalisation. It is also arguably too narrow, since a director may attempt to secure an advantage for an associated person rather than himself. Such procurement is specifically dealt with in the criminal sanctions under Part V of the Companies Act 1980.

Clause 44 fell with the 1978 Bill and was not repeated, along with the remainder of the general statement of directors' duties, in the Companies Act 1980. The question of whether further statutory reform to encompass civil remedies is likely, is considered below.

5 Confidence and unjust enrichment

THE LAW OF CONFIDENCE

So far the question of use of information has been considered from the standpoint of the exploiter, and his liability to the company. It

15 *Cook v Deeks* [1916] 1 AC 554, PC.

should be noted that the law also protects the company by enabling it to require of persons working under service contracts that they observe confidentiality by virtue of their fidelity covenant, expressed or implied. In order to restrain the breach of confidence, a number of elements must be present.

> First, the information itself . . . must have the necessary quality of confidentiality about it. Secondly, that information must have been imparted in circumstances importing an obligation of confidence. Thirdly, there must be an unauthorised use of that information to the detriment of the party communicating it.[16]

The reference to 'detriment of the party communicating it' is a reference, of course, to the company which has made available the information to the employee in the first place. The use of the information by the employee will provide him with a benefit, not a detriment. Later cases have emphasised also the criterion of reasonableness as between the parties, similar to other restrictive covenants.[17] While breach of confidence actions mainly concern trade secrets and intangible industrial property, the protection of price-sensitive information, whether or not amounting to corporate property, is within this jurisdiction.

UNJUST ENRICHMENT

The law of restitution is not well developed in this country, depending as it does upon a number of random cases rather than any coherent set of legal principles.[18] Practitioners have tended not to venture into these unchartered waters when insider dealing is in issue. Nevertheless there exists the general principle that 'a person has a right to have restored to him a benefit gained at his expense if the retention of the benefit by the other would be unjust'.[19] The important point is that no assumption of a pre-existing fiduciary relationship is made. The restitutionary right is based on a basic duty of good faith.[20]

A director is in a position of confidant of company information, whether it is actually inparted to him by another official or he gleans it from the company's books and papers. It is then a matter of judgment whether the information is such that it is reasonable to expect that the director will not disclose it to a third person. Of course, there is no actual disclosure if all the director is doing is buying or selling his own shares, indeed the basis of his personal

16 *Coco v A N Clark (Engineers) Ltd* [1969] RPC 41.
17 *Dunford and Elliot Ltd v Johnson and Firth Brown Ltd* [1977] 1 Lloyd's Rep 505.
18 See Goff and Jones *The Law of Restitution* (3rd edn).
19 Seavy and Scott 'Restitution' 54 LQR 32.
20 *Seager v Copydex Ltd* [1967] 1 WLR 923.

advantage is the *lack* of disclosure to the other party to the transaction. The principle of unjust enrichment, to be useful in this context, should be wide enough to impose liability on a person taking unfair advantage. The principle should also extend to persons who acquire the information from a confidant, i e the director's family, or advisers to the company to whom he has imparted documents in good faith. It is not yet clear how far the judicial process will extend in conferring a remedy equivalent to that of equitable accounting.

6 Reform of civil remedies

Clause 44(3) of the 1978 Bill would, if enacted, have had an effect on transactions involving directors apart from insider dealing in securities. It would have covered, for example, simple exploitation of a company secret such as a confidential list of customers. Nevertheless, it appears that the Government of the day intended civil and criminal sanctions for insider dealing to be complementary, and indeed in the Companies Bill 1973 an alternative code of civil remedies had already appeared. With the passing of the Companies Act 1980 it is an open question whether present or future Governments will feel that the civil side is still in need of reform, or at least clarification. It may be that the Department of Trade lawyers who advised the Government had been pursuaded that to attempt a general codifying statement of directors' duties and liabilities is too complicated, in which event it is thought unlikely that specific legislation on disgorgement of profits for insider dealing would be introduced. On the other hand, the fact that the incidence of such dealing is reduced by the penal statute and by increased self-regulatory surveillance, does not lessen the financial impact on the shareholder or company concerned in the cases which survive. Moreover, as we shall see, the criminal code is itself not complete, since it does not fully cover so-called 'off-market' deals, i e those negotiated otherwise than on a recognised stock exchange.[1]

An alternative to the piecemeal approach would be to bring in an equivalent to the American Securities Exchange Commission to exercise a general monitoring function over the securities industry, and at the same time legislate against 'short-swing' profits made by any person dealing in a company's shares. The American system is considered in chapter 10. However, the political climate at the time of writing is against the establishment of further regulatory bodies

1 Liability is limited to dealings through an 'off-market dealer' as defined by s. 70(3), and does not extend to private treaties.

(except those to be required by future EEC Directives),[2] and there is insufficient evidence of abuse at present to induce a clamour for further far-reaching companies legislation. Both the City Panel on Takeovers and the Stock Exchange have in the past rejected any notion of civil liability in the context of market transactions. However, as an extension to the criminal liability it is just possible that a court before whom a person is convicted under Part V of the 1980 Act may, in addition or in substitution of the statutory penalty, order the person concerned to account to the innocent party for his profit, or the profit that his 'tippees' (i e persons to whom information has been conveyed) have made.[3] The sum would then be recoverable as a civil debt. The Jenkins Committee[4] have in the past recommended that 'the law should protect a person – whether or not a member of the company . . . who suffered loss because a director has taken unfair advantage at his expense of a particular piece of confidential information about the company or any company in the same group in any transaction relating to the securities of such company'. This implies a civil remedy although elsewhere in the Report the question of enforcement was admitted to be difficult.

2 The stock exchange will have a quasi-statutory role under the Sixth Directive (prospectus requirements).
3 Under e g the compensation provisions contained in s. 35 of the Powers of Criminal Courts Act 1973.
4 Cmnd 1749, paras 86–91, 141–147.

7 Registration of holdings

1 Directors

OBLIGATION OF THE COMPANY

The Companies Act 1948, section 195 introduced the requirement that every company should maintain a register, available for inspection, of directors' interests in its shares and debentures. Section 198 provided that it was the duty of a director, or a person deemed to be such, to give written notice to the company of such matters relating to himself as might be necessary for the purposes of section 195. These provisions complemented section 199 which, as discussed,[1] requires a director who is in any way interested in a contract with the company to declare the nature of his interest at a meeting of the board. The allotment of shares to a director or, indeed, his application for shares to be issued to him, certainly constitutes a 'contract or proposed contract with the company', although the sanction of such a limited disclosure to a body of persons who are likely already to be aware of the interest, is weak. It is publicity attendant upon the keeping of a register, that has been regarded as the deterrent to abuse, since if the timing of a transaction is significant in relation to, e g a takeover bid or the publication of results, the director can always be called upon to make a statement justifying his position.[2]

The obligation to record interests notified to the company is now contained in section 29 of the Companies Act 1967, as part of a series of provisions replacing section 195. Every company must keep such a register for the purpose of recording interests which are required to be disclosed under section 27 of the 1967 Act. The register must contain the name of the director giving the information, the information given, and the date when the entry is inscribed. The entries must be in chronological order. The obligation to make the entry must be fulfilled before the expiration

1 Ch 4, pp. 59–62, above.

2 Committee on Company Law Amendment (Cohen Committee) (Cmnd 6659), para 86.

of the period of three days beginning with the day next following that on which it arises, omitting weekends and bank holidays.[3]

OBLIGATION OF COMPANY WITHOUT NOTIFICATION

Whenever it grants to a director a right to subscribe for its shares or debentures, the company must inscribe in the register against his name:

(1) the date upon which the right is granted;
(2) the period during which or time at which it is exercisable;
(3) the consideration for the grant – or lack of it;
(4) the description of shares or debentures involved;
(5) the price to be paid therefor.[4]

When the right to subscribe is actually exercised, the company is obligated to record the following:

(1) the fact of the exercise;
(2) the number or amount of shares or debentures in respect of which the interest is exercised;
(3) whether or not they were registered in his name and, if not, the names of the persons registered and the amounts taken by each of them.[5]

Fines are imposed upon the company and every officer in default for non-compliance.

Section 117 of the Companies Act 1948 provides that no notice of any trust shall be entered on the register of members maintained by the company, and it is an important principle of company law that a company is not bound to recognise any equitable interest or any other right in a share except an absolute right in the registered holder.[6] To preserve this principle section 29(6) of the 1967 Act provides that the company is not affected with notice of, or put upon enquiry as to, the rights of any person in relation to any shares or debentures by reason only of its carrying out its obligations under the section.

MAINTENANCE OF THE REGISTER

The register must be kept either at the registered office, or, if the register of members is kept elsewhere, at the same place, in which case notice must be given of the fact in the prescribed form to the

3 S. 29(4).
4 S. 29(2)(a).
5 S. 29(2)(b).
6 *Re Perkins, ex parte Mexican Santa Barbara Mining Co* (1890) 24 QBD 613; Palmer *Company Law* (22nd edn) vol 1, pp. 540–542.

Registrar of Companies.[7] The register must be open for inspection without charge to members, and other persons (at a fee), in the same way that the register of members is available, so that it is open for at least two hours a day during business hours. Copies must be supplied on application. Unless the register is itself maintained in the form of an index, the company must keep an index of each name and a sufficient indication to enable the information inscribed against it to be readily found. Any necessary alterations must be made within fourteen days.[8]

The register must be produced at the commencement of the company's annual general meeting and remain open and accessible during the continuance of the meeting to any person attending.

The register or index may be in the form of bound books, or looseleaf form provided adequate safeguards are taken to prevent falsification and to facilitate its discovery, upon penalty of fine.[9]

OBLIGATION OF DIRECTOR TO NOTIFY INTEREST

A person who becomes a director of any company must, on appointment, notify the company of any subsisting interest in shares or debentures thereof, or in any other body corporate which is the company's subsidiary or holding company or a subsidiary of the company's holding company. The notification must be in writing and must state:

(1) the number of shares or debentures of each class;
(2) the fact of the subsistence of the interest.[10]

A director shall be under an obligation to notify the company in writing of the occurrence, while he is director, of the following events:

(1) any event in consequence of which he becomes, or ceases to be, interested in shares or debentures of relevant companies;
(2) the entering into by him of a contract to sell any such shares or debentures;
(3) the assignment by him of a right granted by the company to take shares or debentures;
(4) the grant by a relevant company of right to subscribe, or the exercise or the assignment such a right

in each case stating the number or amount, and class, of shares or debentures involved.[11]

7 S. 29(7), (8).
8 S. 29(9).
9 Applying s. 436 of the Companies Act 1948.
10 S. 27(1)(a).
11 S. 27(1)(b).

Where events have to be notified under (1)–(4) above, there are corresponding obligations to indicate the consideration changing hands and certain other particulars. Thus:

(a) for an event under (1) or (2) above, the price paid or received must be shown;
(b) for an event under (3) above, the consideration for the assignment;
(c) for an event under (4) above, either
   (i) (in the case of a grant of a right to subscribe) the date of the grant, the time within which it is exercisable, the consideration and the price to be paid for the securities; or
   (ii) (in the case of an exercise), the number of securities involved, and the persons – including the director – in whose name they are registered; or
   (iii) (in the case of an assignment), the consideration for the assignment.[12]

The director must make his disclosure within a period of five working days from the 'relevant day', the period commencing the day after. In the case of initial notification, where the director is aware of his interest the relevant day is the day he becomes a director. Where he is not so aware, the period runs from the day following his becoming cognisant of the interest.[13] Where the duty involves notification of subsequent events, the relevant day is the date of the event, but in such a case:

(1) the director must be aware of its occurrence, and
(2) he must be aware that its occurrence gives rise to the obligation,

before time begins to run. Otherwise the duty must be complied with within a five-day period commencing from the day following that on which the fact of the occurrence of the event giving rise to the duty comes to the knowledge of the director.[14]

While it is reasonable to exonerate a director from notifying his interest while he is unaware of it, e g because on appointment to the board he has been allotted qualification shares and is not cognisant of that fact, it is less certain why section 27(3)(b) requires that he must be aware that that event *gives rise* to the obligation to register. Ignorance of legal requirements is not a usual source of defence for a director especially if, as is common, company secretaries routinely

12 S. 25(5)–(7).
13 S. 27(3)(a).
14 S. 27(3)(b).

remind directors on appointment or prior to the annual general meeting of their duty to disclose shareholdings and invite them to update any relevant information or confirm its accuracy.

A person who fails to comply with the provisions of section 27, or who in purported compliance makes a statement to the company which he knows to be false or is reckless as to whether it is true or false (i e a fraudulent statement[15]), commits an offence and is liable to a fine or imprisonment. However, prosecutions can only be brought with the consent of the Department of Trade or the Director of Public Prosecutions.[16]

It should be noted that a person in accordance with whose directions or instructions the directors of a company are accustomed to act is deemed to be a director of the company for the purpose of these provisions.[17]

2 Nature of directors' interest

INCLUDED

Section 28 defines what interests are relevant for the purpose of notification under section 27. This also applies in relation to disclosure of substantial share holdings by non-directors under section 33.[18] Thus references to a person's being interested in shares in, or debentures of a company are, as a general principle construed so as not to exclude an interest on the ground of its remoteness or the manner in which it arises or by reason of the fact that the exercise of a right conferred by ownership thereof is, or is capable of being made, in any way subject to restraint or restriction. The rules are difficult to interpret in practice and individual directors or other company officers who are in doubt as to their applicability should, notwithstanding the apparent protection of section 27(3)(b), seek specialist legal advice. What follows is only a general statement of the existing statutory provisions.

Trusts A person who has an interest under a trust whereof the property comprises shares or debentures (other than a discretionary interest) shall be deemed to be interested in the shares or debentures. But a person in receipt of trust income shall not be regarded as being interested in the securities in remainder or reversion.[19]

15 Cf ch 5, p. 89, above.
16 S. 27(8) and (10).
17 S. 27(11).
18 See pp. 124–125, below.
19 S. 28(2) and (7).

Corporate control A person is deemed to be interested in shares or debentures if a body corporate is also interested in them and

(a) that body corporate or its directors are accustomed to act in accordance with his directions or instructions; or
(b) he is entitled to exercise or control the exercise of one-third or more of the voting power at any general meeting of that body corporate.[20]

Joint interest Persons having a joint interest are deemed each of them to have that interest.[1]

Contracts A person is deemed to have an interest if he enters into a contract for shares or debentures.[2]

Order A person is deemed to have an interest if he has a right, otherwise than by virtue of having an interest under a trust, to call for delivery of the shares or debentures to himself or to his order (whether the right is exercisable presently or in the future).[3]

Voting A person is deemed to have an interest if, not being a registered holder of the shares or debentures in question, he is nonetheless entitled to exercise any right conferred by the holding thereof or is entitled to control the exercise of any right to so conferred, other than as a proxy or a representative of another company.[4]

It is suggested that this, last, heading could cover the situation where the right to subscribe for shares is granted at less than market price and renounced or assigned to a company which the director already controls before registration as holder.[5]

EXCLUDED

Certain categories of interest do not require to be notified. Thus an interest held as a bare or custodian trustee, or under an authorised unit trust scheme or other statutory scheme, is to be disregarded.[6] These categories have been extended by Regulations[7] made under the 1967 Act, to include:

20 S. 28(3).
1 Ibid.
2 S. 28(4)(a).
3 S. 28(4)(b).
4 S. 28(4)(c).
5 Rider and Ffrench *The Regulation of Insider Trading* p. 181.
6 S. 28(8)–(10).
7 The Companies (Disclosure of Directors' Interests) (Exceptions) No 1 Regulations 1967 (SI 1967 No 1594) and Nos 2 and 3 Regulations 1968 (SIs 1968 Nos 865 and 1533).

(a) interests of a director who is trustee of a trust or estate of which the public trustee is a co-trustee or co-personal representative;
(b) interests in shares of a private company arising by virtue of the existence of a right of pre-emption under the company's memorandum or articles;
(c) interests in shares or debentures of industrial and provident societies;
(d) interests, whether held as a beneficiary or as a trustee, under certain approved pension schemes;
(e) interests of a director of a wholly owned subsidiary company who is also a director of the holding company and the register of interests is already maintained by the holding company; and
(f) interests in a subsidiary of a company whieh is incorporated outside the United Kingdom.

FAMILY INTERESTS

An interest of the spouse of a director is treated for the purposes of these provisions as the interest of the director himself, as is the interest of an infant child.[8] The obligation to notify remains that of the director. Events such as a contract, assignment, right of subscription, or grant which would, if they related to the director himself, be notifiable under section 27, are still notifiable. The reference to 'child' includes stepchild or adopted child. The effect of this treatment is to prevent a director transferring securities into the name of his wife or holding them upon bare trust for his children, to avoid the possibility of disclosure.

NOTIFICATION TO THE STOCK EXCHANGE

Whenever a company in the case of which shares or debentures are listed on a recognised stock exchange is notified of any matter by a director in consequence of the fulfilment of an obligation imposed on him by sections 27 or 31 of the 1967 Act, and that matter relates to shares and debentures which are also listed, the company is under an obligation to notify the stock exchange of the matter, before the end of the day next following that on which the obligation arises.[9]

The stock exchange concerned is given a discretion whether or not to publish the information which is supplied, and the form that such publication takes. There is a fine on the company 'and every officer who is in default' in the event of non-compliance with this

8 S. 31.
9 S. 25, Companies Act 1976.

requirement; there will, almost certainly, also be a breach of the company's Listing Agreement.[10] If a director has discharged his personal obligation to notify under section 27, he may nevertheless be liable for failing as an officer of the company to ensure that the information is transmitted.

3 Directors: survival of provisions under 1981 Bill

At the time of writing, the Companies (No 2) Bill 1981 is passing through its various stages in Parliament. Part IV of the Bill, if enacted, will make substantial alterations (see next section) to the law relating to disclosure of interests of substantial shareholders. The provisions affecting directors are, however, largely preserved, the main changes being to extend the definition of 'price' in relation to shares or debentures, paid or received to include consideration other than money, and to conform the meaning of 'interest' to that newly-adopted for shareholders' disclosure.[11] The first-mentioned change also operates in relation to restrictions on directors' dealings in share options.[12]

4 Shareholders of public companies

UNDER THE 1967 AND 1976 ACTS

Principally to warn a company's board of share movements likely to result in a change of voting control, rather than to prevent abuse of inside information, a set of provisions basically similar in concept to those governing directors was introduced as section 33 of the Companies Act 1967. The holders of substantial interests in securities, which were defined as holdings of 10 per cent or more in the nominal value of any class of shares carrying unrestricted voting rights, were obliged to notify the company in writing about the occurrence of certain events, e g acquisitions and disposals. Whereas directors of *every* company were bound under the provisions of section 27 to notify, the equivalent obligation of shareholders applied, only in respect of companies having a listing (although not necessarily for the securities in question) on a recognised stock exchange. Debentures were excluded. The notification to the company was required to state the event, the date, and the number of shares involved, the declarant being identified by name

10 The Stock Exchange, Admission of Securities to Listing, para 5(c), n. 27.
11 Companies (No 2) Bill 1981, Sch 3, paras 26, 27. The new definition of interest is considered at p. 130, below.
12 See ch 9, below.

and address. The provisions of section 28 which delineated the nature of directors' interests were in general applied to section 33.

The company was bound to maintain a separate register for these disclosures, which was open to inspection.[13] There was no requirement to notify the stock exchange on which the shares were listed.[14]

Section 26 of the Companies Act 1976 reduced the 10 per cent threshold to 5 per cent 'or such other percentage as may from time to time be prescribed by . . . statutory instrument and different percentages may be so prescribed in relation to companies of different classes or descriptions'.

Although the 1967 Act imposed criminal sanctions for non-compliance, these provisions were essentially 'passive' in character, and there was suspicion that they were not fully effective. Section 27 of the 1976 Act introduced a power enabling a company by notice in writing to require a member within a reasonable time (which was specified in the notice):

(a) to indicate in writing the capacity in which he held the shares; and
(b) if he held them otherwise than as beneficial owner, to indicate in writing so far as it lay within his knowledge the persons who had an interest in them and the nature of that interest.

Any person identified under (b) above could himself be the subject of an inquiry. Information could also be requested concerning any voting agreement or arrangement relating to the shares. An important aspect of section 27 was that it applied to any member, whatever the extent of his shareholding.

FURTHER REFORMS

In February 1980 inspectors were appointed under section 172 of the Companies Act 1948 to investigate the membership of Consolidated Gold Fields Limited following an application by the company to the Department of Trade which resulted from the company's belief that an unknown buyer had secretly acquired approximately 19 per cent of its equity share capital. This was alleged to have been done without the shares purchased being registered, thereby effectively preventing the company from exercising the powers available to its under the Companies Act, to determine the beneficial owners of the shares. De Beers Consolidated Mines Limited then disclosed that it was the mystery buyer and the inspectors limited their inquiry to the circumstances and methods by which De Beers purchased 16.5 million shares in a very short

13 Companies Act 1967, s. 34(5).
14 But see The Stock Exchange, Admission of Securities to Listing, para 5(c).

time on 12 February 1980, in an operation which is known as a 'dawn raid' on the securities market. At the same time as the publication of the inspector's report,[15] the Stock Exchange produced its own report as a result of which member firms were temporarily prohibited from taking part on behalf of clients of share acquisitions of the 'dawn raid' type. The Council for the Securities Industry also decided that further rules needed to be drawn up to govern the conduct of such operations. It treated a 'dawn raid' as an offer, at a price significantly above the existing market price, to acquire voting equity shares amounting to at least 5 per cent of the voting capital which would take the purchaser's holding (including any existing holding) to 15 per cent or more. Offers made to no more than 5 shareholders or open for more than five days were excluded. In December 1980 the Council issued rules governing substantial acquisitions of shares which are considered in the next chapter.

The fragility of the combined statutory and self-regulatory systems resulted in renewed interest in the operation of section 33 of the 1967 Act. The Government published two Consultative Documents, one in August 1980 highlighting the deficiencies[16] and inviting comments, another in May 1981 setting out draft clauses and restating the general policy of the law as follows:[17]

> This policy is that a quoted company, its members and the public at large should be entitled to be informed promptly of the acquisition of a significant interest in its voting shares, whether or not the interest is to be used to influence policy or with a view to subsequent acquisition of a controlling interest, in order that existing members and those dealing with the company may protect their interests and that the conduct of the affairs of the company is not prejudiced by uncertainty over those who may be in a position to influence or control the company.

The principal methods by which the Government proposed that these objectives should be achieved were:

(1) extension of the existing definition of 'interests';
(2) extension of the circumstances in which interests are to be attributed to a person and taken into account as if they were his own in determining disclosure obligations;
(3) requiring more information from a holder of a substantial interest;
(4) extension of the power of a company to investigate interests in its shares;

15 Department of Trade, Consolidated Gold Fields Limited: Investigation under section 172 (HMSO, 1980).
16 Department of Trade, Disclosure of Interest in Shares (August 1980).
17 Department of Trade, Companies (No 2) Bill (May 1981), pp. 1–2.

(5) conferring of a minority shareholder's right to require the company to investigate interests;
(6) conferring of a power on a court to place restrictions on share transfers at the instance of a company when there has been a failure to disclose information, and to limit the circumstances when such restrictions may be removed.

The Companies (No 2) Bill 1981 was originally introduced to implement the requirement of the EEC Fourth Directive on the form of company accounts, to make certain alterations to the law regarding company and business names, and to permit a company to purchase its own securities.[18] The proposals on share disclosure were included at a late stage as Part IV of the Bill and delayed its receiving the Royal Assent. Although one of the Government's subsidiary intentions was to put the existing statutory requirements into a more readily intelligible form, it is not at once apparent that this has happened. The new format replaces sections 28, 33 and 34 of the 1967 Act and sections 26 and 27 of the 1976 Act as regards the disclosure of substantial interests in twenty clauses (clauses 58–78) running to twenty-three pages of Queens Printer's text.[19] Because of the impossibility of summary, these are reproduced in full as Appendix 4 of this work. The following commentary attempts to highlight the ways in which the law has been strengthened rather than to state the rules exhaustively. Emphasis has been given to provisions having greater relevance to insider dealing where possible.

5 The new law

DISCLOSURE OF VOTING INTERESTS IN PUBLIC COMPANIES

A person who knowingly acquires or relinquishes (or becomes aware that he has acquired or relinquished) any interest in relevant share capital of a public company, must disclose it where immediately before or after the relevant time (or both) his interest in the nominal value of the capital exceeds the notifiable percentage.[20] The facts relevant to determining whether a person has such an interest are taken to be what he knows them to be at the relevant time. Any change in circumstances which affects any fact relevant to the application of the notification requirement, triggers an obligation

18 For a general account of the Bill, see e g (1981) 2 Business Law Review (No 4) 99.
19 The following account, however, assumes that the Bill will shortly be enacted in the form in which it was ordered by the Commons to be printed on 9 July 1981.
20 Cl 58(1)–(3).

to make to the company the necessary notification.[21] The notification must comprise particulars of:

(1) the share capital to which it relates;
(2) the number of shares known to be the subject of the interest;
(3) in the case of a cessation of interest, a statement thereof.[1]

The obligation to notify must be performed within the period of five days next following the day upon which it arises. The 'relevant time' is the time of the event or change of circumstance which gives rise to the obligation.[2]

The difference in approach between section 33 and clause 58 concerns the treatment of knowledge of relevant information. Existing provisions base the notification obligation on factual events defined in terms of acquisitions, changes or losses of interest etc. Knowledge of this factual information determines when the notification arises. The view is taken is that it should be enough to prove that a person knew sufficient to be *aware* that he had a substantial interest in share capital in respect of which the obligation arises, rather than to prove knowledge of a particular acquisition. In clause 58 the events causing a notification obligation are generally defined in terms of a known change in interests, not particular known events.

The percentage level at which the disclosure obligation arises is maintained at 5 per cent and the test of significant changes above 5 per cent remains at 1 per cent, after rounding down; the Secretary of State may change the level by statutory instrument.[3]

Illustration X holds 4 per cent of the issued share capital of Y Limited, a public unlisted company. The capital carries class rights giving rights to vote in all circumstances in general meetings ('relevant share capital'). Z, another shareholder, becomes in arrear with calls on shares and forfeits the right to vote at meetings under the Articles. The result is that X now holds more than the notifiable percentage of relevant share capital. If he is also aware of Z's default. X is under an obligation to notify his interest under clause 58(4), notwithstanding that there has been no acquisition or disposal of his interest. This would not have been the case under section 33.

Clause 59 places a new obligation upon a person required to notify under clause 58. The notification is to include details in

21 Cl 58(4).
1 Cl 58(5).
2 Cl 58(9).
3 Cl 58(8), 58(7); cl 59.

writing of the registered holding as a result of which the interest arises, and any known change.

Clause 60 brings in interests of a spouse or child[4] and those of a body corporate in which the person concerned either:

(1) has more than a one-fifth (formerly one-third) interest in its voting shares;
(2) customarily gives directions to the board as to the actions it must take.

The Government opted for the lower level of control because it was felt desirable to improve the mechanism for giving advance warning of acquisition which could block a special resolution or which gives rise to a bid obligation under the City Code on Takeovers and Mergers.

CONCERT PARTIES

Existing requirements do not oblige combinations of persons or companies to aggregate their acquisitions for the purposes of disclosure merely on the ground that they are acting together. Lord Shawcross in his final report as Chairman of the Takeover Panel urged the Government to legislate 'to make it clear beyond doubt, as it is in the USA, that where persons acting in concert' acquire substantial interests, they are subject to disclosure requirements. In the USA the so-called Williams Act in 1968 amended the Securities Exchange Act 1934 to include a broad provision (in section 13(d)(3)) that 'where two or more persons act as a partnership, limited partnership, syndicate, or other group for the purpose of acquiring, holding or disposing of securities, such syndicate or group shall be deemed a "person" ' and consequently subject to all the disclosure requirements applying to a person under securities regulation in the USA.[5] Although the Stock Exchange has recommended that a similar broad provision be introduced into the United Kingdom, it has until now been recognised that there are considerable problems in framing a definition of 'acting in concert' which would successfully identify the element of intention involved. This is confirmed by the experience of the Takeover Panel, which, except in those cases covered by the presumptions stated in the Code, appear to have been able to determine the existence of such a concert party only *ex post facto* and largely on the basis of inferences from circumstantial evidence.

4 As with directors under s. 31 of the 1967 Act.

5 Quoted from Department of Trade, Disclosure of Interests in Shares (August 1980), p. 5. As to securities regulation in the USA, see ch 10, below.

Nevertheless, as a result of its consultations the Government have introduced clauses 62 and 63 into the 1981 Bill. The new statutory provisions operate by attributing to each member the interest of the other members and by requiring them to be taken into account by the member concerned in determining whether he is subject to an obligation to notify a substantial interest under clause 58. This is an attempt to solve a problem which can often have 'insider' connotations. The fact that investors A, B, C are acting in concert in relation to a company's affairs may be unknown to the other shareholders or, indeed, to the company itself, but their conjunction may affect the status of the company or the price at which its securities can be bought and sold. This is particularly the case where the concert party has, as its ultimate objective, a takeover of the company. It is to be noticed that the solution offered by clauses 62 and 63 is different from that of the so-called Williams Act in USA, whose approach of deeming members of a concert party to be a 'person' would, if adopted in statute law in the UK, implicitly impose a similar obligation on members to notify one another of acquisitions of interests. Such an approach would involve an unacceptably strict knowledge requirement, each member of the party being required to notify the company of the interest of his fellow members whether he knew this or not.

INTERESTS TO BE NOTIFIED

Clause 65 replaces section 28 of the 1967 Act and defines when a person is interested in shares for the purposes of clause 58. The definition is extended beyond the view of an interest in shares as only an interest recognised by law as existing in the shares themselves, to include all forms of contract and option and contingent contract to acquire interests, and all forms of arrangements which may confer a present or future right to exercise or control voting powers. The following are included:

(1) interest of any kind whatsoever in the shares;
(2) any interest in shares included in property held upon trust for any beneficiary of that trust;[6]
(3) (a) the entering into of a contract for the purchase of shares (whether for cash or other consideration); or
    (b) the entitlement by a person who is not the registered holder to exercise any right conferred by the holding of the shares or the entitlement to control the exercise of any such right.[7]

6 Cl 65(2).
7 Cl 65(4).

(4) (a) a right to call for delivery of the shares; or
(b) a right to acquire interest in the shares or an obligation to take an interest in the shares.

(Whether in any case the right or obligation is conditional or absolute.) A person is taken to be entitled to exercise or control the exercise of a right if he has a right (whether subject to conditions or not) the exercise of which would make him so entitled.[8]

Persons having a joint interest shall be taken each of them to have that interest. It is immaterial that shares in which a person has an interest are unidentifiable.

As with disclosure of directors' interests under section 27 of the 1967 Act and the Regulations made thereunder,[9] certain interests are disregarded. Additional interests are:

(1) an exempt interest held by a recognised jobber, if he carries on business in the United Kingdom and he holds the interest for the purposes of that business;[10]
(2) an exempt security interest, i e an interest held by a recognised bank or licensed institution under the Banking Act 1979 or an insurance company within the meaning of the Insurance Companies Act 1974, or a trustee savings bank, or a stock broker, or the Post Office, and in each case it is held by way of security only for the purposes of a transaction entered into in the ordinary course of their business in the recognised capacity.[11]

POSITION OF AGENTS

Clause 67, inter alia, places a new requirement upon a person who authorises an agent to deal on his behalf in relevant share capital to secure that the agent informs him immediately of any acquisition or disposal of an interest in shares effected by the agent where the resultant interest will give rise to a notification obligation under clause 58. Without such provision the legislature considered that it would be a simple matter for a principal to arrange for an agent to acquire interests on his behalf without informing him, and thus to evade the requirement to notify. However, the requirement is applied only in respect of those acquisitions or disposals which would give rise to a notification obligation, and will not therefore affect the great majority share dealings through an agent. It is, of course, normal practice for an agent to notify a principal of a deal carried out on his instructions immediately after the event.

8 Cl 65(5) and (6).
9 See p. 122, fn. 7, above.
10 Cl 66(1)(f), (4).
11 Cl 66(1)(g), (5).

REGISTRATION AND INVESTIGATION

By clause 68 every public company is obliged to keep a register for the purposes of clauses 58 and 60, and wherever the company receives information from a person in fulfilment of a notification obligation, it shall itself be under an obligation to mark the register, against the name of that person, with the information and the date of the inscription. Where a company receives a notification which includes a statement that the person notifying (or any other person) has ceased to be a member of a concert party under clause 62, the company must record that information accordingly. The obligations with regard to period of registration, form and maintainance of the register, are the same as for directors.[12] There is the same protection to keeps trust off the title.[13]

A new provision is that where the company ceases to be a public company it is obliged to keep the register and any index for a further period of ten years.[14]

Clause 69 enlarges the provisions enabling a company to require disclosure of beneficial interests in its voting shares. Section 27 of the 1976 Act, already considered, is replaced. The differences of approach are:

(1) the company's investigations need not begin with present registered members but with any person whom the company knows or has reasonable cause to believe to be or to have been interested in its shares;
(2) the company is empowered to seek information of a person whom it knows or has reasonable cause to believe to have acted as agent for someone interested in shares.

These extensions follow closely the existing powers of the Department of Trade to investigate beneficial ownership of companies under section 173 of the Companies Act 1948. Where a company obtains information pursuant to these provisions, it is obliged to register it under clause 70.

A new power is contained in clause 71 which enables a 10 per cent minority membership of a company to requisition the use of the investigative provision. The requisition must:

(a) state that the requisitionists are requiring the company to exercise its powers under clause 69;
(b) specify the manner in which they require those powers to be exercised; and

12 See pp. 118–119, above.
13 Cl 68(4).
14 Cl 68(7).

(c) give reasonable grounds for requiring the company to exercise those powers in the manner specified.[15]

At the conclusion of any investigation carried out by the company in pursuance of such a requisition, the company must prepare a report of the information received and make it available at the registered office within twenty-eight days. The company is not bound to make public the information where disclosure of substantial holdings in bodies incorporated or carrying on business outside the United Kingdom would be harmful.[16] The object of this provision is to enable shareholders to secure information about the interests of others so as to avoid the necessity for a full-scale investigation under the Department of Trade's statutory powers.[17]

PENALTIES

Where information is sought by a company under clause 69 and the addressee fails to give it, the company can apply to the court for an order directing that the shares concerned shall be subject to restrictions imposed by section 174 of the 1948 Act, i e effectively depriving the holder of voting, dividend and other rights until the default has been rectified. An aggrieved person may apply to the court for an order directing that the shares shall cease to be subject to the restrictions.[18] There are also criminal penalties.

A person who fails to fulfil the obligations imposed by clauses 58 to 63 is guilty of an offence, and is liable on conviction on indictment to imprisonment for a term not exceeding two years or a fine or both, and on summary conviction, to imprisonment for a term not exceeding six months or a fine not exceeding the statutory maximum, or both.[19] If a company makes default in acting on requisition of the minority membership under clause 71, the company and every officer is liable to a fine.[20]

6 Official investigation and inspection

DIRECTORS

The Companies Act 1967 empowers the Department of Trade to appoint inspectors if it appears that circumstances suggest a contravention of section 25 (dealing by directors in options for quoted

15 Cl 71(2).
16 Cl 71(6).
17 E g under Companies Act 1948, s. 172.
18 Cl 72(3).
19 Cl 67(3)–(4); as to the 'statutory maximum', see s. 87(1) of Companies Act 1981.
20 Cl 71(10).

securities) or of section 27 (obligation of directors to notify interests).[1] The function of the inspectors is to carry out any necessary investigations to establish whether or not contraventions have occurred, and to report the results to the Department of Trade. To ensure the investigations are effective, the inspectors may utilise powers contained in the Companies Act 1948,[2] to obtain documents and to examine a company's officers and agents on oath.

SHAREHOLDERS

Under section 172 of the Companies Act 1948, where it appears to the Department of Trade that there is good reason to do so, they may appoint inspectors to investigate a company for the purposes of determining the true persons who are or have been financially interested in the success or failure (real or apparent) of the company or able to control or materially to influence its policy. It will be seen at once that the scope of such an investigation is much wider than the mere ownership of shares, and section 172 can be regarded as a most important weapon in the armoury against insider abuse. A more limited power is given under section 173 to investigate the ownership of any securities without the appointment of an inspector, by requiring anyone whom the Department has reasonable cause to believe to have an interest in the securities, to give them relevant information. The statutory powers are commonly used in conjunction with others contained in the Companies Acts, e g sections 164 and 165 dealing in more general terms with a company's state of affairs. Although the inspectors are generally credited with wide powers under section 172, their reports can often be held up or rendered less effective by lack of co-operation and frankness on the part of controllers of overseas companies who have interests in the companies being investigated. This was true of the Pergamon, Lonrho, and Gold Fields investigations. Nevertheless, apart from being an effective sanction against the individuals and companies concerned, inspectors' reports often have the advantage of being able to probe deficiencies in existing regulations or practice which, admittedly after some delay, can produce reforms.[3] A strengthening of the statutory power is imminent.

THE LOWSON AFFAIR[4]

A recent example of the ability of inspectors appointed under statutory powers to uncover instances of insider dealing occurs with the

1 S. 32.
2 S. 167, with modifications.
3 See cll 80–86, Companies (No 2) Bill 1981.
4 For a full discussion see Rider and Ffrench *The Regulation of Insider Trading* p. 188.

Report into the affairs of the late Sir Denys Lowson, a former Lord Mayor of London.[5] The appointment was under section 165 of the 1948 Act, which provides for investigation compulsorily if the company by special resolution, or the court by order, declares that such an investigation ought to take place; alternatively as a matter of discretion if there are circumstances suggesting:

(1) that the company's affairs are being conducted with intent to defraud creditors or otherwise for a fraudulent or unlawful purpose or in a manner unfairly prejudicial to some part of its members, or that any actual proposed act or omission of the company would be so prejudicial etc; or
(2) the persons concerned with its formation or management have been guilty of fraud, misfeasance or rather misconduct; or
(3) that its members have not been given all the information with respect to its affairs which they might reasonably expect.[6]

The investigation centred on the sale in June/July 1972 of a total of approximately 80 per cent of the issued ordinary share capital of National Group of Unit Trusts by First Re-investment Trust, Nelsen Financial Trust and English and Scottish Unit Trust Holdings, and by eight other companies in the Lowson-dominated group, their purchase by Sir Denys, his family and associates, and their subsequent resale in January 1973 at a greatly enhanced price to Triumph Investment Trust. The two reports of Mr Hirst QC and Mr Langdon, in unravelling a complex company structure and series of dealings, drew attention to the dominant position occupied by Sir Denys Lowson and the breaches of duties resulting from conflicts of interest between his position as a director and an individual holder of shares. His dealings on the basis of confidential information constituted insider trading. Sir Denys offered to make restitution of profits but died before this could be carried into effect. Subsequently the companies concerned recovered £7 million from his estate. Summonses under section 199 of the 1948 Act, for conspiracy to defraud and fraud issued by the Director of Public Prosecutions were laid but subsequently withdrawn. On similar facts, it would now be possible to bring proceedings under Part V of the Companies Act 1980, which is considered in detail in chapter 9. Criminal prosecution does not, however, allow the company concerned or any shareholder thereof to recover compensation and in the absence of civil proceedings such as those described in chapter 6 reliance must be placed on the *in terrorem* sanction which

5 Report of the Inspector into the Affairs of First Re-Investment Trust Ltd, Nelsen Financial Trust Ltd, and English and Scottish Unit Trust Holdings Ltd (1974).
6 S. 165(1), as amended by Companies Act 1980, Sch 3.

section 165, section 172 and section 32 of the Companies Act 1967 give rise to. It remains an open question whether these piecemeal arrangements, together with self-regulatory machinery, are a sufficient safeguard of the public interest, or whether the kind of statutory securities regulation existing in the United States, and considered in chapter 10, could not usefully be introduced in the United Kingdom also.

Mention should finally be made of section 109 of the Companies Act 1967 which confers a power upon the Department of Trade, exercised by its Companies Investigation Branch, to call for documents and information from companies and persons associated with them, without the necessity for appointments of inspectors.

8 Self regulation

1 Introduction

In the United Kingdom no one official securities regulatory body exists which corresponds to the Securities Exchange Commission in the United States. The Department of Trade, the Director of Public Prosecutions, the Bank of England, and the courts all exercise authority in particular areas, although none are responsible for co-ordinating policy or maintaining machinery for the orderly working of the capital markets. Emphasis has therefore been placed on the role of the non-statutory, self-regulatory authorities of the City of London which City institutions have, in relatively recent times, developed to ensure fair dealing and to stave off criticism from Government and public which might lead to radical legal intervention. The dominant position of the Stock Exchange in regulating the affairs of its members and of companies who obtain a listing for their securities, is possibly an indication (a) of the regard paid to its integrity and authority, and (b) the success of a flexible internally-enforced system as against a rigid statutory bureaucracy. Nevertheless, critics of self regulation argue that the City tends to reform itself or impose increased disciplinary sanctions only when the level of abuse is causing widespread concern.[1] The recent Gold Fields case which highlighted problems of 'dawn raids' and 'concert parties'[2] produced swift action both from the Stock Exchange and the Council for the Securities Industry, but not before public confidence in the securities market had been affected to the extent that Department of Trade inspectors had been appointed to investigate, and consultations had begun which resulted in new provisions on share disclosure (Part V, Companies Bill 1981). Again, in areas such as takeovers, the organ of self regulation (the City Panel on Takeovers and Mergers) has initially proved itself quite inadequate to thwart the dubious tactics of a determined bidder.[3] While a Conservative Government may be

1 Rider and Ffrench *The Regulation of Insider Trading* p. 207.
2 Discussed in ch 7, pp. 125–126, above.
3 See Davies *The Regulation of Takeovers and Mergers* pp. 42–46.

expected to afford the City repeated opportunities to improve the effectiveness of its policing,[4] an administration of the Left would be under pressure to introduce a more centralised system of control. Meanwhile, the Stock Exchange is about to be invested with, in relation to the contents of company prospectuses, quasi-statutory functions under the terms of the EEC Sixth Directive,[5] a process that may well be extended.[6] In examining the role of City authorities, the following discussion concentrates on those measures aimed directly or indirectly at inhibiting insider dealing in listed securities.[7]

2 The Stock Exchange

LISTING REQUIREMENTS

The Listing Agreement[8] takes the form of a resolution to be passed by the board of directors binding the company to observe rules and procedures in relation to its status as a listed company. (The term 'listing' has replaced altogether the term 'quotation', to draw a distinction with the Unlisted Securities Market.) The Listing Agreement is required to be adopted on the first occasion on which any of the company's securities are admitted to listing.[9] The main object of the Agreement is to secure immediate disclosure of information which might reasonably be expected to have a material effect on market activity and on prices of listed securities. Directors must ensure that dealings do not take place between parties one of whom does not have price-sensitive information in the possession of the other. The Quotations Department (why not now Listing Department?) of the Stock Exchange advises companies in the interpretation of the Agreement, on an individual and confidential basis, through the medium of the company's brokers. It is not thought that the Agreement is directly enforceable at law, although

4 Although it is noteworthy that a Conservative Government was (in 1973) the first to produce a bill on insider dealing and the first (in 1980) to put measures on the statute book.

5 Directive 80/390/EEC; one of three concerning listed securities, which require Member States to nominate a national authority to administer.

6 It is not certain that the Council of the Stock Exchange is necessarily in favour of being invested with this authority, on the basis that it must stand increasingly aloof from the interests of its members.

7 The Draft Directive on reporting of company information (OJ 1979 C29/5) is also relevant to insider dealing.

8 Admission of Securities to Listing, ch 2 ('The Yellow Book').

9 Admission of Securities to Listing, p. 21.

suspension of securities from listing is a powerful deterrent to non-compliance.[10]

Among the matters required to be disclosed by the company are:

(1) Any information necessary to enable shareholders and the public to appraise the company's position and to avoid the establishment of a false market in its securities. This is a very wide provision, giving the Stock Exchange in theory almost unlimited power to require disclosure, a power accordingly to be exercised with great circumspection if companies are not going to find the attractions of de-listing too great.

(2) After board approval, any proposed dividend, distribution, or announcement of profits or losses for the year or half-year. Business on the Stock Exchange is conducted officially until 3.30 p.m. each day, and notification is advised before 3.00 p.m. to ensure immediate release, although the Stock Exchange Market Price Display Service may show the information until 5.00 p.m. It is good practice, therefore, to organise board meetings to approve announcements of offers, results, new issues, acquisitions, disposals, mergers, and other significant matters for 10.00 a.m. or 11.00 a.m.

(3) Any proposed change in capital structure, including any redemption of securities.

(4) Particulars of substantial acquisitions or realisations[11] of assets or businesses, including those in which existing directors or shareholders are interested.

(5) Any information to be notified under section 33 of the Companies Act 1967 (shareholders' interests and register).[12]

(6) Any information required to be disclosed under the provisions of the City Code on Takeovers and Mergers (see below).

(7) Any changes in the directorate or in the general character of the business of the company or any subsidiary. It is a matter of degree as to what amounts to a change in 'general character', and in cases of doubt the company's broker or solicitor should be consulted. Any change which involves altering the objects clause in the memorandum of association is clearly included, but objects clauses are conventionally so widely drawn that it is legally possible to change course from e g a property investment company to a general trading company, with little

10 Gower *Modern Company Law* (4th edn) p. 506, nn. 89, 90. But analagously, members of a club subscribing to its byelaws sometimes have direct rights against each other, see *Clarke v Dunraven* [1897] AC 59.

11 As described in Admission of Securities to Listing, ch 4, and divided into various Classes.

12 Refer now to Part V, Companies (No 2) Bill 1981.

formality.[13] In such a case investors are entitled to be informed of the board's decision, in order to decide whether or not to sell up.

The Company must forward to the Quotations Department copies of proof circulars to shareholders for approval, reports and announcements, and non-routine resolutions; and must circulate much additional information to that required by the Companies Acts, at the time of the Directors' Report.[14] It must adopt rules governing dealings by directors in the listed securities of the company no less exacting than those of the Model Code (see below).

ANNOUNCEMENT OF PRICE-SENSITIVE MATTERS

In April 1977 a Joint Statement was issued by the Stock Exchange and the City Panel on Takeovers and Mergers concerning price-sensitive information.[15] It proceeds on the basis that where evidence of insider dealing has been found, the culprits have usually been tippees or others acting on mere rumour, rather than primary insiders such as directors and connected persons. Accordingly, it was thought desirable to issue guidelines to listed companies ensuring greater confidentiality and security in relation to price-sensitive matters. Four points are emphasised:

(1) companies and those advising them should establish effective internal regimes to ensure secrecy and notify all concerned of their obligations in this regard;[16]
(2) paragraph 1 of the Listing Agreement, requiring disclosure of all necessary information to avoid a false market in the securities, should alert directors to the need for an early warning announcement of matters likely to affect the share price;
(3) where merger or takeover negotiations are proceeding in strict confidence, the Takeover Panel will normally expect an announcement to be made:

13 Unless thereby the 'substratum', i e main object, of the company has gone, see e g *Re German Date Coffee Co* (1882) 20 ChD 169; *Anglo Overseas Agencies Ltd v Green* [1961] 1 QB 1, [1960] 3 All ER 244; but the objects may be construed as independent main objects: *Cotman v Brougham* [1918] AC 514; and of course s. 9 of the European Communities Act 1972 may provide a let-out. See also the dicussion in ch 1, p. 16, above. A change to investment company status may involve different distribution policy, see Companies Act 1980, s. 41.

14 As to the statutory requirements, see Companies Act 1967, s. 16 as amended; ch 4, pp. 66–67, above.

15 Admission of Securities to Listing, pp. 44–46.

16 See rr. 7 and 30 of the City Takeover Code.

(i) where negotiations have reached a stage where an offer is confidently expected; or

(ii) where discussions are about to be enlarged to include, e g major shareholders;

(4) delays in making announcements for any bona fide reason should encourage an application to the Stock Exchange to grant a temporary halt in dealings in the company's securities.[17]

THE MODEL CODE

In 1977 the Stock Exchange promulgated a Model Code for Securities Transactions by Directors of Listed Companies. This has been mentioned in chapter 6[18] and the latest edition[19] is reproduced at Appendix 3. The intention is to provide directors with a set of guidelines to be applied as a minimum standard in their relationship with their companies. The Code is annexed to the Listing Agreement and, as noticed above, must be converted into a set of internal rules by each subscribing company which bind the directors thereof. The manner of adoption is variable, although the simplest courses will be either (i) formal adoption of the Code as a whole by resolution of the board (not the company in general meeting); or (ii) annexing the Code to directors' service contracts and adding a clause thereto requiring them to comply with the spirit and intendment of its terms; or (iii) instructing the company's solicitors to prepare a memorandum (afterwards formally adopted) which states the law on directors' duties including insider dealing, and incorporates the Code by reference or otherwise; or (iv) a combination of (i)–(iii). A specimen memorandum on insider dealing only appears as Appendix 5 of this work.

Neither the Code nor the Listing Agreement specifies what is to happen if the Code is breached by an individual director. It cannot automatically be assumed that such a breach will constitute a breach of the Agreement itself by the company, for which the Stock Exchange could impose a sanction. Indeed it would be harsh if a company were held liable for defaults of its officers, unless the circumstances were such that a majority of the board or even the majority shareholders were aware of the misfeasances and took no steps to remedy them such that an improper motive could be attributed to the company itself. Nor, of course, could the Stock Exchange take any direct action against the officer, since he has not subscribed the Listing Agreement (although, as may be seen from

17 See r. 5, City Takeover Code.
18 See p. 106, above.
19 Admission of Securities to Listing (1981 reprint), pp. 47–53.

Appendix 3, he is required to make a Declaration in the prescribed form and false particulars would invoke censure and adverse publicity). Conversely, the fact that a director abides by the Code 'is not a defence in law and it may therefore be necessary to be satisfied that a proposed dealing would not be in contravention of statutory provisions'.[20] Compliance with Part V of the Companies Act 1980 is considered by the Stock Exchange to be axiomatic.

FORM OF THE CODE

The Code as published appears in four parts. First, there is a preliminary statement emphasising, inter alia, its non-exclusive nature and the importance of flexibility in observing best practice. Second, six basic principles are set out. These are: (1) That directors should not deal in their companies' securities on considerations of a short-term nature. (2) Directors must accept that they will always be thought to be in possession of more information than can at any particular time be made publicly available. Accordingly they are not at all times free to deal in their companies' securities. (3) Notwithstanding the general constraints of (1) and (2), there must be periods in the year when directors can be regarded as free to deal. In choosing a time to deal, directors should embargo transactions for a minimum period of two months[1] prior to the announcement of regularly occurring information, particularly profits, dividends and other distributions, whether or not the information is price-sensitive. Also, dealings should not take place prior to the announcement of matters of an exceptional nature which involve price sensitivity. (4) Because of the particular difficulty of 'matters of an exceptional nature', a director even without knowledge of such matters should be advised, when he notifies an intention to deal,[2] that the transaction may be inappropriate, e g because it would take place after an announcement. (5) All dealings in which a director is, or is deemed to be, interested, should be conducted in accordance with the provisions of the Code.[3] Where he is a trustee of securities, he should observe the same rules, and encourage his fellow trustees (if they are not directors) to do the same. As trustee, he should *not* use confidential information for the benefit of those to whom he owes a fudiciary duty. (6) Where a

20 Admission of Securities to Listing, p. 47.

1 The period defined in r. 3.1 of the Code. In earlier versions, no period was prescribed.

2 Under r. 2.1, which provides notification to the chairman or other designated director.

3 See r. 4.1.

director places investment funds under professional management, the managers should be made subject to the same restrictions (as if they were dealing as insider-principals).[4]

The third part of the Code is constituted by the rules themselves. No detailed commentary is required here, except to remark that rule 6 requires directors to ensure that every employee of the company and every director or employee of a subsidiary company, who is in possession of price-sensitive information, should deal only in accordance with the Code. This is a hard rule to obey, since once the directors have endeavoured to establish a reasonably watertight regime by way of in-house rules or otherwise (see below), there is little else they can do to prevent insider abuse by senior officers or employees. The fourth part is the Director's Declaration, the contents of which is authorised to be disclosed to members of the Stock Exchange.

STOCK MARKET SURVEILLANCE

The Quotations Department of the Stock Exchange has the responsibility for ensuring that the provisions of the Listing Agreement are complied with as regards disclosure of information. Rumours or unusual price movements of larger companies are normally quickly picked up by the market and the Department will make initial investigations through the company's brokers if it is felt that facts are being withheld. This may result in a temporary suspension of listing. Monitoring also takes place through the Market Price Display System, which reveals about 700 listed securities, but it is possible for a little-traded security to fluctuate in price without attracting attention. Where trading has taken place in circumstances suggesting impropriety, an investigating committee will be set up, using the co-operation of jobbers. The rules of the Stock Exchange require member firms to give such information as is requisite. However, where 'warehousing' of shares has taken place over a period of time through nominees, it will be difficult to identify any culprits. The committee will produce a report, which may be circulated to the Takeover Panel or the company concerned, or in rare drastic cases submitted to the Department of Trade or made public. Press comment is one of the most powerful deterrents to abuse, but it is somewhat haphazard. Since the true incidence of insider activity is not known,[5] it is likewise impossible to gauge the tenacity of the investigating committee structure.

4 But it is not clear how this is to be procured or enforced.

5 In its Report for 1972–73, the Takeover Panel expressed the view 'that the incidence of such dealing has been much exaggerated'.

About twenty investigations a year are made, a quarter of which find evidence of abuse. It is unlikely that Governments of both complexions would have pressed ahead with criminal sanctions against insider dealing if this was the extent of the problem. It is, however, the maximum extent that the Stock Exchange can intervene without fundamentally changing the way it operates.[6]

3 The City Takeover Panel

ORIGINS OF THE PANEL

Insider abuse and other sharp practices during the period of economic growth and takeover activity that characterised the Macmillan Government, prompted that Government to eoncourage City institutions to work together to produce 'Revised Notes on Company Amalgamations' (1963), the object of which was to secure fair dealing and timely disclosure in relation to bids. Further outside criticism led to the establishment of the City Panel on Takeovers and Mergers, whose authority depended more on the reputation of its chairman (Lord Shawcross) than the extent of its powers: and which was soon shown to lack the means to check the excesses of certain determined individuals.[7] The Panel has from time to time been reconstituted, so it now has a full-time executive and an Appeals Committee. The City Code, which it administers, has been clarified and less reliance placed on exhortations to observe the 'spirit' of the rules as a substitute for faulty drafting.[8] Nevertheless there remain severe weaknesses in its functioning:[9]

The Council of the Stock Exchange expects companies whose securities are listed to comply with the City Code[10] and gives full support to the Panel. Among the remedies it can employ are:

(1) public statements of censure;
(2) reference to the Department of Trade for action under the Prevention of Fraud (Investments) Act 1958 or the Companies Acts;
(3) reference to professional disciplinary bodies of persons found to be in breach of the Code; and
(4) request to the Stock Exchange to suspend or de-list.

6 The Stock Exchange is also responsible for the regulation of the Unlisted Securities Market.

7 Among the worst examples was Pergamon Press; see Davies 'An Affair of the City' 36 Modern Law Review 457.

8 See Davies *Regulation of Takeovers and Mergers* p. 40.

9 For example, its inability to compel witnesses, and lack of qualified privilege in relation to possible libel suits.

10 Note 24, para 5(b), Admission of Securities to Listing, p. 28.

It has no powers to initiate civil or criminal proceedings of any kind.

THE CITY CODE AND INSIDER DEALING

The Code was first produced in 1958 and has passed through five editions.[11] It is supplemented by Panel Memoranda of Interpretation and Practice.[12] The provisions of the Code fall into two categories, General Principles and Rules, there being fourteen of the former and thirty-nine of the latter, as well as eight Practice Notes. The Code seeks principally to protect shareholders of a target company, not by prescribing the contents of takeover documents[13] but by regulating in detail the timetable and procedure for a bid. It is capable of applying to public companies doing business on the Unlisted Securities Market and to private companies where the takeover of a public company is involved.[14] The governing principle is set out as General Principle 5:

> It must be the object of all parties to a takeover or merger transaction to use every endeavour to prevent the creation of a false market in the shares of the offeror or offeree company.

This, of course, is in similar terms to paragraph 1 of the Stock Exchange Listing Agreement.[15] Its generality is made more potent by the fact that General Principle 1 states that 'the General Principles and the spirit of the Code will apply in areas or circumstances not explicitly covered by any Rule'.

Other relevant General Principles can be summarised shortly. GP3 expresses that no relevant information is to be withheld from shareholders, the test of relevancy being such evidence, facts and opinions as are necessary to make an adequate judgement. It must, for example, be relevant (and hence disclosable) to the shareholder of a target company that the directors of it, in recommending an acceptance of an offer, are to receive shares or service agreements after the merger. Under GP9, if offers are made only to particular shareholders, any subsequent general offer by the offeror or persons acting in concert, must be made on not less favourable terms.[16] Under GP10, and save as therein set out, during the course

11 It is printed both separately and as pp. 81 – 133 of the current reprint of Admission of Securities to Listing.
12 As to which see Palmer *Company Law* (22nd edn) vol 2, Part D.
13 These are contained in the Licensed Dealers (Conduct of Business) Rules 1960 (SI 1960 No 1216) under the Prevention of Fraud (Investments) Act 1958.
14 City Code, Practice Note No 1.
15 See p. 139, above.
16 See also GP13, and the definition of 'acting in concert' on pp. 81 – 82 of Admission of Securities to Listing; cf discussion on statutory control of 'concert parties', ch 7, pp. 129 – 130, above.

of takeover negotiations, neither the offeror or offeree company nor their advisers are to furnish information to some shareholders which is not made available to all the others. Thus, if a merchant bank acting for a bidder discloses to the major shareholders of the target, in confidence, that its principal will in no circumstances increase the bid price for the shares, that itself is price-sensitive information (because it may encourage the major shareholders to accept or sell at once, ánd not 'hang on') and should be disclosed to the others. In such a case it may be better not to communicate the intention at all. The first paragraph of GP11 deals with directors. They are, when advising their shareholders, enjoined from acting other than directors and to disregard their personal or family shareholdings or their personal relationships with the company.

The following rules apply to the present discussion:

Rule 7
The vital importance of absolute secrecy before an announcement must be emphasised.

Rule 13(1)
There must be included in every offer document a statement whether or not any agreement arrangement or understanding exists between the offeror or any person acting in concert with it and any of the directors, or recent directors, or shareholders or recent shareholders of the offeree company having any connection with or dependence upon the offer, and full particulars of any such agreement, arrangement or understanding.

Rule 17(1) and (2) (summarised)
The offer document must state:
(a) the shareholdings of the offeror and its directors in the offeree;
(b) the shareholdings in either company of persons acting in concert with the offeror, or those who have already agreed to accept the offer.

The advice document of the offeree company must state similar.

Rule 17(4)
If any party referred to (in sub-rules (1) and (2) above) has dealt for value in the shares in question during the period commencing 12 months prior to the beginning of the offer period and ending with the latest practicable date prior to the posting of the offer document, the details, including dates and prices, must be stated. If no such deals have been made this fact should be stated.

Rule 30
All persons concerned with the consideration and discussion of any proposed offer must treat the information related to the potential offer as secret and must not pass it to any other person unless it is necessary to do so. Furthermore, such persons must conduct themselves so as to minimise the chances of an accidental leak of information. No dealings of any kind (including option business) in the securities of the offeree company

by any person, not being the offeror, who is privy to the preliminary takeover or merger discussions or to an intention to make an offer may take place between the time when there is reason to suppose that an approach or an offer is contemplated and the announcement of the approach or offer or the termination of the discussions.

No such dealings shall take place in the securities of the offeror except where the proposed offer is not deemed price sensitive in relation to such securities.

(The remainder of rule 30 defines 'privy' in a similar sense to 'connected' for the purposes of section 68 of the Companies Act 1980.)[17]

Rule 36

Except with the consent of the Panel, the offeror or persons acting in concert with it may not enter into arrangements to deal or make purchases or sales of shares of the offeree company, either during an offer or when one is reasonably in contemplation, if such arrangements to deal, purchases or sales have attached thereto favourable conditions which are not being extended to all shareholders.

It will be seen that these rules fall naturally into three groups. First, those which require absolute confidentiality during discussions and an embargo on use of price-sensitive information during that time. Second, those which require full disclosure of material facts at the first available opportunity, including details of shareholders and directors' interests. Third, those which demand equality of treatment, both as to offers and disclosure, between all groups of shareholders of the target company. Rule 30 is the most important inhibitor of insider dealing, and is considerably strengthened as against the 1974 Code version.[18] Nothing in the rules, however, prevents an offeror company from acquiring shares in the offeree during the negotiation period if the only price-sensitive information it has is its own intentions.[19] Information received confidentially from the offeree or its directors or advisers, however, may prevent dealing. Rule 31 provides that in principle it is considered undesirable to fetter the market.

PANEL DECISIONS

The City Takeover Panel publicises the results of its investigations by issuing Statements, identified either by date or with the name of the company concerned. Where evidence of insider dealing is found pressure is brought to bear (without any legal compulsion) on the culprit to restore his illicit profit by making a suitable donation to charity, etc. Many cases involve breach of rule 30, or, where no

17 See p. 154, below.
18 See Rider and Ffrench *The Regulation of Insider Dealing* p. 163.
19 Subject to r. 31 and Practice Note 7.

specific abuse can be traced, the more general provisions of rule 7 (need for secrecy during negotiations).

In *A Gun (Holdings) Ltd*,[20] an insider gratuitously leaked the fact of merger negotiations at a party, to a tippee who immediately purchased the securities concerned and made a profit of £1,100. The insider was in breach of rule 7 but the tippee, who was a complete outsider without fiduciary responsibilities towards the company, was excused. In *Tootal Ltd and Trutax Ltd*[1] share purchases were mysteriously effected in the vicinity of the company's premises on bid rumours, even though the management of the company was itself unware of the rumours. Since no individuals could be blamed for passing price-sensitive information, there was held merely to be a breach of rule 7. In *D F Lyons & Co Ltd*[2] the offeror company had dealt after having obtained information about the intentions of a third party, and was in breach of rule 30. In *C H Johnson & Sons Ltd*[3] a bank employee acquired inside information through his employer's involvement in negotiations for a public offer. This was in breach of rule 30 since he was 'privy' within the meaning of that rule, and he was ordered to repay his profit.

4 Internal and professional rules

IN-HOUSE RULES

As discussed, the Stock Exchange requires, through the medium of its Listing Agreement, that companies establish internal rules and procedures to minimise the risk of insider activity, both by compelling secrecy and prohibiting the taking of a personal advantage which is inconsistent with one's duty. Since the Model Code is less than four years old, however, its universal acceptance is still distant. Company secretaries and other advisers should check to see what, if any, regime is in force for their directors and senior employees, and whether existing memoranda need updating in the light of the Companies Act 1980 and the Companies Bill 1981. A specimen memorandum on insider dealing appears at Appendix 5, but this is intended only as a guide as to the *type* of reminders that should be made available, since different companies have different requirements.

The position of those who professionally advise companies, is generally regulated by the professional bodies concerned (see

20 Statement, 11 February 1976.
1 Statement, 2 October 1975.
2 Statement, 2 October 1972.
3 Statement, 28 November 1977. There are many other instances.

below). Banking houses, however, who are often brought in at sensitive moments in a public company's life, have special problems as insiders, since no special constraints are imposed on them the breach of which involves disciplinary professional action. The City Takeover Panel has therefore addressed itself to the question of bankers' conflicts of interest.[4]

The Panel recommended that a number of principles be adhered to:

(1) All clients of the bank should be made aware of the conflict of interest and of the need for complete segregation (the so-called 'Chinese Wall').
(2) No inside information which a bank has access to should be used in forming any investment decisions, unless it is already available to independent outsiders, e g brokers or analysts.
(3) While banks are bound by the City Code, they are not precluded from buying shares in their client's company on their own account.
(4) The number of persons within the bank having price-sensitive information should be as restricted as possible.
(5) Security should periodically be reviewed.
(6) Banks should prohibit staff from dealing on their own account except through the bank itself.
(7) The standard for judging the propriety of any dealings is whether the bank is prepared to justify it subsequently at a public inquiry.

PROFESSIONAL RULES

Rule 16 of the Stock Exchange's Rules and Regulations provides for heavy penalties for Members violating the Rules, or the City Code.

The Law Society has issued guidelines to solicitors to the effect that it is improper for a solicitor to use for his own advantage, or that of any client, any trust or communicate any information which is confidential.[5] Most firms of solicitors issue specific rules to their staff on insider dealing.

5 The Council for the Securities Industry

Following consultations with the Secretary of State for Trade and the professional organisations concerned, the Bank of England

4 Annual Report of the City Panel on Takeovers and Mergers (1970), Appendix 1.
5 Practice Notes, Council Statement, 71 Law Society's Gazette 395.

announced on 30 March 1978 the decision to establish a Council for the Securities Industry. Its objectives are:

(a) to maintain the highest ethical standards in the conduct of business within the securities industry;
(b) to keep under constant review the evolution of the securities industry, market practice and related codes of conduct and to scrutinise the effectiveness of existing forms of regulation and the machinery for their administration;
(c) to maintain arrangements for the investigation of cases of alleged misconduct within the securities industry and breaches of codes of conduct or best practice keep these arrangements under review;
(d) to initiate new policies and codes as necessary concerning activities in the securities industry other than those properly within the domestic province of each individual constituent member;
(e) to resolve differences on matters of principle between constituent parts of the securities industry;
(f) to consider the need for changes in legislation affecting the activities of the securities industry and to examine any proposals for such legislation;
(g) to ensure liaison with the European Commission on securities industry matters and the implementation of the EEC Capital Markets Code of Conduct.[6]

Membership of the Council consists of leading representatives of City institutions all of whom have agreed to accept the rulings of the Council and to assist its operation. The Council's existence is derived from an increased awareness of the need to co-ordinate the machinery of self-regulation, and to monitor the capital markets in the light of the secondary banking crisis of 1973/74.

The Council has taken responsibility for revisions of the City Code and the February 1981 reprint (CSI No 3, blue cover) is issued under its authority. The Council also issues documents bearing upon particular aspects of the industry.[7]

The Council is financed from contributions made by the bodies represented thereon and from a levy on contract notes of securities exchange transactions.

Almost immediately after its formation the Council tackled the problem of insider dealing.[8] The Council's position is that it is

6 Report for year to 31 March 1979, p. 5.
7 E g Guidelines for Personal Dealings by Fund Managers (CSI No 4), March 1981.
8 Report for year to 31 March 1979, Appendix A.

contrary to good business ethics that a man holding a position of trust should use confidential information for his personal benefit. It endorsed the Stock Exchange's Model Code for Directors and made comments on the statutory proposals resulting in Part V of the Companies Act 1980. In its report for the year to 31 March 1981 (Appendix B) the council made a statement to indicate how the self-regulatory bodies proposed to complement the narrow statutory code. However, the only direct recommendation seems to be that organisations, other than listed companies, should consider whether they should not prepare a code of conduct for their members based on the Model Code, where they do not already have one.[9] It remains to be seen whether any further measures are contemplated, particularly with regard to restitution of windfall profits and improved inquisitorial powers of the Takeover Panel to ferret out evidence of insider abuse. It must be noted that the Council has been roundly criticised for its relatively tame attitude to certain problems of securities regulation, but it is too early to assess whether this is well-founded.

9 Appendix B, para 9.

9 Statutory prohibition of insider dealing

1 Timing and application

TIMING

The Companies Act 1980 received the Royal Assent on 1 May 1980. Part V, which contains provisions outlawing the use by an insider of unpublished price-sensitive information in relation to a company's quoted securities, came into operation on 23 June, 1980.[1] Accordingly, any transaction occurring on or after that date is one to which the Act can apply and periods of connection with a company[2] can be ante-dated for the purposes of establishing insider status to 23 December 1979.

APPLICATION

The prohibitions under Part V apply only to individuals. The word 'individual' is used instead of the word 'person' in order to exclude companies or other corporate bodies, e g local authorities. A limited company registered under the Companies Acts 1948/80, whose officers or staff acquired confidential information acting e g as bankers to another company, could not have attributed to it the quality of an insider and is not capable of being prosecuted directly under Part V. To have provided otherwise it would have required companies to construct an artificial 'Chinese wall' among their operating divisions to stem the flow of information. However, an individual director, officer or employee of a body corporate may have relevant information and as such he will be prohibited from dealing himself or from counselling or procuring another person to deal,[3] who could be his employer or an associated company of the employer.

The company whose securities are covered means any company whether registered under the Companies Act or not. Accordingly

1 Companies Act 1980 (Commencement) Order 1980 (SI 1980 No 745).
2 E g under s. 68(1).
3 S. 68(6).

foreign companies, unregistered companies, companies incorporated by private act of Parliament and companies incorporated by Royal Charter are included.[4] Where Part V refers to a 'related company', e g in treating a director thereof as a person connected with the subject company,[5] the reference is to any body corporate which is the first company's subsidiary or holding company, or is another subsidiary of that company's holding company.

Illustration X buys shares in P Limited. X is a director of H Limited, which is a partially-owned subsidiary of J Limited. P Limited is also a subsidiary of J Limited. H Limited will be a 'related company' of P Limited, and X as an officer of such company will be deemed to be connected with P Limited, whether he actually has inside information affecting the price of its shares, or not.

As to territorial jurisdiction, actions taken in the United Kingdom in connection with overseas companies having a Stock Exchange listing, will be subject to sanction. Actions taken outside the United Kingdom which would result in the commission of an offence if they were taken here, may still so result if the individual concerned returns within the jurisdiction.

Illustration X is prohibited from dealing by virtue of his connection with Y Limited under Part V. He flies to South Africa and instructs a broker in London to deal, and then returns home. Alternatively he procures some other individual in South Africa to give the necessary instructions. In either case he will be liable to prosecution. Since Part V is concerned with 'counselling or procuring' as well as actual dealing, the important venue for jurisdiction is the place where the instruction or suggestion originates.

2 Prohibition of dealing

THE STATUTORY INSIDER

Insiders are identified in different ways under the Act. Restrictions are principally imposed on dealings by an individual who is, or has at any time within the previous six months, 'knowingly connected with a company'.[6]

4 S. 73(5).
5 For 'connected individuals', see s. 73(1).
6 S. 68(1).

Connection can arise in one of two ways:

(1) an individual is a director of the company or of a related company;
(2) an individual occupies a position as an officer (other than director) or employee of, or has a professional relationship with, a company or a related company which might reasonably be expected to give him access to unpublished price-sensitive information about the securities of either company and which he would not reasonably be expected to disclose except for the proper performance of his functions.[7]

To establish a connection under (2) of the above, it will be noticed that a number of separate, cumulative criteria have to be met. First, the individual must either be (i) an office holder, or (ii) an employee, or (iii) have a professional relationship. It is not settled whether the officer must be designated as such, e g company secretary or general manager, or whether the exercise of a function within the organisation such as a senior bookkeeper, would be sufficient.[8] If the bookkeeper is an employee, he will be covered under (ii). The term 'officer' is defined in the Companies Act 1948[9] to include manager. A borderline case might be a part-time accounts assistant engaged under a contract for services, unless it can be said he has established a professional relationship within (iii). A solicitor or broker is clearly within this latter category; but does 'professional' refer only to the status of the person providing the services to the company, or would anyone in business, e g supplying computer software or advertising material, be so classified? It appears that the draftsman of section 73(1)(b) intended the categories to be exhaustive.

Second, the position occupied has to be shown to be one 'which might reasonably be expected to give him access to unpublished price-sensitive information'. It is not necessary to show that the individual actually acquired the information, or that he had the opportunity to acquire it, merely that his relationship with the company was of a kind that an impartial observer would regard as in some way being confidential or privileged. It is, of course, possible that a person be afforded access to company books and papers for a certain purpose, but succeed in acquiring information unconnected with that purpose. For example, personnel consultants in attendance at a company's premises on staff duties

7 S. 73(1)(b).
8 Joffe suggests that it would; Joffe *The Companies Act 1980* para 11.10.
9 S. 455; 'officer' is also treated as a separate category in s. 56(2) of the 1980 Act (Disclosure of interest).

may overhear discussions concerning matters which, if disc... would be 'price-sensitive'. It is submitted that a court would find little difficulty in showing that the test of 'constructive access' had been satisfied in such a case.

Third, it has to be shown that the individual is 'knowingly' connected. The requirement of knowledge peppers section 68, occasionally confusingly, but in this context is used to exonerate an individual who is 'unwittingly connected with the company because, for example, of labyrinthine group holdings.[10] 'Knowledge' is probably limited to actual knowledge or recklessness, and it will not be sufficient to show that he ought to have known of his connection with the subject company, even if his ignorance is negligent. It may possibly be too easy for a defendant to deny in the witness box that he was cognisant of the relationship.

The other types of insider are Crown servants and tippees. These are separately treated below.[11]

INSIDE INFORMATION

Information has the quality of being confidential for the purposes of Part V if:

(a) it is held by virtue of the connection with the company;[12]
(b) it is information that ought not reasonably to be disclosed by the individual except for the proper performance of his functions;[13]
(c) the individual knows that it is unpublished price-sensitive information in relation to the securities;[14] and
(d) it relates to any transaction (actual or contemplated) involving the company with which the individual is connected and the company whose securities are concerned or to the fact that such a transaction is no longer contemplated.[15]

Each of these aspects require some discussion:

(a) *Reason for holding* Information of an external kind[16] is generated in the capital markets and any regulation of insider dealing must be delicately balanced so as not to substantially interfere with the workings of those markets. Information may be price-

10 Prentice *The Companies Act 1980* p. 122.
11 See p. 64.
12 S. 68(1)(a).
13 S. 68(1)(b).
14 S. 68(1)(c).
15 S. 68(1)(d).
16 Considered in ch 6, p. 103, above.

sensitive and also unpublished in the sense that not every shareholder has instant access to the records or figures upon which it is based, but it is of a quality that is incapable of realistic protection. Accordingly only information acquired by virtue of the insider's office is considered relevant. If an insider such as a director is told over a business lunch by an investment analyst that his company could be heading for takeover since there has been a gradual build-up of interest in the listed securities (a prolonged 'dawn raid' of the type RTZ were experiencing in the late summer of 1981), then unless that information is as a result of a tip by a prohibited person, in which case both the analyst and the director will be tippees and themselves prohibited, the information or rumour does not of itself restrict the director. Whether this is to be regarded as a weakness in the drafting of section 68 remains to be seen.[17]

(b) *Unreasonable to disclose* An objective test is imposed on the insider to determine whether it is proper for him to make known to a third party the information which he has acquired by virtue of his position. It is hard to see what category of disclosure this covers, since there can be few cases where a director or employee can legitimately divulge information except in the performance of their contractual or fiduciary duties, and perhaps not even then. One commentator[18] suggests that section 68(1)(b) is drawing a distinction between proper and improper usages of information, but it is submitted that the only occasion for proper disclosure is in performance of functions, at least in the case of a director or employee. It would be unwise for anyone giving guidance on the impact of Part V to advise a company or its staff or associates that there were any occasions when confidential information could properly be used for self-dealing or transmitted to an outsider for such use.

(c) *Unpublished and price-sensitive* These words are considered below:

PRICE-SENSITIVITY ETC

Section 73(2) defines 'unpublished price-sensitive information' as information which:

(a) relates to specific matters relating or of concern (directly or indirectly) to that company, that is to say, is not of a general nature relating to or of concern to that company;

17 In the US the proposed Federal Draft Securities Law makes no distinction between the Internal Company Information and Market Information; ALI FED SEC Code, para 1603, Comment 2 (j).

18 Prentice *The Companies Act 1980* para 301.

(b) is not generally known to those persons who are accustomed or would be likely to deal in those securities but which would if it were generally known to them, be likely to affect the price of those securities.

This definition is a minefield. The first problem is to distinguish specific and general information. In debate the Government described the difference as being between 'day-to-day knowledge' and 'knowledge of important factors which, when revealed to the market, will shift the price' of the securities. It may be that the distinction involves a rationalisation from other elements of the definition, since if information is not generally known to outsiders but would, if it were known, affect the market price, it might well possess the quality of being 'specific'. Approaching the matter subjectively, however, it would appear that information is general if it is of a kind which can be obtained from an examination of the company's continuous records. Thus investment analysts and brokers relying on published results and statistics would not be affected. Specific information is anything else, e g knowledge of a particular factory closure or sale of a particular unprofitable subsidiary.

The information must be 'not generally known to those persons who are accustomed or would be likely to deal'. Generally known means known or available to all of them.[1] As to whether a person is accustomed or likely to deal, are assessments of fact which a court would have to consider in a particular case.

It is also necessary to show that, if the information were known, it would have a material bearing on the price of the securities in question. A distinction must be drawn between price and value. The price of a security is that which the market can be persuaded to pay for it, no doubt on the basis of a variety of factors some of which are nothing to do with the company at all (e g international political instability or economic recession). 'Internal' factors, such as writing up or down assets in the company's books, may affect the underlying value of the security but not the price at which it is traded. If an insider uses information which is not price-sensitive according to this test, tending very much to have an immediate impact, then he is not acting unlawfully.

RECOGNISED STOCK EXCHANGE

The section 68 prohibition is in relation to dealing in the securities of a particular company on a recognised stock exchange. For these purposes, any person who (whether as principal or agent) buys or

1 See discussion at ch 6, p. 103, above.

sells or agrees to buy or sell any securities is treated as 'dealing' in security.[2] Dealing is thus not a course of established trading, it can consist of one isolated transaction. The securities that may not be dealt in are listed securities and, in the case of a company within the meaning of the 1948 Act or a company registered under Part VIII of that Act or an unregistered company, any shares, debentures or rights to subscribe whether or not the same are listed.[3] A 'recognised stock exchange' is any body of persons which is for the time being a recognised stock exchange for the purposes of the Prevention of Fraud (Investments) Act 1958.[4] Section 73(3) extends the definition to include dealings in securities through an investment exchange, i e an organisation maintaining a system whereby an offer to deal in securities made by a subscriber to the organisation is communicated, without his identity being revealed, to other subscribers to the organisation, and whereby any acceptance of that offer by any of those other subscribers is recorded and confirmed.[5] It will be seen that the prohibitions are extended to other advertised securities the subject of off-market transactions.[6]

3 Group transactions

An individual who is, or at any time in the preceding six months has been, knowingly connected with a company shall not deal on a recognised stock exchange in securities of *any other company* if he has information which satisfies certain conditions. The first three conditions are the same as those applying under section 68(1), i e there must be a connection with the first company, it must be unreasonable to expect the individual to make the disclosure, and he must be aware of the unpublished price-sensitive nature of the information. Additionally, there is a requirement that such information

> relates to a transaction (actual or contemplated) involving both the first and that other company or involving one of them and securities of the other or to the fact that such transaction is no longer contemplated.[7]

The prohibition applies both where the other company is independent of the company with which the individual is connected, and also where it is a subsidiary.

2 S. 73(3).
3 S. 73(5).
4 See s. 87(5) and Companies Act 1948, s. 455(1).
5 S. 73(5).
6 See pp. 163–164, below.
7 S. 68(2).

Illustration D is a director of E Limited. E Limited and F Limited, a free-standing company, participate in a joint venture operation which involves the setting up of a 50:50 company, G Limited. Because of the size of the operation, the joint venture agreement is considered to be price-sensitive on the securities both of E Limited and F Limited. D will be unable to deal in shares of F Limited under section 68(2).

The wording of the extra condition is wide enough to cover various sorts of arrangements between one company and another. It could, for example, cover an informal 'concert party' between free-standing companies,[8] having the object of encroaching upon the securities of a target company with a view to ultimate control. The directors of both parties would be prohibited from dealing in the shares of the other. It does not extend, however, to the shares of the target. (Compare the provisions of section 68(4) discussed below.)

An individual who is connected with a company is not prevented from dealing in the securities of a subsidiary of another company to which section 68(2) applies, unless he knows that the information relates to a transaction involving the subsidiary and the company with which he is connected.[9]

4 Involvement of other persons

COUNSELLING

An individual who is for the time being prohibited from dealing on a recognised stock exchange in any securities, whether that individual is a person connected with a company or merely someone who has received information from an insider (the tippee), is not allowed to counsel or procure any other person to deal in those securities, knowing or having reasonable cause to believe that that person would himself deal in them on a recognised stock exchange.

It is obvious that if the prohibition on insider dealing were confined to the primary insider, e g director, shareholder, or professional adviser, it would be an easy matter to arrange for some nominee to deal for the benefit of the insider, or for his family and associates to deal. This provision prevents such an arrangement. It is not necessary that any information be communicated, merely that the outsider be encouraged to trade in his own right on a recognised stock exchange. It is also of no consequence that the primary

8 As to the disclosure requirements of which, see ch 7, pp. 129–130, above.
9 Joffe *The Companies Act 1980* para 11.108.

insider receives no benefit for the advice he tenders; he is just as much liable under section 63(6) if he is asked for a tip over a business lunch', as if he procures his agent to buy and sell securities and is to receive the bulk of any profit.

The onus of proof on the prosecution is relatively high under this provision. It has to be shown that the counsellor knows or thinks it likely that the tippee will deal on a recognised stock exchange. Thus, if the tippee sells shares by private treaty or concludes an 'off-market' transaction, there is no liability. Moreover, if the advice given is simply to refrain from dealing, knowing that the share price is going to rise because of some material event, the insider is not liable. It is in fact one of the major weaknesses of Part V that a connected person escapes prosecution if all that he does is sit tight. Liability does not attach to *misuse* of information as such, but to dealing upon the basis of information given or received.

It is important to note that the 'counselling and procuring' provision, as also the provision prohibiting the *communication* of price-sensitive information (see below), may have a foreign element. Under section 70(2) a person who is precluded himself from dealing shall not counsel or procure any other person to deal in the knowledge or with reasonable cause to believe that such other person will deal outside Great Britain on any stock exchange other than a recognised stock exchange.

COMMUNICATION

An insider is prohibited from communicating unpublished price-sensitive information to any other person if he knows or has reasonable cause to believe that that person, or indeed any other, will make use of the information for the purposes of dealing, or even of counselling or procuring anyone else to deal, on a recognised stock exchange in the securities concerned.[10] The unlawful act is the communication; it is not necessary to establish that anyone actually dealt as a result of information received.

Illustration D an insider, tells T that D's company Y Limited, is about to declare a large profit in its half-yearly results. T has no money and does not buy shares in Y Limited himself, but he passes the information on to U. U advises his uncle, V to buy shares on the Stock Exchange, in anticipation of the price rising. D will be guilty of a offence under section 68(7) if he has a reasonable belief either that T will deal, or that T will pass on the information to a third person who may himself deal or counsel or procure a fourth person to do so.

10 S. 68(7).

As has been pointed out, however,[11] if the information has a genuine price-sensitive quality and is accepted with enthusiasm by the tippee, 'it will be difficult for the person disclosing it to rebut the natural inference that it would be exploited for trading purposes'. Under section 70(2) an individual who is prohibited from dealing in securities must not communicate the information which he holds to any other person in knowledge or with reasonable cause to believe that that other person will make use of the information for the purposes of dealing, or counselling or procuring any other to deal, in the securities in question outside Great Britain on any stock exchange other than a recognised stock exchange.

TIPPEES

A tippee is an outsider to whom price-sensitive information is communicated, or who is counselled or procured to deal in securities, by a person connected with the company.

Where an individual has information which he obtained from another whom he knows is connected with the particular company (or has been connected within six months) and he also knows or has reasonable cause to believe that the insider obtained the information by virtue of his position, then

(1) he must not himself deal on a recognised stock exchange in securities of the company if he knows that the information is unpublished price-sensitive information; and
(2) he must not deal in securities of any other company if he knows the information is unpublished and price-sensitive in relation to those securities and;
    (a) such information relates to any transaction (actual or contemplated) involving the first company and the other company, or
    (b) such information relates to any transaction involving one company and securities of the other, or
    (c) such information relates to the fact that any such transaction as is mentioned in (a) or (b) above is no longer contemplated.[12]

Liability is only established if the tippee knows or has reasonable cause to believe that, because of the insider's connection and position, it would be reasonable to expect him not to disclose the information except for the proper performance of the functions attaching to that position.

11 Prentice *The Companies Act 1980* para 310.
12 S. 68(3).

The mental element is crucial here. The tippee is only liable if:

(a) he knows the insider is a connected person;[13]
(b) he knows or reasonably believes that the information being offered arises by virtue of the connection; and
(c) he knows or reasonably believes that it would be reasonable to expect him not to disclose the information except for the proper performance of the functions attaching to his position.

This threefold hurdle, it is submitted, will make prosecutions against tippees difficult to sustain unless a certain amount of inference is drawn as to the likelihood of the conditions being fulfilled.

The tippee will not be liable if he does not receive information, but is simply counselled to deal in the securities of a company by the insider. This is because in such a case he cannot know of the 'unpublished price-sensitive' quality of the tip. However, as explained above, the insider himself will be guilty of an offence, since by counselling or procuring he is in breach of section 68(6).

Because section 68(3)(a) refers to information obtained ('directly or indirectly') from another individual who is connected it appears that the provision is broad enough to catch sub-tippees as well as the person who receives a 'hot' tip from the primary insider. At each stage down the line there is a responsibility not to deal, and not to divulge.

5 Takeover offers

Because the offer to acquire shares of another company is the most price-sensitive matter an insider is concerned with, there is now a battery of self-regulatory and statutory controls to prevent profit-taking during the fluid takeover period.[14] The statutory code inhibits dealing in two ways. As discussed, actual or contemplated transactions between the insider's company and another (or the securities of another), amount to information which the insider cannot exploit by virtue of section 68(2). In addition, there is a provision[15] which operates against non-insiders who are about to make a bid, creating price-sensitive information of their own. Thus, where an individual is contemplating making a takeover offer (as defined)[16] in a particular capacity, he must not deal on a recognised

13 Actually s. 68(3) speaks of 'knowingly obtained' (directly or indirectly from another individual), but it is submitted that the knowledge is to be imputed not to the obtaining of the information but to the status of the insider.

14 As to the City Code on Takeovers and Mergers, see pp. 145–147, below.

15 S. 68(4).

16 S. 73(5).

stock exchange in the target company's securities *in another capacity*, if he is aware of the price sensitivity of his actions.

Although this is an adroit attempt to solve a major problem, commentators have focused on two difficulties.[17] First, the restriction only applies to 'individuals', and thereby excludes most of the persons who will in fact make bids for companies, i e other companies. It is therefore an empty sanction unless, e g directors, employees and other agents can be said to be 'contemplating' on behalf of their principals, and thus themselves stopped from dealing. Again, it is not clear how the issue of capacity is to apply. If someone acquires price-sensitive confidential information 'in a particular capacity', e g acting for Company X (the offeror), almost any transaction he engages in other than on the instructions of Company X (and whether for his own or a third party's account) should be thought of as being in 'another capacity'. It is therefore suggested that section 68(4) is designed to cover the following type of situation:

> **Illustration** PQ, a banking house, goes in search of a company for RS Ltd to acquire. A director of PQ has discussions in confidence with TU Ltd, a potential target, and meanwhile on the instructions of RS Ltd acquires shares in the market of TU Ltd. VW, another client, asks for investment advice and the director acquires shares in TU Ltd for VW as well. Later, RS Ltd makes a bid, and VW makes a profit. Assuming RS Ltd is 'contemplating' a bid when the director deals for VW, such director is dealing 'in another capacity' (albeit as agent) and is guilty of an offence under the provision.

Even on this interpretation it is not beyond doubt whether, in the example, the fact that PQ as a corporate entity or another department thereof entered into the transactions instead of the director as an individual, or whether VW did its own dealing on advice, would produce a different result. If so, section 68(4) may be too narrowly drawn. There is also the problem that even if the motive of contemplating a bid can be attributed at the relevant time to RS Ltd, the same is not necessarily true of PQ's director, who may take a more sanguine view of his negotiations with TU's board.

6 Deals off market

Both because of the development of securities trading otherwise than on the Stock Exchange[18] and to discourage circumvention of

17 See Prentice *The Companies Act 1980* p. 128; Joffe *The Companies Act 1980* para 11.112.

18 The Over-the-Counter Market and the Unlisted Securities Market.

section 68, section 70 of the Companies Act 1980 renders unlawful dealing 'off market' through the medium of a dealer making a market in advertised securities. Strictly, the term 'off market' is a misnomer, since there is an element of public exchange involved. Indeed section 70(4) states:

> For the purposes of this section an off-market dealer shall be taken to deal in advertised securities if he deals in such securities or acts as an intermediary in connection with deals made by other persons in such securities. . .

On the other hand, since private face-to-face transactions are excluded altogether from Part V, 'off market' comes to mean 'off the stock market' or, strictly, otherwise than on a recognised exchange.

Exactly the same prohibitions apply here as in the principal section. Thus the insider must not counsel or procure;[19] or communicate,[20] and the tippee must not take advantage of his tip.[1] The securities in respect of which dealings are banned are 'advertised securities' which are

> in relation to a particular occurrence . . . listed securities or securities in respect of which, not more than six months before that occurrence, information indicating the prices at which persons have dealt or were willing to deal in those securities has been published. . .[2]

7 Special categories of persons

CROWN SERVANTS

Section 69 prohibits a Crown servant or former Crown servant from trading on a recognised stock exchange in securities on the basis of information which he knows is unpublished price-sensitive information and which he obtained by virtue of his official position. A 'crown servant' is any individual who holds office under, or is employed by, the Crown,[3] and therefore somewhat anomalously local government officers and employees of nationalised industries are not affected.

The Crown servant may not counsel or procure another to deal, nor communicate any information, nor may anyone who obtains

19 S. 70(1)(b).
20 S. 70(1)(c).
1 S. 70(2).
2 S. 70(3). This would certainly cover Messrs Nightingale & Co, whose share prices are quoted in the daily papers.
3 S. 73(5).

information from him use it if he reasonably believes that his informant came by the information officially.[4]

The prohibition also extends to off-market deals.

LIQUIDATORS, RECEIVERS, AND TRUSTEES IN BANKRUPTCY

Persons by law administering the affairs of another, or a company which is winding-up, may be by virtue of such function seised of confidential information relating to the affairs of outside organisations. Thus, a liquidator of Company X who discovers it is possible to sell the Company's property much more profitably than expected, so as to yield a final dividend to shareholders, might be able to buy shares in Company X's holding company in anticipation of a rise. He will be protected from liability only in 'the exercise in good faith of his functions',[5] which seems to state the obvious as any departure from the strict duties of office are unlikely to be in good faith.

JOBBERS

The provisions of section 68 do not prohibit an individual by reason of his having any information from doing anything, if the information

(a) was obtained by him in the course of a business as a jobber, and
(b) was of a description which it would be reasonable to expect him to obtain in the ordinary course of the business,

and in either case he acts in good faith in the course of the business.[6]

The jobbers' exemption is necessary by virtue of their continuous contact with the market, and their unique capacity to generate market movements, which would otherwise infringe Part V.

TRUSTEES AND PERSONAL REPRESENTATIVES

These fiduciaries were given complete exemption when insider trading legislation was first drafted in the Companies Bill 1973, but now a series of rather uncertain hurdles must be jumped. The provisions as to trustees are very important and active steps should be taken by legal advisers to ensure that they are made aware of their liabilities. The problem is one of there being a conflict between two

4 S. 69(2).
5 S. 68(8)(b).
6 S. 68(8)(c).

beneficial interests (apart from their own), i e the trust and the company, conflict resolved in common law in the company's favour,[7] at least as far as actual profiteering is concerned. Where, however, a fiduciary is in possession of confidential company information which, if he does *not* disclose it, his beneficiaries will suffer loss, effectively he is obliged to choose between the lesser of two breaches of duty. It is submitted that, as a matter of general principle, a trustee could never be held liable where he chooses an option (i e non-disclosure) which is likely to avoid the commission of a criminal offence by the tippee beneficiary.[8]

Where a trustee[9] would otherwise be liable under section 68 if he dealt or counselled, he will be treated as acting independently of any intention to make a profit or avoid a loss, and hence able to claim a defence under section 68(8)(a) (see below), provided he acts on the advice of a person who

(a) appeared to him to be an appropriate person from whom to seek advice; and
(b) did not appear to be a person prohibited from dealing, i e an insider or tippee.[10]

It is clear this defence only applies to the trustee in a tippee situation, and not where he is a primary insider, where there remains a total prohibition. Trustees invariably rely on agents and advisers to assist in the administration of the trust fund,[11] and where investment advice is tendered to them and accepted by them in accordance with (a) and (b) above, it is immaterial if the adviser is acting in contravention of section 68(3), (6), or (7). The 'appearance' of suitability is in each case a subjective matter: there is no requirement that the trustee acts with reasonable care in selecting his adviser (provided that, as a matter of general law, he does so in good faith).

Illustration A, B, and C are trustees of a company pension fund, and D is a corporate investment adviser to the fund. D acts for another client in takeover negotiations and acquires price-sensitive information, making D a prohibited person. The fund holds shares in the target company and D advises A, B, and C to acquire more. Unless the circumstances are such as to put the trustees on enquiry, e g because of the size of the proposed purchase in relation to the fund's existing portfolio, they will be

7 See above, ch 6, pp. 107–110.
8 Prentice *The Companies Act 1980* para 326.
9 Or personal representative, or individual acting for a corporate trustee or personal representative.
10 S. 68(11).
11 This is expressly recognised by ss. 23(1) and 30(1) of the Trustee Act 1925.

protected. This is so even if it is clear they are acting to make a profit, since section 68(1) is merely a deeming provision.

There is a line to be drawn, however, between accepting spontaneous advice and soliciting information. If the adviser offers a particular security, mentioning that he thinks that company is ripe for a takeover, the trustees may legally deal. But if (in breach of confidence) the adviser says 'we are acting for XYZ in relation to the acquisition of ABC', the trustees can infer without difficulty that he has inside information and they must not initiate a request to purchase.[12]

8 General defences

LACK OF COMMERCIAL INTENTION

It is a defence under Part V of the Act to show that an individual acted otherwise than with a view to the making of a profit or the avoidance of a loss (whether for himself or another person) in his use of confidential information.[13] This is designed to exonerate forced sales, e g to pay back tax or satisfy pressing trade creditors of a business. In one sense there is no legitimate reason why this defence should be allowed, since improvidence in handling one's business affairs such as to require panic realisations of assets, is hardly a matter for sympathy. Conversely, a prohibition on dealing could imply, in the case of an individual who regularly is in possession of price-sensitive information, that funds are tied up indefinitely in securities and can never be turned into cash. The court will have to distinguish between long- and short-term motives, and problems will arise where these are mixed.[14]

The burden of proof is on the particular insider to show the genuineness or otherwise of his intentions. The onus shifts from the prosecution once possession of insider information is established. It would, for example, be a legitimate defence that a portfolio was changed round on a regular basis or that a proportion of a trust fund was kept liquid, necessitating realisations prior to payments out to beneficiaries.

COMPLETION OF TRANSACTIONS

Provided he does so to facilitate the completion or carrying out of a transaction, an individual to whom section 68 applies is not thereby

12 See Gower *Modern Company Law* (4th edn, Supp, 1981) para (f) to rider on pp. 636–638.
13 S. 68(8)(a).
14 The provisions of the Model Code for Directors contemplate a stricter regime: see below, Appendix 3, p. 230.

precluded from engaging in a securities transaction.[15] This permits, e g the finalising of a transaction (such as the execution of a share transfer) where, since the bargain for sale was struck, he has come into possession of price-sensitive information.

9 International bond issues

Shortly before Part V was enacted the Government, on request, added an exemption affecting the Eurobond market. There is evidence of some rather hurried draftmanship.

The London Eurobond market exists for professional investors, who buy and sell bonds both as principals and brokers as a result of an issue through a lead bank. The issue managers will invariably be in possession of price-sensitive information, and indeed one of their functions is to participate in or 'make' the market so as to stabilise the price. In such a case, the general prohibition on dealing does not apply to anything done in good faith by the issue manager in connection with that issue not later than three months after the issue date or where he is merely making a market for the securities.[16]

International bond issue is a defined term.[17] It is to be extended to cover, by approval of the Secretary of State, a wide variety of issues of international securities.

The main criticism of this provision is that where securities are denominated in sterling, not less than 50 per cent in nominal value of them must be offered to overseas investors.

10 Contravention

Prosecutions are in the hands of the Director of Public Prosecutions or the Secretary of State for Trade.[19] This implies that only serious malpractices are going to be punished. The sanction for contravention is a fine, or up to two years imprisonment. The substantial burden of proof on the prosecution to show the requisite state of knowledge of the defendant, and his connection with the company, diminish the chances of swift action. But company advisers should notify their boards that penalties are heavy, and on this basis the Act should have a substantial deterrent effect.

No civil remedies are available. The Act expressly provides that no transaction shall be void or voidable by reason only that it was entered into in breach of the statutory code.[20]

15 S. 68(10).
16 S. 71(1). Employees of the manager are also protected.
17 S. 71(2).
18 Companies (No 2) Bill 1981, NC 24.
19 S. 72(2).
20 S. 72(3).

10 The American experience

This chapter offers a brief outline of securities regulation in the United States as it affects the issues raised in chapters 6 to 9. The increased federal involvement in capital markets dates from President Roosevelt's 'New Deal' and the Securities Act 1933 (initial disclosure) and the Securities Exchange Act 1934 (regulation of subsequent dealing) have exercised powerful influences on American corporate activity ever since. The federal statutes are supplemented by state laws (the so-called 'Blue Sky Laws') which are achieving increasing uniformity between states but whose effectiveness is still hampered by jurisdictional boundaries. Persons or corporations engaged in securities transactions in the United States must comply both with local and federal laws. To appreciate the federal position, to which the present discussion is confined, some knowledge is required of the basic mechanism of regulation provided by the Securities Exchange Commission ('the Commission').[1]

1 The Commission

The Commission was set up by the Securities Exchange Act 1934 ('the Exchange Act'), and is composed of five members, the chairman being designated by the president. It has nine regional offices throughout the US, and five operating divisions, i e

(a) the Division of Corporate Finance;
(b) the Division of Market Regulation;
(c) the Division of Enforcement;
(d) the Division of Corporate Regulation; and
(e) the Division of Investment Management.

1 Much of the material for this chapter is taken from Spiers *Doing Business in the US* vol 3 (1978). See also Rider and Ffrench *The Regulation of Insider Trading* chs 2–4.

The Commission conducts both formal and informal investigations of non-compliance with the securities laws. It may issue injunction proceedings, refer matters for prosecution by the US Attorney General, and take administrative proceedings against local securities exchanges, brokers, associations, and others, subject in each case to a right of appeal to the federal courts. Its role includes that of overseeing state and federal self-regulatory bodies as well as equivalent investigatory functions of the UK Department of Trade. It is, however, much more of an umbrella organisation than anything in the UK e g offering advice to the public on particular transactions (the so-called 'no action' letter procedure)[2] and appearing as *amicus curiae* in civil litigation in US district courts. As a result, there exists a much more cohesive but flexible system of control than London has so far been able to devise.

2 The Securities Act 1933

INITIAL DISCLOSURE

This legislation was enacted to protect investors in the 'new issues' market as opposed to markets for the day-to-day trading of securities. The purpose of the Act is to compel full, accurate disclosure of material information concerning securities and the persons issuing them where it is proposed to make a distribution of securities. Registration by the issuer prior to a public offering is required, either by the issuer or his controller. A prospectus must be filed as part of the registration process. As soon as a public offering is contemplated, the issuer and those connected with him must guard against engaging in any activity that may be regarded as conditioning the market to the offering. The mere fact of the proposed issue may be a price-sensitive matter and the subject of insider information. Offers may only be made after a registration statement is filed. Advance promotions, known as 'beating the gun', are illegal. The term 'prospectus' is very widely defined to include 'any notice, circular, advertisement, letter, or communication, written or by radio or television, which offers any security for sale or confirms the sale of any security'.[3]

There is exemption from registration in the case of certain securities, e g US Government bonds and those of small businesses, and certain transactions, e g private offerings. Even after registration there can be no sale of the securities during a period of twenty days, to enable the market to 'absorb' the information contained in the registration statement, which is very detailed.

2 *Spiers* para 42.02(3).
3 Securities Act 1933, s. 2(10).

3 Disclosure under the 1934 Act

DIVISIONS OF THE ACT

The Securities Exchange Act 1934 deals with post-issue trading in securities, including disclosure requirements. The broad divisions of the Act are:

(1) the requirement to register every non-exempt security, if the equity is to be held by more than 500 registered shareholders and the issue of the security exceeds $1,000,000; or else the company is engaged in interstate commerce;
(2) periodic reports must be filed with the Commission once the company's securities have been registered in the first instance.
(3) solicitation of proxies is forbidden except pursuant to Regulations made by the Commission under the Act;
(4) provisions are directed against certain activities arising out of the sale and purchase of securities, namely insider trading, manipulation and fraud.

DISCLOSURE PROVISIONS

No member, broker or dealer may effect any transaction in any security (other than an exempt security) on a National Securities exchange, unless a registration statement is operative for that security.[4]

Information must be provided with regard to directors, and members holding more than 10 per cent of any class of security, as to their interests or material contracts with the issuing company. The registration provisions have been extended by the Commission to interstate corporations of a certain size whose securities are *not* listed on any exchange, but sold privately or on the 'over-the-counter' market (which is much more developed than in the UK).

Every issuer of a security registered pursuant to section 12 must file reports with the Commission to ensure that the information originally tendered is kept current.[5] The revisions must be 'timely', i e filed within ten days after the end of any month during which relevant events occurred, and made in duplicate to the local securities exchange. The information required includes any change in control of the company, unusual acquisitions or dispositions, changes in capital, and any *other* information in support so as to render the remainder not misleading.[6] Tables must be submitted showing the legal and beneficial ownership of shares held as to

4 Securities Exchange Act 1934, s. 12(a).
5 S. 13.
6 See the requirements of Form 10K and Form 10Q. *Rider and Ffrench* pp. 11–12.

more than 10 per cent by any person. Directors' holdings must be shown, without necessarily identifying them individually. Transactions affecting directors, and benefits received by them, are recorded, whether in relation to the company making the registration or any subsidiary. Interests of spouses are included.

Issuing companies are also required to make annual and quarterly returns.

Mention was made in chapter 8 of the so-called Williams Act, designed to provide disclosure of concentrations of shares prior to a takeover.[7] The Act adds new clauses to sections 13 and 14 of the 1934 Act, not to tip the balance of regulation either in favour of management or in favour of the takeover bidder, but to ensure that shareholders are afforded full and fair disclosure of all facts before making a decision whether to tender their securities. (In the US, a reference to 'cash tender offer' is much more common than a 'takeover bid'.) The Williams Act amendment requires disclosure of pertinent information not only where there is a block acquisition by outsiders, but where a company repurchases its own equity securities.

Any person who acquires directly or indirectly, a security of a class of equity securities that is registered pursuant to section 12 and who becomes, directly or indirectly, the beneficial owner of more than 5 per cent of the securities of that class, must prepare a Schedule 13D information statement describing his or her ownership.[8] The Schedule 13D statement must contain the following information:

(a) identification of the class of security;
(b) identification of the purchasers and their backgrounds;
(c) the source and amount of the funds, including borrowing;
(d) if the purchaser seeks to acquire control of the company, a description of any plans or proposals that there may be with respect to it, e g liquidation, sale of assets, merger etc;
(e) accounting of the number of shares benefically owned or as to which there is a right to acquire;
(f) information as to any contract, arrangements or understandings with any person with respect to the company's securities.

The information statement must be sent to the company and to each exchange where the security is traded, and copies filed with a Commission within ten days after the purchase. It has been noticed

7 Act of 29 July 1968.
8 S. 13(d).

that section 13(d)(3) includes in the definition 'person' two or more persons who act together.[9]

Certain transactions are exempted from these filing requirements. Where a bidder would, after finalisation of a tender offer, beneficially own more than 5 per cent of that class of equity security, an information statement must be filed with a Commission at the same time the tender offer is transmitted to security holders. This provision applies only to securities that are part of a class of securities registered under section 12 of the Act.[10] Schedule 14D contains the information that must be filed, requiring essentially the same information called for by Schedule 13D plus additional items including:

(a) previous transactions by the offeror with the target company if they were of significant size;
(b) identification of all persons employed by the bidder to make solicitations for the tender offer;
(c) financial statements of the offeror with such information as is material to decide whether to accept the offer; and stating how the tender offer will be affected by the anti-trust laws etc.

All supplementary materials involved in either the tender offer or its solicitation must be filed as part of the statement and sent to the issuing company concurrently with its transmission to security holders. These disclosure requirements form the basis of the protection available to a target company and its directors who may be trying to fend off a bid.

PROXIES

The primary method of shareholder voting in the United States is by proxy. Consequently, it is common practice for shareholders who plan to attend the meeting, or else the management of the company, to solicit non-attending shareholders for their vote. In order to ensure fair voting and complete disclosure in the course of a proxy solicitation, section 14(a) has been added to the Securities Exchange Act. This section prohibits the solicitation for any proxy with respect to a security registered under section 12 (other than an exempted security) in contravention of Commission Rules and Regulations. These require that the proxy solicitor furnish each person solicited with a written proxy statement containing the information required by Schedule 14A, and, in the case of a solicitation by or on behalf of management for an annual meeting at

9 See p. 129, above.
10 S. 14(d).

which directors are to be elected, also require that the proxy statement be accompanied or preceded by a annual report to shareholders.

The primary purpose of section 14 is to protect the investor by preventing management or others from obtaining authorisation for corporate action by means of deceptive or inadequate disclosure. The rules also have relevance for insider trading, because Schedule 14A requires that the proxy statement must identify substantial shareholders holding more than 10 per cent of the outstanding voting securities of the issuer, beneficially or nominally.

4 Accounting for profits

SECTION 16

Every person who directly or indirectly owns more than 10 per cent of any class of equity security registered pursuant to section 12 of the Exchange Act and every director and officer of an issuing company that has an equity security that is so registered, must file a statement of ownership with the Commission. In order to prevent the unfair use of information that may have been obtained by corporate insiders, section 16(b) makes such beneficial owners and directors liable for any profit realised by them from any purchase and sale of the security (other than an exempted security) within any period of less than six months. It is a crucial feature of this provision that liability does not depend upon proof that the insider make unfair use of confidential or price-sensitive information, but only that the 'short swing' transaction has the potential for speculative abuse. It will also be noticed that the requirement to register under section 16(a) is an individual requirement, and is quite distinct from the issuing company's obligation under sections 12 and 13. References in section 16(a) to 'directly or indirectly owns' are references to beneficial ownership, and the Commission is much exercised in interpreting this provision to ensure that the right people have to make disclosure. Thus wherever there is a relationship which gives benefits to another person substantially equivalent to ownership, the term 'beneficial owner' would be apt to apply, and this is, of course not confined to family relationships.

Persons under a statutory obligation to disclose must do so both with regard to their initial acquisitions, and also upon subsequent change. The Initial Statement of Beneficial Ownership of Securities is in Form 3. The Statement would also have to be filed in respect of existing holdings where the issuing company had become a registered public company, or the date upon which a security statement under section 12 became effective. Form 4 is used to report changes, and must be filed within ten days following the end of the month in which the change took place. There is no obligation to report where transactions in total do not exceed $3,000 in a six month period, and in certain other cases. Filed reports are publicly available at the Commission's offices, and also at the various stock exchanges upon which the particular issuer's securities are listed. The Commission also prepares an Official Summary of Securities Transactions, which are widely circulated, to enable shareholders to see at a glance what dealings have taken place, and if necessary to obtain further details of them.

APPLICATION OF THE SHORT-SWING PROFITS RULE

Section 16(b) is the only statutory provision in the US specifically directed at insider dealing, and it is drafted in very wide terms. Unlike the UK requirement to prove intention,[11] the policy of the American law is to side step the burden of having to prove that the director or insider intended, at the time he bought, to get out on a short swing, instead making the assumption that there is a breach of confidence. That breach can also extend beyond the period of holding office as a director; for whereas with 10 per cent *share-holders* the Act specifically provides that liability is conditional upon the person being such a holder both at the time of the purchase and at the time of the sale, a director or officer purchasing securities during his time of office but selling within six months out of office, remains liable.

In assessing the profit realised and hence, the damages to be paid to the company, US courts take a severe view. The rule of thumb used in the computation of the award is the 'lowest price in, highest price out' within six months. The process has been described as follows:

> Listed in one column are all the purchases made during the period which recovery of profits is sought. In another column are listed all of the sales during that period. Then the shares purchased at the lowest price are matched against an equal number of the shares sold at the highest price within six months of such purchase, and the profit computed. After that the next lowest price is matched against the next highest price and that profit is computed. Then, the same process is repeated until all the shares in the purchase column which may be matched against shares sold for higher prices in the sales column have been matched off. When necessary for accurate computation it would seem proper to split a larger denomination or lot of shares in order to match off part of the lot against

11 See ch 9, p. 167, above.

an equal amount on the other side. The gross recovery is the sum of the profits thus determined.[12]

The right to recover damages is vested in the corporate issuer, or in default a stockholder suing on behalf and in the name of the issuer. No regard is paid to the fact that this is a 'windfall' profit received by the company.

The transactions that are encompassed by section 16(b) include not only deals on a stock exchange, but on the over-the-counter market. To constitute a 'sale and purchase' at all, some consideration must be exchanged. Thus the mere conversion of an equity security into another security is exempted, although a share exchange consequent upon a merger would be included because the consideration need not consist of cash. In recent years US courts have tended to reject a purely mechanistic view of purchases and sales in this context. The proper approach is to see whether the purchase and subsequent exchange lends itself to the type of speculative abuse which section 16(b) was designed to prevent.[13]

EXEMPTIONS AND RELIEFS

The following are the principal transactions exempted from section 16(b):

(1) transactions by registered investment companies;
(2) transactions entered into in connection with the primary or secondary distribution of a substantial block of securities among syndicate members;
(3) acquisitions of shares, stock, stock options under certain stock bonus, stock options, or similar schemes. These would cover, for example, employee share plans;
(4) certain transactions by public utility holding companies;
(5) transactions in which securities are received by redeeming other securities;
(6) long-term profits incident to sales within six months of the exercise of an option. A transaction involving the purchase and disposition of an equity security where the purchase consists of the exercise of an option acquired more than six months before such exercise is exempt provided the profits earned do not exceed the difference between the proceeds of

12 Rubin and Feldman 'Statutory Inhibitions Upon Unfair Use of Corporate Information by Insiders' 95 U Pa L Rev 468 (1947).

13 *Newmark RKO Inc* 425 F 2d 348 (2nd Cir 1970); *Kern Country Land Co v Occidental Petroleum Corpn* 411 US 582.

the sale and the lowest market price of any security of the same class within six months before or after the date of the sale;

(7) security transactions involved in mergers or consolidations involving an 85 per cent-owned subsidiary or a company that owned more than 85 per cent of the combined assets prior to the merger.

(8) transactions involving the deposit or withdrawal of equity securities under a voting trust or deposit agreement.

(9) transactions involving the conversion of equity securities, unless there has been a purchase of a convertible security and a sale of the underlying security, or a sale of the convertible security and a purchase of underlying security, within a period of less than six months, including the conversion date.

(10) sales of subscription rights which have been acquired without payment of consideration.

Because of the impact of section 16(b), there is a limitation period. No suit may be brought more than two years after the date that the 'profit' was realised. It is thought that the period begins to run from the date of the last transaction used to compute the amount of the profit.[14]

ASSESSMENT OF SECTION 16(b)

There has been much criticism of this provision, and particularly its scope, although many of the critics are anti-control insiders who feel it is too effective a sanction! Independent commentators have, however, pointed to the harsh computation of accountable profits (which may, indeed, exceed the amount of the insider's actual gain) and the absolute nature of the liability in which lack of intention to make a profit or ignorance of the relevant circumstances, is no defence whatsoever. There is no remedy for the individual shareholder. The Commission does not intervene enough as *amicus curiae* and so different courts approach the complex statutory provisions in different ways. Tippees are not covered, unlike the UK legislation. Finally, it can sometimes be needlessly costly for a shareholder to sue on behalf of the issuing company to recover the short swing profit, and there is no guarantee that compensation or refund of expense will be made by the court. Attorneys' fees in the US are very high and this will operate as a disincentive to action, where abuse has clearly taken place. In such cases the deterrent effect of section 16(b) must be regarded as more important than the legal consequences flowing from a breach of it.

14 Rider and Ffrench *The Regulation of Insider Trading* p. 42.

SHORT SALES AND SALES AGAINST THE BOX

Section 16(c) prohibits an insider from engaging in a 'short sale' or a 'sale against the box'. In a short sale, a seller enters into a contract of sale, through a broker, to sell securities which the seller does not currently own. At delivery time, since the seller does not own the securities under the contract of sale, the broker will purchase in the market the necessary shares to cover the contract. The broker will thereafter debit the purchase from a sellers account. A 'sale in the box' occurs when the seller, owning the securities for which a contract of sale has been entered into, refuses to deliver. As in the short sale, the broker must purchase the necessary securities in the market to cover the sale. By employing either of these devices, a corporate insider could avoid having his or her involvement with the sale of the corporation's securities recorded in the corporate books.

Section 16(c) requires the seller to own the securities sold and to deliver such securities within twenty days after the sale, or to deposit the securities in the mail or other usual channels of transportation within five days after the sale. Inability to make delivery must be supported by proof of a good faith attempt to make delivery or deposit or by proof that to make delivery or deposit would cause undue inconvenience or expense.[15]

5 Rule 10(b)–5

ORIGINAL PURPOSE

Section 17(a) of the Securities Act 1933, the anti-fraud provision of that statute, has since its adoption provided a basis for Commission administrative and injunction actions, and criminal prosecutions, against fraudulent offers and sales of securities. The absence of a comparable provision against fraudulent *purchases* in the securities laws was remedied in 1942 by the adoption of Rule 10(b)–5 under section 10(b) of the Exchange Act. Section 10(b) provides that it is unlawful

> to use or employ in connection with the purchase or sale of any security registered on a National Securities Exchange or any security not so registered, any manipulative or deceptive device or contrivance in contravention of such rules and regulations as the Commission may prescribe as necessary or appropriate in the public interest or for the protection of investors.

15 Spiers *Doing Business in the US* vol 3, para 44.03[17].

Rule 10(b) – 5, states:

> It shall be unlawful for any person directly or indirectly by use of any means or instrumentality of interstate commerce, or of the mails, or of any facility of any National Securities Exchange,
> (1) to employ any device, scheme, or artifice to defraud,
> (2) to make any untrue statement of a material fact or to omit to state a material fact necessary in order to make the statements made, in the light of the circumstances under which they were made, not misleading, or
> (3) to engage in any act, practice, or course of business which operates or would operate as a fraud or deceit upon any person, in connection with the purchase or sale of any securities.

The rule was primarily designed as an administrative tool of the Commission, being used mainly in cases of dealer/broker fraud rather than insider dealing, which was considered to be adequately covered by section 16(b). Rule 10(b) – 5 was drafted by the simple device of copying most of the language from section 17(a) of the Securities Act 1933 and adding to that the phrase 'in connection with the purchase or sale of any security', taken from section 10(b).

It was not until some years after its adoption that private litigants began to find that Rule 10(b) – 5 was a flexible weapon in the courts against general company misconduct, including insider dealing. In *Kardon v National Gypsum*[16] it was held that a seller of shares had a right to maintain a private action to recover damages on the basis that non-compliance of Rule 10b amounted to a statutory tort. The *Kardon* principle has since then been widely applied throughout the United States as a civil remedy in a manner which the originators of the Rule could not have contemplated.

SCOPE OF THE RULE

In relation to insider dealing,

> the essence of the Rule is that anyone who, trading for his own account in the securities of a corporation has access directly or indirectly, to information intended to be available only for a corporate purpose and not for the personal benefit of anyone, may not take advantage of such information knowing it is unavailable to those with whom he is dealing, that is, the investing public.[17]

It is clear that this covers any person with a fiduciary relationship with the company, e g directors, officers or shareholders, or the

16 69 F Supp 512 (1947).
17 *SEC v The Texas Gulf Sulphur Co* 401 F 2d 833 (1968) at 848.

company itself. In the *Texas Gulf Sulphur* case, an employee having a contractual relationship with the company was held to be included. Other categories, for example financial consultance, underwriters, solicitors, accountants and others acting in a more general capacity would now also fall within the Rule.

Where Rule 10(b) – 5 scores over section 16(b) is in stretching out a restraining arm on those who communicate information and the persons to whom such is communicated, as well as those who are in a direct relationship with the company. This takes us into the categories of 'tipper, tippee, and sub-tippee' (acquiring the tip secondhand).[18] The tipper's liability is established on the basis of aiding and abetting a violation of the Rule by another person. There is, however, a doubt as to the extent of the liability. The first-generation tippee is clearly caught.[19] The sub-tippee is probably outside the present scope of judicial interpretation of the Rule, but bearing in mind recent UK developments, his days are probably numbered.

6 Common law liability

Brief mention may be made of the extent to which US common law has offered a remedy to a company against an agent who acts on inside information. The matter is not without interest since a developed doctrine is always liable to be imported into the UK to supplement the limited rules as to fiduciary relationships that exist here.

The leading case is *Diamond v Oreamuno*.[20] The facts were:

> MA Inc had servicing obligations to customers in respect of computer hardware supplied by it which it subcontracted to IBM. IBM increased its charges for servicing which MA Inc was obliged to pay, which greatly affected its monthly earnings figure. Two directors of MA Inc sold their shares in the company before the monthly figures were announced. Later the share price fell considerably. The plaintiffs were shareholders of the company, suing derivatively to recover the profit (i e the avoided loss) on the basis of misuse of confidential information.

It was held that the use of the information as to the company's prospects was a breach of fiduciary duty and the directors were liable to account for the profits. It was not necessary for the

18 See ch 6, pp. 161 – 162, above.
19 *Ross v Licht* 263 F Supp 395 (SDNY 1967).
20 248 NE Reporter 2nd Series 910 (1969).

company to show that it had suffered actual loss. There had been misappropriation of a corporate asset.[1] The court relied on the concepts underlying section 16(b) and Rule 10(b)–5 of the Securities Exchange Act as a basis for the decision, holding that the purpose of the Federal Code would be frustrated if parallel equitable remedies were not also developed. Although it is unlikely that UK courts will accept Part V of the Companies Act 1980 as a source for new equities, the reasoning in *Diamond v Oreamuno* is bound to be found persuasive.[2]

1 Compare the discussion in ch 6, pp. 107–110, above.

2 Indeed Gower *Modern Company Law* (4th edn) p. 595, n. 70 treates it virtually as a UK precedent.

Appendices

Appendix 1
Companies Act 1980, Parts IV & V

Part IV

DUTIES OF DIRECTORS AND CONFLICTS OF INTERESTS

Duty in relation to employees

46. Directors to have regard to interests of employees.—(1) The matters to which the diretors of a company are to have regard in the performance of their functions shall include the interests of the company's employees in general as well as the interests of its members.

(2) Accordingly, the duty imposed by subsection (1) above on the directors of a company is owed by them to the company (and the company alone) and is enforceable in the same way as any other fiduciary duty owed to a company by its directors.

Particular transactions giving rise to a conflict of interest

47. Contracts of employment of directors.—(1) Subject to subsection (6) below, a company shall not incorporate in any agreement a term to which this section applies unless the term is first approved by a resolution of the company in general meeting and, in the case of a director of a holding company, by a resolution of that company in general meeting.

(2) This section applies to any term by which a director's employment with the company of which he is the director or, where he is the director of a holding company, his employment within the group is to continue, or may be continued, otherwise than at the instance of the company (whether under the original agreement or under a new agreement entered into in pursuance of the original agreement), for a period exceeding five years during which the employment—

(a) cannot be terminated by the company by notice; or
(b) can be so terminated only in specified circumstaces.

(3) In any case where—

(a) a person is or is to be employed with a company under an agreement which cannot be terminated by the company by notice or can be so terminated only in specified circumstances; and

(b) more than six months before the expiration of the period for which he is or is to be so employed, the company enters into a further agreement (otherwise than in pursuance of a right conferred by or by virtue of the original agreement on the other party thereto) under which he is to be employed with the company or, where he is a director of a holding company, within the group,

subsection (2) above shall apply as if to the period for which he is to be employed under that further agreement there were added a further period equal to the unexpired period of the original agreement.

(4) A resolution of a company approving a term to which this section applies shall not be passed at a general meeting of the company unless a written memorandum setting out the proposed agreement incorporating the term is available for inspection, by members of the company both—

(a) at the registered office of the company for not less than the period of 15 days ending with the date of the meeting; and

(b) at the meeting itself.

(5) A term incorporated in an agreement in contravention of this section shall to the extent that it contravenes this section be void; and that agreement and in a case where subsection (3) above applies the original agreement shall be deemed to contain a term entitling the company to terminate it at any time by the giving of reasonable notice.

(6) No approval is required to be given under this section by any body corporate unless it is a company within the meaning of the 1948 Act or registered under Part VIII of that Act or if it is, for the purposes of section 150 of that Act, a wholly owned subsidiary of any body corporate, wherever incorporated.

(7) In this section—

(a) 'employment' includes employment under a contract for services; and

(b) 'group', in relation to a director of a holding company, means the group which consists of that company and its subsidiaries.

48. Substantial property transactions involving directors, etc.—(1) A company shall not enter into an arrangement—

(a) whereby a director of the company or its holding company or a person connected with such a director is to acquire one or more non-cash assets of the requisite value from the company; or

(b) whereby the company acquires one or more non-cash assets of the requisite value from such a director or a person so connected;

unless the arrangement is first approved by a resolution of the company in general meeting and, if the director or connected person is a director of its holding company or a person connected with such a director, by a resolution in general meeting of the holding company.

(2) For the purposes of this section a non-cash asset is of the requisite value if at the time the arrangement in question is entered into its value is not less than £1,000 but, subject to that, exceeds £50,000 or ten per cent of the amount of the company's relevant assets, and for those purposes the amount of the company's relevant assets is—

(a) except in a case falling within paragraph (b) below, the value of its net assets determined by reference to the accounts prepared and laid under section 1 of the 1976 Act in respect of the last preceding accounting reference period in respect of which such accounts were so laid;

(b) where no accounts have been prepared and laid under that section before that time, the amount of its called-up share capital.

(3) An arrangement entered into by a company in contravention of this section and any transaction entered into in pursuance of the arrangement (whether by the company or any other person) shall be voidable at the instance of the company unless—

(a) restitution of any money or any other asset which is the subject-matter of the arrangement or transaction is no longer possible or the company or the person nominated by it has been indemnified in pursuance of subsection (4)(b) below by any other person for the loss or damage suffered by it; or

(b) any rights acquired bona fide for value and without actual notice of the contravention by any person who is not a party to the arrangement or transaction would be affected by its avoidance; or

(c) the arrangement is, within a reasonable period, affirmed by the company in general meeting and, if it is an arrangement for the transfer of an asset to or by a director of its holding company or a person who is connected with such a director, is so affirmed with the approval of the holding company given by a resolution in general meeting.

(4) Without prejudice to any liability imposed otherwise than by this subsection, but subject to subsection (5) below, where an arrangement is entered into with a company by a director of the company or its holding company or a person connected with him in

contravention of this section, that director and the person so connected, and any other director of the company who authorised the arrangement or any transaction entered into in pursuance of such an arrangement, shall (whether or not it has been avoided in pursuance of subsection (3) above) be liable—

(a) to account to the company for any gain which he had made directly or indirectly by the arrangement or transaction; and

(b) (jointly and severally with any other person liable under this subsection) to indemnify the company for any loss or damage resulting from the arrangement or transaction.

(5) Where an arrangement is entered into by a company and a person connected with a director of the company or its holding company in contravention of this section, that director shall not be liable under subsection (4) above if he shows that he took all reasonable steps to secure the company's compliance with this section, and, in any case, a person so connected and any such other director as is mentioned in that subsection shall not be so liable if he shows that, at the time the arrangement was entered into, he did not know the relevant circumstances constituting the contravention.

(6) No approval is required to be given under this section by any body corporate unless it is a company within the meaning of the 1948 Act or registered under Part VIII of that Act, or, if it is, for the purposes of section 150 of that Act, a wholly-owned subsidiary of any body corporate, wherever incorporated.

49. Prohibition of loans, etc., to directors and connected persons.—(1) Except as provided by section 50 below—

(a) a company shall not—

(i) make a loan to a director of the company or of its holding company;

(ii) enter into any guarantee or provide any security in connection with a loan made by any person to such a director; and

(b) a relevant company shall not—

(i) make a quasi-loan to a director of the company or of its holding company;

(ii) make a loan or a quasi-loan to a person connected with such a director;

(iii) enter into a guarantee or provide any security in connection with a loan or quasi-loan made by any other person for such a director or a person so connected.

(2) Except as provided by that section, a relevant company shall not—

(a) enter into a credit transaction as creditor for such a director or a person so connected;

(b) enter into any guarantee or provide any security in connection with a credit transaction made by any other person for such a director or a person so connected.

(3) A company shall not arrange for the assignment to it or the assumption by it of any rights, obligations or liabilities under a transaction which, if it had been entered into by the company, would have contravened subsection (1) or (2) above; but for the purposes of this Part of this Act the transaction shall be treated as having been entered into on the date of the arrangement.

(4) A company shall not take part in any arrangement whereby—

(a) another person enters into a transaction which, if it had been entered into by the company, would have contravened subsection (1), (2) or (3) above; and

(b) that other person, in pursuance of the arrangement, has obtained or is to obtain any benefit from the company or its holding company or a subsidiary of the company or its holding company.

50. Exceptions from s. 49.—(1) Where a director of a relevant company or of its holding company is associated with a subsidiary of either of those companies, subsection (1)(b)(ii) and (iii) of section 49 above shall not by reason only of that fact prohibit the relevant company from—

(a) making a loan or quasi-loan to that subsidiary; or

(b) entering into a guarantee or providing any security in connection with a loan or quasi-loan made by any person to that subsidiary.

(2) Subsection (1)(b) of that section shall not prohibit a relevant company ('the creditor') from making a quasi-loan to one of its directors or to a director of its holding company if—

(a) the quasi-loan contains a term requiring the director or a person on his behalf to reimburse the creditor his expenditure within two months of its being incurred; and

(b) the aggregate of the amount of that quasi-loan and of the amount outstanding under each relevant quasi-loan does not exceed £1,000.

For the purposes of this subsection, a quasi-loan is relevant if it was made to the director by virtue of this subsection by the creditor or by its subsidiary or, where the director is a director of the creditor's holding company, any other subsidiary of that company;

and 'amount outstanding' has the same meaning as in section 56(8) below.

(3) Subsection (2) of that section shall not prohibit a company's entering into—

(a) any transaction for any person if the aggregate of the relevant amounts does not exceed £5,000; or

(b) any transaction for any person if—

(i) the company enters into the transaction in the ordinary course of its business; and

(ii) the value of the transaction is not greater, and the terms on which it is entered into, are no more favourable in respect of the person for whom the transaction is made than that or those which it is reasonable to expect the company to have offered to or in respect of a person of the same financial standing as that person but unconnected with the company.

(4) Subject to the following provisions of this section, each of the following is excepted from the prohibitions in section 49 above, that is to say—

(a) a loan, or quasi-loan by a company to its holding company or a company's entering into a guarantee or providing any security in connection with a loan or quasi-loan made by any person to its holding company;

(b) a company's entering into a credit transaction as creditor for its holding company or entering into a guarantee or providing any security in connection with any credit transaction made by any other person for its holding company;

(c) a company's doing any thing to provide any of its directors with funds to meet expenditure incurred or to be incurred by him for the purposes of the company or for the purpose of enabling him properly to perform his duties as an officer of the company or a company's doing anything to enable any of its directors to avoid incurring such expenditure;

(d) a loan or quasi-loan made by a money-lending company to any person or a money-lending company's entering into a guarantee in connection with any other loan or quasi-loan.

(5) The exception specified in subsection (4)(c) above operates only if one of the following conditions is satisfied, that is to say—

(a) the thing in question is done with prior approval of the company given at a general meeting at which the purpose of the expenditure incurred or to be incurred or which would otherwise be incurred by the director and the amount of the funds to be provided by the company and the extent of the company's liability under any transaction which is or is connected with that thing are disclosed;

(b) that thing is done on condition that, if the approval of the company is not so given at or before the next following annual general meeting, the loan shall be repaid or any other liability arising under any such transaction discharged within six months from the conclusion of that meeting;

but that exception does not authorise a relevant company to enter into any transaction if the aggregate of the relevant amounts exceeds £10,000.

(6) The exception specified in subsection (4)(d) above operates only if both the following conditions are satisfied, that is to say—

(a) the loan or quasi-loan in question is made by the company or it enters into the guarantee in the ordinary course of the company's business; and

(b) the amount of the loan or quasi-loan or the amount guaranteed is not greater, and the terms of the loan, quasi-loan or guarantee are not more favourable, in the case of the person to whom the loan or quasi-loan is made or in respect of whom the guarantee is entered into than that or those which it is reasonable to expect that company to have offered to or in respect of a person of the same financial standing as that person but unconnected with the company;

but that exception does not authorise a relevant company which is not a recognised bank to enter into any transaction if the aggregate of the relevant amounts exceeds £50,000.

In determining for the purposes of this subsection the aggregate of the relevant amounts, a company which a director does not control shall be deemed not to be connected with him.

(7) The condition specified in subsection (6)(b) above shall not of itself prevent a company from making a loan to one of its directors or a director of its holding company—

(a) for the purpose of facilitating the purchase, for use as that director's only or main residence, of the whole or part of any dwelling-house together with any land to be occupied and enjoyed therewith;

(b) for the purpose of improving a dwelling-house or part of a dwelling-house so used or any land occupied and enjoyed therewith;

(c) in substitution for any loan made by any person and falling within paragraph (a) or (b) above,

if loans of that description are ordinarily made by the company to its employees and on terms no less favourable than those on which the transaction in question is made, and the aggregate of the relevant amounts does not exceed £50,000.

51. Relevant amounts.—(1) The following provisions of this section shall have effect for the purpose of defining the amounts relevant for determining whether any transaction or arrangement (a 'proposed transaction or arrangement') falls within the exception provided by subsection (3)(a) or (4)(c) or (d) of section 50 above, and for that purpose 'the relevant exception' in subsection (2) below means that exception.

(2) The relevant amounts in relation to a proposed transaction or arrangement are—

(a) the value of the proposed transaction or arrangement;

(b) the value of any existing relevant arrangement falling within subsection (3) or (4) of section 49 and entered into by virtue of the relevant exception by the company or by a subsidiary of the company or, where the proposed transaction or arrangement is to be made for a director of its holding company or a person connected with such a director, by a subsidiary of its holding company;

(c) the amount outstanding under any other relevant transaction made by virtue of the relevant exception by the company or by a subsidiary of the company or, where the proposed transaction or arrangement is to be made for a director of its holding company or a person connected with such a director, by a subsidiary of its holding company.

(3) For the purposes of this section, a transaction is relevant if it was made—

(a) for the director for whom the proposed transaction or arrangement is to be made or for any person connected with that director; or

(b) where the proposed transaction or arrangement is to be made for a person connected with a director of a company, for that director or any person connected with him;

and an arrangement is relevant if it relates to a relevant transaction.

(4) For the purposes of this section, a transaction entered into by a company which is (at the time that transaction was entered into) a subsidiary of the company which is to make the proposed transaction or is a subsidiary of that company's holding company, is not a relevant transaction if at the time of the determination referred to in subsection (1) above it no longer is such a subsidiary.

(5) The amount outstanding under any transaction within subsection (2)(c) above is the value of the transaction less any amount by which that value has been reduced.

52. Civil remedies for breach of s. 49.—(1) Where a company enters into a transaction or arrangement in contravention of section 49 the transaction or arrangement shall be voidable at the instance of the company unless—

(a) restitution of any money or any other asset which is the subject matter of the arrangement or transaction is no longer possible, or the company has been indemnified in pursuance of subsection (2)(b) below for the loss or damage suffered by it; or

(b) any rights acquired bona fide for value and without actual notice of the contravention by any person other than the person for whom the transaction or arrangement was made would be affected by its avoidance.

(2) Without prejudice to any liability imposed otherwise than by this subsection but subject to subsection (3) below, where an arrangement or transaction is made by a company for a director of the company or its holding company or person connected with such a director in contravention of section 49, that director and the person so connected and any other director of the company who authorised the transaction or arrangement shall (whether or not it has been avoided in pursuance of subsection (1) above) be liable—

(a) to account to the company for any gain which he has made directly or indirectly by the arrangement or transaction; and

(b) (jointly and severally with any other person liable under this subsection) to indemnify the company for any loss or damage resulting from the arrangement or transaction.

(3) Where an arrangement or transaction is entered into by a company and a person connected with a director of the company or its holding company in contravention of section 49, that director shall not be liable under subsection (2) above if he shows that he took all reasonable steps to secure the company's compliance with that section, and, in any case, a person so connected and any such other director as is mentioned in that subsection shall not be so liable if he shows that, at the time the arrangement or transaction was entered into, he did not know the relevant circumstances constituting the contravention.

53. Criminal penalties for breach of s. 49.—(1) A director of a relevant company who authorises or permits the company to enter into a transaction or arrangement knowing or having reasonable cause to believe that the company was thereby contravening section 49 above shall be guilty of an offence.

(2) A relevant company which enters into a transaction or arrangement for one of its directors or for a director of its holding

company in contravention of section 49 above shall be guilty of an offence.

(3) A person who procures a relevant company to enter into a transaction or arrangement knowing or having reasonable cause to believe that the company was thereby contravening section 49 above shall be guilty of an offence.

(4) A relevant company shall not be guilty of an offence under subsection (2) of this section if it shows that, at the time the transaction was entered into, it did not know the relevant circumstances.

(5) A person guilty of an offence under this section shall be liable—

(a) on conviction on indictment, to a term of imprisonment not exceeding two years or a fine, or both; and

(b) on summary conviction to a term of imprisonment not exceeding six months or a fine not exceeding the statutory maximum, or both.

Disclosure of transactions involving directors and others

54. Substantial contracts, etc., with directors and others to be disclosed in accounts.—(1) Subject to subsections (5) and (6) and to section 58 below, group accounts prepared by a holding company in accordance with the requirements of section 1 of the 1976 Act in respect of a financial year (the 'relevant period') ending on or after the appointed day shall contain the particulars specified in section 55 below of—

(a) any transaction or arrangement of a kind described in section 49 above entered into by the company or by a subsidiary of the company for a person who at any time during the relevant period was a director of the company or was connected with such a director;

(b) an agreement by the company or by a subsidiary of the company to enter into any such transaction or arrangement for a person who at any time during the relevant period was a director of the company or was connected with such a director; and

(c) any other transaction or arrangement with the company or with a subsidiary of the company in which a person who at any time during the relevant period was a director of the company had, directly or indirectly, a material interest.

(2) Subject as aforesaid, accounts so prepared by any company other than a holding company in respect of a financial year (the

'relevant period') ending on or after the appointed day shall contain the particulars specified in section 55 below of—

(a) any transaction or arrangement of a kind described in section 49 above entered into by the company for a person who at any time during the relevant period was a director of the company or of its holding company or was connected with such a director;

(b) an agreement by the company to enter into any such transaction or arrangement for a person who at any time during the relevant period was a director of the company or of its holding company or was connected with such a director; and

(c) any other transaction or arrangement with the company in which a person who at any time during the relevant period was a director of the company or of its holding company had, directly or indirectly, a material interest.

(3) Where by virtue of section 150(2) of the 1948 Act a company does not produce group accounts in relation to any financial year, subsection (1) above shall have effect in relation to the company and that financial year as if the word 'group' were omitted.

(4) For the purposes of subsections (1)(c) and (2)(c) above—

(a) a transaction or arrangement between a company and a director of the company or of its holding company or a person connected with such a director shall (if it would not otherwise be so treated) be treated as a transaction, arrangement or agreement in which that director is interested; and

(b) an interest in such a transaction or arrangement is not material if in the opinion of the majority of the directors (other than that director) of the company which is preparing the accounts in question it is not material (but without prejudice to the question whether or not such an interest is material in any case where those directors have not considered the matter).

(5) Subsections (1) and (2) above do not apply, for the purposes of any accounts prepared by any company which is, or is the holding company of, a recognised bank, in relation to a transaction or arrangement of a kind described in section 49 above, or an agreement to enter into such a transaction or arrangement, to which that recognised bank is a party.

(6) Subsections (1) and (2) above do not apply in relation to the following transactions, arrangements and agreements—

(a) a transaction, arrangement or agreement between one company and another in which a director of the first or of its subsidiary or holding company is interested only by virtue of his being a director of the other;

(b) a contract of service between a company and one of its directors or a director of its holding company;

(c) a transaction, arrangement or agreement which was not entered into during the relevant period for the accounts in question or which did not subsist at any time during that period;

(d) a transaction, arrangement or agreement which was made before the appointed day and which does not subsist on or after that day.

(7) Subsections (1) and (2) above apply whether or not—

(a) the transaction or arrangement was prohibited by section 49 above;

(b) the person for whom it was made was a director of the company or was connected with a director of the company at the time it was made;

(c) in the case of a transaction or arrangement made by a company which at any time during a relevant period is a subsidiary of another company, it was a subsidiary of that other company at the time the transaction or arrangement was made.

55. Particulars required to be included in accounts by s. 54.—(1) The particulars of a transaction, arrangement or agreement which are required by section 54 to be included in the annual accounts prepared by a company are particulars of the principal terms of the transaction, arrangement or agreement and (without prejudice to the generality of the foregoing provision)—

(a) a statement of the fact either that the transaction, arrangement or agreement was made or subsisted, as the case may be, during the financial year in respect of which those accounts are made up;

(b) the name of the person for whom it was made, and, where that person is or was connected with a director of the company or of its holding company, the name of that director;

(c) in any case where subsection (1)(c) or (2)(c) of section 54 applies, the name of the director with the material interest and the nature of that interest;

(d) in the case of a loan or an agreement for a loan or an arrangement within section 49(3) or (4) above relating to a loan—

(i) the amount of the liability of the person to whom the loan was or was agreed to be made, in respect of principal and interest, at the beginning and at the end of that period;

(ii) the maximum amount of that liability during that period;
(iii) the amount of any interest which, having fallen due, has not been paid; and
(iv) the amount of any provision (within the meaning of Schedule 8 to the 1948 Act) made in respect of any failure or anticipated failure by the borrower to repay the whole or part of the loan or to pay the whole or part of any interest thereon;

(e) in the case of a guarantee or security or an arrangement within section 49(3) above relating to a guarantee or security—
(i) the amount for which the company (or its subsidiary) was liable under the guarantee or in respect of the security both at the beginning and at the end of the financial year in question;
(ii) the maximum amount for which the company (or its subsidiary) may become so liable; and
(iii) any amount paid and any liability incurred by the company (or its subsidiary) for the purpose of fulfilling the guarantee or discharging the security (including any loss incurred by reason of the enforcement of the guarantee or security); and

(f) in the case of any other transaction, arrangement or agreement, the value of the transaction or arrangement, or, as the case may be, the value of the transaction or arrangement to which the agreement relates.

56. Particulars of amounts outstanding to be included in accounts.—(1) This section applies in relation to the following classes of transactions, arrangements and agreements—

(a) loans, guarantees and securities relating to loans, arrangements of a kind described in subsection (3) or (4) of section 49 relating to loans and agreements to enter into any of the foregoing transactions and arrangements;
(b) quasi-loans, guarantees and securities relating to quasi-loans, arrangements of a kind described in the said subsection (3) or (4) relating to quasi-loans and agreements to enter into any of the foregoing transactions and agreements;
(c) credit transactions, guarantees and securities relating to credit transactions, arrangements of a kind described in the said subsection (3) or (4) relating to credit transactions and agreements to enter into any of the foregoing transactions and arrangements.

(2) The group accounts of a holding company and the accounts of any other company prepared in accordance with the requirements of section 1 of the 1976 Act in respect of a financial year (the 'relevant period') ending on or after the appointed day, shall contain a statement in relation to transactions, arrangements and agreements made by the company and, in the case of a holding company, by a subsidiary of the company for persons who at any time during the relevant period were officers of the company (but not directors) of the aggregate amounts outstanding at the end of the relevant period under transactions, arrangements and agreements within paragraphs (a), (b) and (c) respectively of subsection (1) above, and the numbers of officers for whom the transactions, arrangements and agreements falling within each of those paragraphs were made.

(3) Subsection (2) above shall not apply in relation to any transaction, arrangement or agreement made by a recognised bank for any of its officers or for any of the officers of its holding company.

(4) The group accounts of a company which is, or is the holding company of a recognised bank, and the accounts of any other company which is a recognised bank, prepared in accordance with the requirements of section 1 of the 1976 Act in respect of a financial year (the 'relevant period') ending on or after the appointed day, shall contain a statement in relation to transactions, arrangements and agreements made by the company preparing the accounts, if it is a recognised bank, and (in the case of a holding company) by any of its subsidiaries which is a recognised bank, for persons who at any time during the relevant period were directors of the company or were connected with a director of the company, of the aggregate amounts outstanding at the end of the relevant period under transactions, arrangements and agreements within paragraphs (a), (b) and (c) respectively of subsection (1) above, and the numbers of persons for whom the transactions, arrangements and agreements falling within each of those paragraphs were made.

(5) For the purposes of the application of subsection (4) above in relation to loans and quasi-loans made by a company to persons connected with a person who at any time is a director of the company or of its holding company, a company which a person does not control is not connected with him.

(6) Where by virtue of section 150(2) of the 1948 Act a company does not produce group accounts in relation to any financial year, subsections (2) and (4) above shall have effect in relation to the company and that financial year as if the word 'group' were omitted.

(7) Subsections (2) and (4) above do not apply in relation to a transaction, arrangement or agreement which was made before the

appointed day and which does not subsist on or after that day.

(8) For the purposes of this section, 'amount outstanding' means the amount of the outstanding liabilities of the person for whom the transaction, arrangement or agreement in question was made, or, in the case of a guarantee or security, the amount guaranteed or secured.

57. Further provisions relating to recognised banks.—(1) Subject to section 58 below, a company which is, or is the holding company of, a recognised bank shall maintain a register containing a copy of every transaction, arrangement or agreement of which particulars would, but for subsection (5) of section 54 above be required by subsection (1) or (2) of that section to be disclosed in the company's accounts or group accounts for the current financial year and for each of the preceding ten financial years or, if such a transaction or arrangement is not in writing, a written memorandum setting out its terms.

(2) Subject to section 58 below, a company which is, or is the holding company of, a recognised bank shall before its annual general meeting make available, at the registered office of the company for not less than the period of 15 days ending with the date of the meeting, for inspection by members of the company a statement containing the particulars of transactions, arrangements and agreements which the company would, but for subsection (5) of section 54 above, be required by subsection (1) or (2) of that section to disclose in its accounts or group accounts for the last complete financial year preceding that meeting, and such a statement shall also be made available for inspection by the members at the annual general meeting.

(3) It shall be the duty of the auditors of the company to examine any such statement before it is made available to the members of the company in accordance with subsection (2) above and to make a report to the members on that statement; and the report shall be annexed to the statement before it is made so available.

(4) A report under subsection (3) above shall state whether in the opinion of the auditors the statement contains the particulars required by subsection (2) above and, where their opinion is that it does not, they shall include in the report, so far as they are reasonably able to do so, a statement giving the required particulars.

(5) Subsection (2) above shall not apply in relation to a recognised bank which is for the purposes of section 150 of the 1948 Act the wholly-owned subsidiary of a company incorporated in the United Kingdom.

(6) Where a company fails to comply with subsection (1) or (2) above, every person who at the time of that failure is a director of

the company shall be guilty of an offence and liable on conviction on indictment to a fine and on summary conviction to a fine not exceeding the statutory maximum.

(7) It shall be a defence in proceedings against a person for an offence under subsection (6) above for him to prove that he took all reasonable steps for securing compliance with subsection (1) or (2) above, as the case may be.

(8) For the purposes of the application of this section in relation to loans and quasi-loans made by the company to persons connected with a person who at any time is a director of the company or of its holding company, a company which a person does not control is not connected with him.

58. Transactions, etc., excluded from ss. 54 and 57.—(1) Subsections (1) and (2) of section 54 above do not apply, in relation to the accounts prepared by a company in respect of a relevant period, to transactions of the kind mentioned in subsection (2) below which are made by the company or by a subsidiary of the company for a person who at any time during the relevant period was a director of the company or of its holding company or was connected with such a director, if the aggregate of the values of each transaction, arrangement or agreement so made for that director or any person connected with him, less the amount (if any) by which the liabilities of the person for whom the transaction or arrangement was made has been reduced, did not at any time during the relevant period exceed £5,000.

(2) The said transactions are—

(a) credit transactions;

(b) guarantees provided or securities entered into in connection with credit transactions;

(c) arrangements within subsection (3) or (4) of section 49 above relating to credit transactions;

(d) agreements to enter into credit transactions.

(3) Subsections (1)(c) and (2)(c) of section 54 above do not apply, in relation to the accounts prepared by a company in respect of a relevant period, to any transaction or arrangement made by the company or by a subsidiary of the company for a person who at any time during the relevant period was a director of the company or of its holding company or was connected with such a director, if the aggregate of the values of each transaction or arrangement within the said subsection (1)(c) or (2)(c), as the case may be, so made for that director or any person connected with him, less the amount (if any) by which the liabilities of the person for whom the transaction or arrangement was made had been reduced, did not at any time during the relevant period exceed £1,000 or, if more, did not exceed

£5,000 or one per cent of the value of the net assets of the company which is preparing the accounts in question as at the end of the relevant period for those accounts, whichever is the less.

(4) Section 57 above does not apply in relation to transactions or arrangements made or subsisting during a relevant period by a company or by a subsidiary of a company for a person who at any time during that period was a director of the company or of its holding company or was connected with such a director, or to any agreement made or subsisting during that period to enter into such a transaction or arrangement, if the aggregate of the values of each transaction or arrangement made for that person and of each agreement for such a transaction or arrangement, less the amount (if any) by which the value of those transactions, arrangements and agreements has been reduced, did not exceed £1,000 at any one time during the relevant period.

59. Duty of auditors of company in breach of ss. 54 or 56.—If in the case of any group or other accounts of a company the requirements of section 54 or 56 above are not complied with, it shall be the duty of the auditors of the company by whom the accounts are examined to include in their report on the balance sheet of the company, so far as they are reasonably able to do so, a statement giving the required particulars.

60. Disclosure by directors of interests in contracts, etc.—(1) Any reference in section 199 of the 1948 Act (disclosure by a director of a company of his interest in a contract with the company) to a contract shall be construed as including a reference to any transaction or arrangement (whether or not constituting a contract) made or entered into on or after the appointed day.

(2) For the purposes of the said section 199, a transaction or arrangement of a kind described in section 49 above made by a company for a director of the company or a person connected with such a director shall, if it would not otherwise be so treated (and whether or not prohibited by that section), be treated as a transaction or arrangement in which that director is interested.

61. Extension of s. 26 of 1976 Act.—(1) In subsection (1) of section 26 of the 1967 Act (disclosure of director's service contract with company) the following paragraph shall be inserted after paragraph (b)—

'(c) in the case of each director who is employed under a contract of service with a subsidiary of the company, a copy of that contract or, if it is not in writing, a written memorandum setting out the terms of that contract,'

(2) The following subsection shall be inserted after subsection (3) of that section—

'(3A) Subsection (1) above shall not apply in relation to a director's contract of service with the company or with a subsidiary of the company if that contract required him to work wholly or mainly outside the United Kingdom, but the company shall keep a memorandum—

(a) in the case of a contract of service with the company, setting out the name of the director and the provisions of the contract relating to its duration;

(b) in the case of a contract of service with a subsidiary of the company, setting out the name of the director, the name and place of incorporation of the subsidiary and the provisions of the contract relating to its duration,

at the same place as copies and the memorandums are kept by the company in pursuance of subsection (1) above.'.

(3) Each reference in subsection (4), (5) and (7) of that section to subsection (1) shall be construed as including a reference to subsection (3A) of that section; the reference in subsection (7) of that section to a contract of service with a company shall be construed as including a contract of service with a subsidiary of a company; and in subsection (8) of that section, paragraph (a) shall cease to have effect.

Supplemental

62. Power to increase financial limits under Part IV.—(1) The Secretary of State may by order made by statutory instrument substitute for any sum of money specified in this Part of this Act a larger sum specified in the order.

(2) An order under this section shall be subject to annulment in pursuance of a resolution of either House of Parliament.

(3) An order under this section shall not have effect in relation to anything done or not done before the coming into force of the order and, accordingly, proceedings in respect of any liability (whether civil or criminal) incurred before that time may be continued or instituted as if the order had not been made.

63. Shadow directors.—(1) Subject to subsections (2) and (5) below, a person in accordance with whose directions or instructions the directors of a company are accustomed to act ('a shadow director') shall be treated for the purposes of this Part of this Act as a director of the company unless the directors are accustomed so to act by reason only that they do so on advice given by him in a professional capacity.

(2) A shadow director shall not be guilty of an offence under section 57(6) above by virtue only of subsection (1) above.

(3) Section 199 of the 1948 Act (disclosure by a director of a company of his interests in a contract, transaction or arrangement with the company) shall apply in relation to a shadow director of a company as it applies in relation to a director of a company, except that the shadow director shall declare his interest, not at a meeting of the directors, but by a notice in writing to the directors which is either—

(a) a specific notice given before the date of the meeting at which, if he had been a director, the declaration would be required by subsection (2) of that section to be made; or

(b) a notice which under subsection (3) of that section (general notices) falls to be treated as a sufficient declaration of that interest or would fall to be so treated apart from the proviso;

and section 145 of that Act (minutes of proceedings of meetings) shall have effect as if the declaration had been made at the meeting in question and had accordingly formed part of the proceedings at that meeting.

(4) A shadow director of a company shall be treated for the purposes of section 26 of the 1967 Act (directors' service contracts, etc., to be open to inspection by a company's members) as a director of the company.

(5) A body corporate shall not be treated as the director of any of its subsidiary companies by reason only of subsection (1) above.

64. Connected persons.—(1) For the purposes of this Part of this Act, a person is connected with a director of a company if, but only if, he is—

(a) that director's spouse, child or step-child; or

(b) except where the context otherwise requires, a body corporate with which the director is associated; or

(c) a person acting in his capacity as the trustee (other than as trustee under an employees' share scheme or a pension scheme) of any trust the beneficiaries of which include the director, his spouse or any of his children or step-children or a body corporate with which he is associated or the terms of which confer a power on the trustees that may be exercised for the benefit of the director, his spouse or any of his children or step-children or any such body corporate; or

(d) a person acting in his capacity as partner of that director or of any person who, by virtue of paragraph (a), (b) or (c) above, is connected with that director,

unless that person is also a director of the company.

(2) In subsection (1) above a reference to the child or step-child of any person includes a reference to any illegitimate child of that person, but does not include a reference to any person who has attained the age of 18 years.

(3) For the purposes of this Part of this Act—

(a) a director of a company is associated with a body corporate if, but only if, he and the persons connected with him, together, are interested in shares comprised in the equity shares capital of that body corporate of a nominal value equal to at least one-fifth of that share capital or are entitled to exercise or control the exercise of more than one-fifth of the voting power at any general meeting of that body; and

(b) a director of a company shall be deemed to control a body corporate if, but only if—

(i) he or a person connected with him is interested in any part of the equity share capital of that body or is entitled to exercise or control the exercise of any part of the voting power at any general meeting of that body; and

(ii) that director, the persons connected with him and the other directors of that company, together, are interested in more than one-half of that share capital or are entitled to exercise or control the exercise of more than one-half of that voting power.

For the purposes of this subsection, a body corporate with which a director is associated and a trustee of a trust the beneficiary of which is or may be such a body corporate shall be regarded as if they were not connected with that director.

(4) The rules set out in section 28 of the 1967 Act (interest in shares) shall have effect for the purposes of subsection (3) above with the substitution of the words 'more than one-half' for the words 'one-third or more' in subsection (3)(b) of that section; and in subsection (3) above—

(a) 'equity share capital' has the same meaning as in section 154 of the 1948 Act; and

(b) references to voting power the exercise of which is controlled by a director shall, without prejudice to the other provisions of that subsection, include references to voting power the exercise of which is controlled by a body corporate controlled by that director.

65. Interpretation of Part IV.—(1) In this Part of this Act—

'guarantee' includes indemnity, and cognate expressions shall be construed accordingly;

'money-lending company' means a company the ordinary business of which includes the making of loans or quasi-loans or the giving of guarantees in connection with loans or quasi-loans;

'recognised bank' means a company which is recognised as a bank for the purposes of the Banking Act 1979;

'relevant company' means any company which—

(a) is not a private company; or

(b) is a subsidiary of a company which either is itself not a private company or has another subsidiary which is not a private company; or

(c) has a subsidiary which is not a private company;

'services' means anything other than goods or land.

(2) For the purposes of this Part of this Act—

(a) a quasi-loan is a transaction under which one party ('the creditor') agrees to pay, or pays otherwise than in pursuance of an agreement, a sum for another ('the borrower'), or agrees to reimburse, or reimburses otherwise than in pursuance of an agreement, expenditure incurred by another party for another ('the borrower')—

(i) on terms that the borrower (or a person on his behalf) will reimburse the creditor; or

(ii) in circumstances giving rise to a liability on the borrower to reimburse the creditor;

(b) any reference to the person to whom a quasi-loan is made is a reference to the borrower; and

(c) the liabilities of a borrower under a quasi-loan include the liabilities of any person who has agreed to reimburse the creditor on behalf of the borrower.

(3) For the purposes of this Part of this Act, a credit transaction is a transaction under which one party ('the creditor'),—

(a) supplies any goods or sells any land under a hire-purchase agreement or conditional sale agreement;

(b) leases or hires any land or goods in return for periodical payments;

(c) otherwise disposes of land or supplies goods or services on the understanding that payment (whether in a lump sum or instalments or by way of periodical payments or otherwise) is to be deferred.

(4) For the purposes of this Part of this Act the value of a transaction or arrangement is—

(a) in the case of a loan, the principal of the loan;

(b) in the case of a quasi-loan, the amount, or maximum amount, which the person to whom the quasi-loan is made is liable to reimburse the creditor;

(c) in the case of a transaction or arrangement, other than a loan or quasi-loan or a transaction or arrangement within paragraph (d) or (e) below, the price which it is reasonable to expect could be obtained for the goods, land or services to which the transaction or arrangement relates if they had been supplied at the time the transaction or arrangement is entered into in the ordinary course of business and on the same terms (apart from price) as they have been supplied or are to be supplied under the transaction or arrangement in question;

(d) in the case of a guarantee or security, the amount guaranteed or secured;

(e) in the case of an arrangement to which subsection (3) or (4) of section 49 above applies, the value of the transaction to which the arrangement relates less any amount by which the liabilities under the arrangement or transaction of the person for whom the transaction was made have been reduced.

(5) For the purposes of subsection (4) above, the value of a transaction or arrangement which is not capable of being expressed as a specific sum of money (because the amount of any liability arising under the transaction is unascertainable, or for any other reason) shall, whether or not any liability under the transaction has been reduced, be deemed to exceed £50,000.

(6) For the purposes of this Part of this Act, a transaction or arrangement is made for a person if—

(a) in the case of a loan or quasi-loan, it is made to him;

(b) in the case of a credit transaction, he is the person to whom goods or services are supplied, or land is sold or otherwise disposed of, under the transaction;

(c) in the case of a guarantee or security, it is entered into or provided in connection with a loan or quasi-loan made to him or a credit transaction made for him;

(d) in the case of an arrangement within subsection (3) or (4) of section 49 above, the transaction to which the arrangement relates was made for him; and

(e) in the case of any other transaction or arrangement for the supply or transfer of goods, land or services (or any interest therein), he is the person to whom the goods, land or services (or the interest) are supplied or transferred.

(7) This Part of the Act, except sections 54, 56 and 57, does not apply to arrangements or transactions entered into before the appointed day but, for the purposes of determining whether an arrangement is one to which section 49 (3) or (4) applies, the transaction to which the arrangement relates shall, if it was entered into before the appointed day, be deemed to have been entered into after that day.

(8) For the purposes of this Part of this Act it is immaterial whether the law which (apart from this Act) governs any arrangement or transaction is the law of the United Kingdom, or of a part of the United Kingdom, or not.

66. Consequential repeals and savings.—(1) Section 190 of the 1948 Act (prohibition on loans to directors) shall cease to have effect.

(2) Section 197 of the 1948 Act (particulars in accounts of loans to officers, etc.) and section 16(1)(c) of the 1967 Act (particulars in the director's report of contracts in which a director has a significant and material interest) shall, except—

(a) in relation to accounts and directors' reports prepared in respect of any financial year ending before the appointed day; and

(b) in relation to accounts and directors' reports prepared in respect of the first financial year ending after the appointed day but only in relation to loans and contracts entered into before the appointed day which do not subsist on or after that day,

cease to have effect.

67. Application of ss. 54 to 58 and 62 to 66 to unregistered companies.—Section 435 of and Schedule 14 to the 1948 Act (which provide for the application of certain provisions of that Act to unregistered companies) shall have effect as if sections 54 to 58 and 62 to 66 above were provisions of that Act and were included among the provisions of that Act specified in that Schedule which relate to accounts and audit; and the reference in the last entry in column 3 of that Schedule to provisions applied by virtue of the foregoing entries in that Schedule shall be construed accordingly.

Part V

INSIDER DEALING

68. Prohibition on stock exchange deals by insiders, etc.—(1) Subject to subsection (8) below, an individual who is, or at any time in the preceding six months has been, knowingly connected with a company shall not deal on a recognised stock exchange in securities of that company if he has information which—

(a) he holds by virtue of being connected with the company;
(b) it would be reasonable to expect a person so connected and in the position by virtue of which he is so connected not to disclose except for the proper performance of the functions attaching to that position; and
(c) he knows is unpublished price sensitive information in relation to those securities.

(2) Subject to subsections (8) and (10) below, an individual who is, or at any time in the preceding six months has been, knowingly connected with a company shall not deal on a recognised stock exchange in securities of any other company if he has information which—

(a) he holds by virtue of being connected with the first company;
(b) it would be reasonable to expect a person so connected and in the position by virtue of which he is so connected not to disclose except for the proper performance of the functions attaching to that position;
(c) he knows is unpublished price sensitive information in relation to those securities of that other company; and
(d) relates to any transaction (actual or contemplated) involving both the first company and that other company or involving one of them and securities of the other or to the fact that such transaction is no longer contemplated.

(3) Subject to subsections (8) and (10) below, where—

(a) any individual has information which he knowingly obtained (directly or indirectly) from another individual who is connected with a particular company, or was at any time in the six months preceding the obtaining of the information so connected and who the former individual knows or has reasonable cause to believe held the information by virtue of being so connected; and
(b) the former individual knows or has reasonable cause to believe that, because of the latter's connection and position, it would be reasonable to expect him not to disclose the information except for the proper performance of the functions attaching to that position;

then, the former individual—

(i) shall not himself deal on a recognised stock exchange in securities of that company if he knows that the information is unpublished price sensitive information in relation to those securities; and

(ii) shall not himself deal on a recognised stock exchange in securities of any other company if he knows that the information is unpublished price sensitive information in relation to those securities and it relates to any transaction (actual or contemplated) involving the first company and the other company or involving one of them and securities of the other or to the fact that any such transaction is no longer contemplated.

(4) Subject to subsections (8) and (10) below, where an individual is contemplating, or has contemplated, making, whether with or without another person, a takeover offer for a company in a particular capacity, that individual shall not deal on a recognised stock exchange in securities of that company in another capacity if he knows that information that the offer is contemplated or is no longer contemplated is unpublished price sensitive information in relation to those securities.

(5) Subject to subsections (8) and (10) below, where an individual has knowingly obtained (directly or indirectly), from an individual to whom subsection (4) above applies, information that the offer referred to in subsection (4) is being contemplated or is no longer contemplated, the former individual shall not himself deal on a recognised stock exchange in securities of that company if he knows that the information is unpublished price sensitive information in relation to those securities.

(6) Subject to subsections (8) and (10) below, an individual who is for the time being prohibited by any provision of this section from dealing on a recognised stock exchange in any securities shall not counsel or procure any other person to deal in those securities, knowing or having reasonable cause to believe that that person would deal in them on a recognised stock exchange.

(7) Subject to subsections (8) and (10) below, an individual who is for the time being prohibited as aforesaid from dealing on a recognised stock exchange in any securities by reason of his having any information, shall not communicate that information to any other person if he knows or has reasonable cause to believe that that or some other person will make use of the information for the purpose of dealing, or of counselling or procuring any other person to deal, on a recognised stock exchange in those securities.

(8) The provisions of this section shall not prohibit an individual by reason of his having any information from—

(a) doing any particular thing otherwise than with a view to the making of a profit or the avoidance of a loss (whether for himself or another person) by the use of that information;

(b) entering into a transaction in the course of the exercise in good faith of his functions as liquidator, receiver or trustee in bankruptcy; or

(c) doing any particular thing if the information—

(i) was obtained by him in the course of a business of a jobber in which he was engaged or employed; and

(ii) was of a description which it would be reasonable to expect him to obtain in the ordinary course of that business;

and he does that thing in good faith in the course of that business.

(9) In subsection (8) above 'jobber' means an individual, partnership or company dealing in securities on a recognised stock exchange and recognised by the Council of the Stock Exchange as carrying on the business of a jobber.

(10) An individual shall not, by reason only of having information relating to any particular transaction, be prohibited—

(a) by subsection (2), (3) (ii), (4) or (5) above from dealing on a recognised stock exchange in any securities; or

(b) by subsection (6) or (7) above from doing any other thing in relation to securities which he is prohibited from dealing in by any of the provisions mentioned in paragraph (a) above;

if he does that thing in order to facilitate the completion or carrying out of the transaction.

(11) Where a trustee or personal representative, or, where a trustee or personal representative is a body corporate, an individual acting on behalf of that trustee or personal representative, who, apart from subsection (8) (a) above, would be prohibited by this section from dealing, or counselling or procuring any other person to deal, in any securities deals in those securities, or counsels or procures any other person to deal in them, he shall be presumed to have acted as mentioned in that paragraph if he acted on the advice of a person who—

(a) appeared to him to be an appropriate person from whom to seek such advice; and

(b) did not appear to him to be prohibited by this section from dealing in those securities.

69. Prohibition on abuse of information obtained in official capacity.—(1) This section applies to any information which—

(a) is held by a Crown servant or former Crown servant by virtue of his position or former position as a Crown servant or is knowingly obtained by an individual (directly or indirectly) from a Crown servant or former Crown servant who he knows or has reasonable cause to believe held the information by virtue of any such position;

(b) it would be reasonable to expect an individual in the position of the Crown servant or former position of the former Crown servant not to disclose except for the proper performance of the functions attaching to that position; and

(c) the individual holding it knows it is unpublished price sensitive information in relation to securities of a particular company (relevant securities).

(2) This section applies to a Crown servant or former Crown servant holding information to which this section applies and to any individual who knowingly obtained any such information (directly or indirectly) from a Crown servant or former Crown servant who that individual knows or has reasonable cause to believe held the information by virtue of his position or former position as a Crown servant.

(3) An individual to whom this section applies—

(a) shall not deal on a recognised stock exchange in any relevant securities;

(b) shall not counsel or procure any other person to deal in any such securities, knowing or having reasonable cause to believe that that other person would deal in them on a recognised stock exchange; and

(c) shall not communicate to any other person the information held or, as the case may be, obtained by him as mentioned in subsection (2) above if he knows or has reasonable cause to believe that that or some other person will make use of that information for the purpose of dealing, or of counselling or procuring any other person to deal, on a recognised stock exchange in any such securities.

(4) Section 68(8) and (11) above shall apply for the purposes of this section as they apply for the purposes of that section.

(5) An individual shall not, by reason only of having information relating to a particular transaction, be prohibited by any provision of this section from doing anything if he does that thing in order to facilitate the completion or carrying out of the transaction.

70. Off-market deals.—(1) Subject to section 71 below, sections 68 and 69 above shall apply in relation to—

(a) dealing otherwise than on a recognised stock exchange in the advertised securities of any company—

(i) through an off-market dealer who is making a market in those securities, in the knowledge that he is an off-market dealer, that he is making a market in those securities and that the securities are advertised securities; or

(ii) as an off-market dealer who is making a market in those securities or as an officer, employee or agent of such a dealer acting in the course of the dealer's business;

(b) counselling or procuring a person to deal in advertised securities in the knowledge or with reasonable cause to believe that he would deal in them as mentioned in paragraph (a) above;

(c) communicating any information in the knowledge or with reasonable cause to believe that it would be used for such dealing or for such counselling or procuring,

as they apply in relation to dealing in securities on a recognised stock exchange and to counselling or procuring or communicating any information in connection with such dealing.

(2) An individual who, by reason of his having information, is for the time being prohibited by any provision of section 68 or 69 above from dealing in any securities shall not—

(a) counsel or procure any other person to deal in those securities in the knowledge or with reasonable cause to believe that that person would deal in the securities outside Great Britain on any stock exchange other than a recognised stock exchange; or

(b) communicate that information to any other person in the knowledge or with reasonable cause to believe that that or some other person will make use of the information for the purpose of dealing or of counselling or procuring any other person to deal in the securities outside Great Britain on any stock exchange other than a recognised stock exchange.

Sections 68(8) and (11) and 69(5) shall have effect as if any reference therein to either of those sections included a reference to this subsection.

(3) In this section—

'advertised securities', in relation to a particular occurrence, means listed securities or securities in respect of which, not more than six months before that occurrence, information indicating the prices at which persons have dealt or were willing to deal in those securities has been published for the purpose of facilitating deals in those securities;

'off-market dealer' means a person who—

(a) holds a licence under section 3 of the Prevention of Fraud (Investments) Act 1958 (principals' and representatives' licences for dealers in securities); or

(b) is a member of a recognised stock exchange or recognised association of dealers in securities within the meaning of that Act; or

(c) is an exempted dealer within the meaning of that Act.

(4) For the purposes of this section an off-market dealer shall be taken to deal in advertised securities if he deals in such securities or acts as an intermediary in connection with deals made by other persons in such securities; and references in this section to such a dealer's officer, employee or agent dealing in such securities shall be construed accordingly.

(5) For those purposes an individual shall be taken to deal through an off-market dealer if the latter is a party to the transaction, is an agent for either party to the transaction or is acting as an intermediary in connection with the transaction.

71. International bonds.—(1) Section 68 above shall not by virtue of section 70 above prohibit an individual from doing anything in relation to any debenture if—

(a) that thing is done by him in good faith in connection with an international bond issue—

(i) not later than three months after the issue date, or

(ii) in a case where the international bond issue is not proceeded with, before the date on which it is decided not to proceed with the issue,

and he is an issue manager for that issue or is an officer, employee or agent of an issue manager for that issue; or

(b) he is or was an issue manager for an international bond issue who is making a market in that debenture, or is an officer, employee or agent of such an issue manager, and that thing is done by him in good faith as a person making a market in that debenture or as an officer, employee or agent of such a person;

and in either case the unpublished price sensitive information by virtue of which section 68 would but for this section apply in relation to that thing is information which he holds by virtue of his being (or having been) such an issue manager or an officer, employee or agent of such an issue manager, and is information which it would be reasonable to expect him to have obtained as an issue manager, or as such officer, employee or agent.

(2) In subsection (1) above—

'international bond issue' means an issue of debentures of a company (the 'issuing company')—

(a) all of which are offered or to be offered by an off-market dealer to persons (whether principals or agents) whose ordinary business includes the buying or selling of debentures, and

(b) where debentures are denominated in sterling, not less than 50 per cent, in normal value of the debentures are so offered to persons who are neither citizens of the United Kingdom and Colonies nor companies incorporated or otherwise formed under the law of any part of the United Kingdom;

'issue date' means the date on which the first of those debentures is issued by the issuing company; and

'issue manager' means—

(a) an off-market dealer acting as an agent of the issuing company for the purposes of an international bond issue; or

(b) where the issuing company issues or proposes to issue the debentures to an off-market dealer under an arrangement in pursuance of which he is to sell the debentures to other persons, that off-market dealer.

72. Contravention of ss. 68 and 69.—(1) An individual who contravenes the provisions of section 68 or 69 above shall be liable—

(a) on conviction on indictment to imprisonment for a term not exceeding two years or a fine, or both; and

(b) on summary conviction to imprisonment for a term not exceeding six months or a fine not exceeding the statutory maximum, or both.

(2) Proceedings for an offence under this section shall not be instituted in England and Wales except by the Secretary of State or by, or with the consent of, the Director of Public Prosecutions.

(3) No transaction shall be void or voidable by reason only that it was entered into in contravention of section 68 or 69 above.

73. Interpretation of Part V.—(1) For the purposes of this Part of this Act, an individual is connected with a company if, but only if,—

(a) he is a director of that company or a related company; or

(b) he occupies a position as an officer (other than director) or employee of that company or a related company or a position involving a professional or business relationship between himself (or his employer or a company of which he is a director) and the first company or a related company which in either case may reasonably be expected to give him access to information which, in relation to securities of either company, is unpublished price sensitive information, and which it would be reasonable to expect a person in his position not to disclose except for the proper performance of his functions.

(2) Any reference in this Part of this Act to unpublished price sensitive information in relation to any securities of any company is a reference to information which—

(a) relates to specific matters relating or of concern (directly or indirectly) to that company, that is to say, is not of a general nature relating or of concern to that company; and

(b) is not generally known to those persons who are accustomed or would be likely to deal in those securities but which would if it were generally known to them would be likely materially to affect the price of those securities.

(3) For the purposes of this Part of this Act a person deals in securities if (whether as principal or agent) he buys or sells or agrees to buy or sell any securities; and references in this Part of this Act to dealing in securities on a recognised stock exchange shall include references to dealing in securities through an investment exchange.

(4) For the purposes of this Part of this Act, an off-market dealer shall be taken to make a market in any securities if in the course of his business as an off-market dealer he holds himself out both to prospective buyers and to prospective sellers of those securities (other than particular buyers or sellers) as willing to deal in them otherwise than on a recognised stock exchange.

(5) In this Part of this Act, except where the context otherwise requires—

'company' means any company, whether a company within the meaning of the 1948 Act or not;

'Crown servant' means an individual who holds office under, or is employed by, the Crown;

'debenture' has the same meaning in relation to companies which were not incorporated under the 1948 Act as it has in relation to companies which were so incorporated;

'investment exchange' means an organisation maintaining a system whereby an offer to deal in securities made by a subscriber to the organisation is communicated, without his identity being revealed, to other subscribers to the organisation, and whereby any acceptance of that offer by any of those other subscribers is recorded and confirmed;

'listed securities', in relation to a company, means any securities of the company listed on a recognised stock exchange;

'related company', in relation to any company, means any body corporate which is that company's subsidiary or holding company, or a subsidiary of that company's holding company;

'securities' means listed securities and, in the case of a company within the meaning of the 1948 Act or a company registered under Part VIII of that Act or an unregistered company, the following securities (even if they are not listed securities), that is to say, any shares, any debentures or any right to subscribe for, call for or make delivery of a share or debenture;

'share' has the same meaning in relation to companies which were not incorporated under the 1948 Act as it has in relation to companies which were so incorporated;

'take-over offer for a company' means an offer made to all the holders (or all the holders other than the person making the offer and his nominees) of the shares in the company to acquire those shares or a specified proportion of them, or to all the holders (or all the holders other than the person making the offer and his nominees) of a particular class of those shares to acquire the shares of that class or a specified proportion of them; and

'unregistered company' means any body corporate to which the provisions specified in Schedule 14 to the 1948 Act apply by virtue of section 435 of that Act (application of provisions to unregistered companies).

Appendix 2

The Conduct of Company Directors

(Department of Trade White Paper, Cmnd 7037, 1977)

1. The Government announced in a statement by the Secretary of State for Trade to the House of Commons on 28 July 1977 that it was preparing legislative proposals to make insider dealing in securities a criminal offence and to remedy weaknesses in the law which had been demonstrated by recent company investigations, notably in connection with loans to directors and the private interests of directors. This White Paper describes the action which the Government intends to take to improve and strengthen the law on these subjects.

Duties of directors

2. Consideration of all the topics in this paper must begin with the legal responsibilities and duties of company directors. Directors are appointed to act in the interests of the company and an important area of their legal responsibilities derives from trust law – the fiduciary duty to act in the interests of the company. They are also under a duty to exercise care and skill in the discharge of their functions. These duties are part of common law and are not defined in statute. The Government believes that it is desirable to include a general statement of the duties of directors in statute law.

3. For the statutory definition of fiduciary duty the Government will introduce a provision requiring a director to observe the utmost good faith towards his company in all of his actions and to act honestly in the exercise of the powers and in the discharge of the duties of his office. It will also be provided that a director shall not make use of any money or property belonging to his company to benefit himself; nor of any information acquired by him or opportunity afforded to him by virtue of his position as a director of a company, if by doing so he gains an advantage for himself where there may be a conflict with the interests of the company.

4. The standard of skill and care which the law expects of a company director in the performance of his duties derives from case law.[1] He is required to perform his duties with reasonable care, exercising that degree of skill which may reasonably be expected of a person of his knowledge and experience. The law thus appears to draw a distinction between the standard of skill and the standard of care. For the standard of care, an objective test is set, namely that to be expected of a reasonable man; the standard of skill, on the other hand, is a subjective test under which the level required depends upon the knowledge and experience possessed by each director. The Government has decided that the present requirements of the law should be codified in legislation which will require a director to exercise that degree of care and diligence that a reasonably prudent person would exercise in comparable circumstances and the degree of skill which may reasonably be expected of a person of his knowledge and experience.

5. The Government also believes that employees should be given legal recognition by company law. The statutory definition of the duty of directors will require directors to take into account the interests of employees as well as of shareholders. They will also be required to send the annual report and accounts to all employees as well as to shareholders. This will be an additional financial and administrative burden to companies, but the Government believes that employees as well as shareholders are entitled to the information in company reports and accounts and that these should be made available to both on an equal footing.

6. The Bullock Committee recommended that there should be 'one place where a director, and particularly the new employee representative, can see a statement of the basic duties he owes to the company as a result of his membership of the board'.[2] The Government agrees that it would be useful to bring together in one place a comprehensive statement of the various legal responsibilities of directors, but this would seen more appropriate to a hand-book than to the statute itself. The Government intends to consult with the CBI and the TUC about the preparation of such a handbook.

7. The Bullock Report also drew attention to the case of *Parke v The Daily News Limited*[3] in 1962, where the family controlling the company which purchased *The Daily News* wished to distribute the whole of the purchase price among the employees who would

1 *Re City Equitable Fire Insurance Co Ltd* [1925] 1 Ch 407.
2 *Report of the Committee of Inquiry on Industrial Democracy* (Cmnd 6706) Chapter 8, paragraph 36.
3 *Supra cit* Chapter 7, paragraphs 11 and 12.

become redundant. A shareholder of *The Daily News* contested this proposed action and the Court found that there was no lawful basis for it. It is not certain that the requirement which we propose to introduce that directors should take into account the interests of employees as well as of shareholders would be held to extend to the actions of directors in the course of winding up a company, or to former employees. The Government, therefore, intends to make it lawful for directors to make provision for employees or former employees when closing down the whole or any part of the business.

Loans to directors

8. The definition of the fiduciary duty of directors, proposed in paragraph 3, will broadly give statutory form to the existing common law that a director may not make use of his company's money to further his private interests, and loans by companies to their directors are prohibited, with certain important exceptions, by section 190 of the Companies Act 1948. Nevertheless there have been a number of serious cases where directors have sought to circumvent the law in order to obtain large sums of money from their companies, and inspectors in recent company investigations have recommended that Section 190 should be strengthened.

9. The Government propose to reform the law relating to loans to directors in the following ways:

(i) For public companies and private companies which belong to a group of which a public company is also a member:

(a) to widen the scope of Section 190 to prohibit, subject to certain exceptions, loans to directors' families and to companies in which a director has an interest as well as loans to directors themselves; and to make breach of these provisions a criminal offence;

(b) to introduce limitations on the scale and terms on which loans to directors may be made when they are permitted under the specific exemptions.

(ii) For all companies:

(a) to ensure that there is greater disclosure of loans to directors by amending Section 197 of the 1948 Act.

The following paragraphs discuss these proposals in greater detail.

10. Section 190 provides that it shall not be lawful for a company to make a loan, or to enter into a guarantee or provide any security for a loan, to a person who is its director or a director of its holding company. In the case of public companies and private companies that belong to a group of which a public company is also a member it is proposed to extend this prohibition to include a director's spouse, son or daughter, and to prohibit the making of a loan to any company which a director or his family controls or in which he or his family has a major financial interest, defined as 20 per cent or more of any of the classes of capital or of the company's long- or medium-term loan debts. Loans to trusts of which the director or any member of his family is a trustee, other than a bare trustee, or a beneficiary, will similarly be prohibited.

11. There are at present three exceptions to the general prohibition on loans to directors: a subsidiary company may make a loan to its holding company where the latter is its director: a company may provide, subject to certain safeguards, funds to a director to meet expenses incurred for the purposes of the company; and finally there is the 'banking exemption' which provides that, in the case of a company whose ordinary business includes the lending of money, a loan may be made to a director where such loan is in the ordinary course of the company's business. Alleged abuses of the second and particularly the third exemption have given rise to considerable concern.

12. It has been suggested that the meaning of 'in the ordinary course of business' should be defined more closely. It is, however, difficult to formulate a definition which would be satisfactory in all circumstances. We therefore propose instead to require that such loans must be on normal commercial terms as to interest rate, repayment terms, security and otherwise; they are to be subject to an overall limit of £50,000 and are to be disclosed in the accounts; and to make a breach of the new provision subject to criminal penalties. It will, however, be permissible for a director to obtain a low interest loan for house purchase from his company provided that this is done under a scheme which is available to employees of the company and on the same terms; the limit of £50,000 will, nevertheless, still apply and the loans must be disclosed.

13. In order not to obstruct legitimate inter-company lending, there will be an exemption to the provisions in paragraphs 10 to 12 for loans by one company to another within the same group defined as a holding company and its subsidiaries. However, where such loans would otherwise have been caught by the rules on prohibition, limitation or disclosure details of the loans must be disclosed separately in the accounts of the lending company.

14. The new disclosure provisions to replace those in Section 197 will cover all loans made to directors, including those to their families and associated companies, and will require for each loan:

a statement of the identity of the borrower, and the name of the director concerned if he is not the borrower;

a statement of the terms of the loan, including interest rate and security;

a statement of the amount outstanding at the beginning and the end of the period, and the highest amount outstanding during the period if this is a higher amount;

a statement as to whether any interest due has not been paid, and whether any provision had been made in the accounts for non-recovery of the loan.

This information will be part of the accounts and will be subject to audit.

15. There are other ways, besides the receipt of a loan, by which a director may become indebted to his company, such as trade credit. It is considered that where such indebtedness is significant it is a matter of legitimate concern to the shareholders, and it is intended that in future companies should be required to show, separately from any loans, the amount of other indebtedness of each director to the company, or his family or associated company, where such indebtedness exceeds £5,000. It is also proposed to limit to £10,000 the advances which can be made by a company to its director to cover expenses.

Directors' conflicts of interest

16. The general fiduciary duty of a director to his company also needs to be strengthened by specific statutory provisions covering transactions, other than loans, in which the director's duty to his company conflicts or may conflict with his private interests or those of his family. In general, it is not possible to lay down in law what directors may or may not do in particular circumstances: the variety of situations is too great. There are, however, two specific types of contract where the possibility of conflict is so clear that the approval of the shareholders should be sought before the contract is valid: one concerns long-term contracts of service, the other significant purchases by the company of assets from or sales to, a director or a company in which the director has an interest. The Stock Exchange listing agreement already provides that, for listed companies, certain of these contracts must be authorised by the shareholders. The Government propose that for all companies directors' service contracts for periods longer than 5 years shall not be valid unless approved by the company in general meeting, and intend to introduce a requirement that significant contracts involving the transfer of assets between a company and a director, his family, or another company in which a director has an interest, shall require the prior approval of the company in general meeting.

17. For other transactions involving possible conflicts of interest it is proposed to provide for fuller disclosure of transactions in the annual accounts of companies, and to strengthen the rights of shareholders to take legal action where they consider that their interests have been harmed by the actions of the directors. The new disclosure provisions will be along similar lines to those already in operation for listed companies, which provide that details of contracts of significance, defined as contracts involving in aggregate more than 1 per cent of the company's purchases or receipts, shall be disclosed. It is considered that this information should be provided in the form of a note to the accounts, rather than in the directors' report, and will therefore be subject to audit.

18. Hitherto, directors who have pursued their private interests at the expense of the company have had little to fear from the shareholders, even when the latter have the necessary information. In private companies in particular, this may be considered as one aspect of the need to improve the position of minority shareholders, and it is intended to introduce legislation to amend Section 210 of the 1948 Act to enable minority shareholders to take action more readily to protect their interests by providing that they may petition the Court on the grounds that the affairs of the company are being conducted in a manner unfairly prejudicial to their interests. Such amendment will of course help to deal with a wider range of abuses than those involving contracts in which the directors have a personal interest.

Non-executive directors

19. Non-executive directors can perform a useful function in helping to resolve problems of conflicts of interest as well as in other ways. In recent years there has been growing interest in the role of non-executive directors on company boards. The report of the Company Affairs Committee of the CBI, *The Responsibilities of the British Public Company*, published in 1973 (the Watkinson Report) concluded that 'the inclusion on the board of public companies of non-executive directors is highly desirable . . . by virtue of the fact that unlike executive directors they are not closely involved in the day-to-day affairs of the company and they are in a better position to see the company as a whole and to take a critical view of it'. Despite this, only 35 per cent of companies in *The Times 1000 1975–76* had more than two non-executive directors. Twenty-five per cent had none.

20. Non-executive directors can bring to the board a breadth of knowledge and experience which the company's own management may not possess. Even more important, they can increase the element of independence and objectivity in board decision-making. Not being involved in day-to-day management they are able to take a detached look at the way in which the company is being run and at its medium- and long-term policies. They should provide independent supervision of the company's management. In order to do this effectively, however, the non-executive directors need free access to management information and there need to be enough of them. One or two non-executive directors on a board which is 20 strong are unlikely to exercise real influence.

21. In the United States and Canada a practice has developed in recent years whereby the boards of public companies appoint an audit committee composed wholly or mainly of non-executive directors. The duties of the audit committee are flexible depending on the needs of the company, but the core functions are to review the financial statements and to review the audit arrangements and the company's internal financial controls. The audit committee works closely with the auditors who are normally invited to attend its meetings. It has been found in the United States and Canada that audit committees play a useful role in strengthening the influence of non-executive directors and the position of the auditors. Public companies registered under the Canadian Business Corporations Act 1973 are required to have an audit committee and this will also be a requirement from 1 July 1978 for companies listed on the New York Stock Exchange. The time may come when it will be appropriate to legislate in this field, but the Government believes initially at least it will be better for companies, investors and their representative bodies to work out schemes which can benefit from a degree of flexibility which the law could not provide. It has been found in North America that one of the conditions for the successful operation of audit committees is that the board should contain a sufficient number of strong and independent non-executive directors to serve on them. This means that companies must be willing to allow members of their senior management or directors to serve as non-executive directors on the boards of other companies, to the general advantage of industry. The Consultative Committee of Accountancy Bodies, in a memorandum to the Secretary of State for Trade, has supported experiments with audit committees by UK companies. The Government welcomes this and also the consideration which is currently being given to them by the Confederation of British Industries and The Stock Exchange.

Insider dealing

22. Insider dealing is understood broadly to cover situations where a person buys or sells securities when he, but not the other party to the transaction, is in possession of confidential information which affects the value to be placed on those securities. Furthermore the confidential information in question will generally be in his possession because of some connection which he has with the company whose securities are to be dealt in (eg he may be a director, employee or professional adviser of that company) or because someone in such a position has provided him, directly or indirectly, with the information. Public confidence in directors and others closely associated with companies requires that such people should not use inside information to further their own interests. Furthermore, if they were to do so, they would frequently be in breach of their obligations to the companies, and could be held to be taking an unfair advantage of the people with whom they were dealing.

23. There are at present in this country no legal sanctions aimed specifically at discouraging insider dealing although, for example, both the 1967 and the 1976 Companies Acts contain provisions requiring disclosure of dealings by directors and substantial shareholders. In addition, the Stock Exchange regulations and the City Code on Take-overs and Mergers contain provisions against insider dealing and the Stock Exchange has recently announced details of 'a model code' which it intends to introduce as part of its Listing Agreement; this lays down principles to be observed by directors and employees wishing to deal in their company's securities. The Government has looked carefully at the issues involved and has paid attention both to what is done in other countries and to the views expressed by various organisations in this country. The question of what should be done about insider dealing has attracted considerable debate here and overseas and this has served to clarify the issues and to identify the conflicting considerations which have to be balanced. That insider dealing is wrong is widely accepted and the Government has concluded that this should be underlined by statutory provisions which would make insider dealing in certain circumstances a criminal offence. It will not be possible to produce a perfect answer to the problem which will enable the immediate identification and conviction of every wrongdoer but the Government intends to establish as soon as possible that insider dealing is an offence and to create penalties which will be sufficient in most cases to deter those who are tempted to use inside information for their own personal gain. If the provisions proposed prove insufficient in the light of experience, the Government will not hesitate to modify and refine them.

24. The Government believes that market transactions in quoted securities should be treated differently from other transactions. In the former, with the jobbing system and market structure, it will not generally be practicable to identify a victim who has suffered as a result of insider dealing. This rules out any adequate civil law remedy that would compensate the victim and is a further reason why criminal sanctions are called for. In other cases there will be a direct contractual relationship between the parties and it is, therefore, possible to build on existing civil law remedies with some strengthening of the criminal and civil law on fraud and misrepresentation (see paragraph 30). The Government is considering into which category the ARIEL system and the over-the-counter market should fall.

25. The Government's principal proposal is that it shall be a criminal offence for an insider to deal on the market in quoted securities in certain circumstances where he has inside information. We intend, however, that this offence should not be one of absolute liability. The prosecution will need to show that the insider knew or had reasonable grounds to believe that the information was not generally known and was price sensitive and that he dealt nevertheless. Also, it will be possible for a person to offer as a defence that his purpose in dealing was not to make a profit or avoid a loss by the use of his inside information.

26. In making these proposals the Government has recognised that the creation of insider dealing as an offence must not be such as to inhibit dealings which are not under criticism. It has particularly in mind that the directors and employees of a company will not infrequently hold shares in the company for which they work. By the very nature of their employment they will usually be in possession of confidential information and they could be inhibited from dealing perfectly innocently unless their special position was recognised. The difficulty is a real one, but the Government believes that the defence set out in the preceding paragraph will afford a suitable measure of protection in relation to innocent dealings by directors and employees. While the Government welcomes the initiative taken by the Stock Exchange in producing the 'model code' referred to in paragraph 23, the Government does not consider that it would be practicable or desirable to provide in legislation that compliance with the 'model code' should of itself be a defence to the proposed criminal offence. Furthermore, in the Government's view, the wide variety of possible factors to be considered make it impossible to lay down, whether in legislation or in some statutory code, more specific guidance about the circumstances in which, under the provisions set out above, it would be lawful to deal.

27. In defining an insider it would be possible either to list in the legislation specific classes of persons who together with defined associates would be treated as insiders (principally directors, employees, substantial shareholders and persons with a professional or business relationship with the company) or to adopt a wider approach, as in the United States, that an insider is anyone who has inside information. The principal advantage of the wider approach is that it might avoid some of the anomalies as to who is and who is not within the defined category of insider. However, it would be difficult to enforce in practice and could bring within the prohibition on dealing a much wider range of individuals who would be in some doubt at to whether they were committing a criminal offence by dealing or not. Since this would be unsatisfactory, we think it best to adopt the approach of listing specific classes of persons.

28. However, in addition to the specific list of persons who are to be treated as insiders, the Government proposes that anyone who receives information which he knows to be price sensitive and not generally available and which he realises has come directly or indirectly from an insider should also refrain from dealing. It is not proposed to restrict this provision to those who are in some specified relationship with the insider. The Government recognises that a broad definition may inhibit some transactions but believes that its proposals for a defence against the criminal charge will provide an adequate protection for the innocent. If in a few cases a person is not clear whether he falls within the definition, the prudent course will be for him to refrain from dealing. The alternative of setting out in the legislation those who are in specified family or business relationships with the insider would necessarily introduce arbitrary distinctions and could on occasion exclude from the crime persons who were knowingly behaving in an improper manner.

29. It is not proposed that companies themselves should be capable of prosecution for insider dealing. The provisions required to bring companies within the scope of the offence would be very complex and we do not think that by focusing solely on individuals we should be likely to miss any culpable person who should be brought within the net. Also the main aim of the legislation will be to set out in the statute standards by which people can measure their behaviour. However, we would propose to make it an offence for anyone who should not deal to procure dealings by any other person and in this case companies would be included in the definition of person. This provision is necessary to prevent evasion of the legislation by, for example, a person dealing through a company of which he is the major shareholder.

30. Where a market transaction is not involved and there are face to face dealings between vendor and buyer the insider would be put under an obligation, to be enforced by criminal sanctions, to reveal his status to the other party involved in the transaction. Although the latter probably has already sufficient grounds for a civil action where this is not done, we intend to provide specifically that default would give grounds for action to rescind the contract in question and recover any loss caused by the failure to disclose.

31. Where insider dealing takes place in market transactions in quoted securities there are substantial problems in linking buyers and sellers which seem to rule out civil actions by those who claim to have made losses through buying or selling shares at a critical time. Indeed one of the main arguments for creating the criminal offence of insider dealing is precisely that there is usually no effective civil remedy. With the establishment of criminal sanctions criminal penalties will be the natural way of making insiders pay for illicit gains. In addition there would be nothing in the statute which would prevent civil remedies being sought in any suitable case under the present law. The Courts have general power now under the Powers of the Criminal Courts Act 1973 to order a convicted person to pay compensation, and this would apply to convictions for insider dealing. However, such an order has to be made in favour of an identified person, and in market transactions it will not normally be possible to identify such a person. There may be some scope for the use of these powers in the more straight forward cases, where the victim is identified and the extent of his loss is clear. It is often argued, however, that it would be wrong to allow the insider to retain the financial benefit of his actions and that the company itself should be allowed to sue for 'disgorgement'. There will be cases in which the company will already have a right to recover profits obtained from the misuse of information acquired by directors or employees by virtue of their position or which has been entrusted to persons in confidence. To extend the law so as to enable the company to sue for disgorgement where it has no right to do so at present would bring with it a windfall profit resulting from the criminal behaviour of one of its employees but would mean that the insider did not keep any illicit gains. The arguments for and against some provision to ensure that an insider is deprived of such gains are finely balanced and the Government has not yet reached a firm conclusion: further discussion of this subject would be welcome.

32. The preceding paragraphs set out the main principles on which the forthcoming legislation on insider dealing will be based. This legislation will also deal with a number of questions of a more detailed nature, such as the position of trustees and the arrangements within financial institutions for restricting access to the confidential information held by certain departments. These raise important and sometimes difficult issues, and will be the subject of further consideration and consultation.

Appendix 3

Model Code for Securities Transactions by Directors of Listed Companies

The Stock Exchange regards it as highly desirable that directors of listed companies should hold securities in their own companies. Directors wishing to buy or sell such securities must first have regard to the statutory provisions in Part V of the Companies Act 1980 on insider dealing. It is regarded as axiomatic that directors of listed companies will not deal in their companies securities when prohibited from doing so by those statutory provisions. The statutory provisions are not confined to directors of listed companies but concern themselves more widely with individuals 'connected with a company'.

The Stock Exchange believes that special considerations apply to directors of listed companies. There are occasions where, even though not expressly prohibited by the statutory provisions, it would be undesirable for a director to buy or sell his company's securities.

These occasions are:—

(i) where a director is himself unaware of a price sensitive matter under discussion (perhaps because it has not yet been made known to the board) which is likely ultimately to call for an exceptional announcement and where for his own protection he should be told not to deal; and

(ii) the periods prior to the regular announcements of results and dividends.

The purpose of the model code remains primarily to give guidance on these two occasions so as to enable companies to establish an agreed procedure which would provide general protection against misinformed criticism both for the company and for the individual directors, given that, under the statutory provisions, a director might otherwise be free to deal. The Stock Exchange sees the model code (including the basic principles set out below) as setting a minimum standard of good practice against which companies should measure their own company codes. The model code should therefore be seen as setting guidelines rather than rigid rules to be followed in every detail.

Two further aspects should be mentioned:—

(i) compliance with the model code is not a defence in law and it may therefore be necessary to be satisfied that a proposed dealing would not be in contravention of the statutory provisions. It should not, for example, be assumed that compliance with the procedure set out in basic principle 4 (to establish the time at which an intended acquisition by a company should be deemed price sensitive information) or that dealing under the extenuating circumstances indicated in rule 3.1 (where a pressing financial commitment has to be met) would necessarily preclude contravention of the statutory provisions. Basic principle 4 and rule 3.1 are intended as guidance for the Chairman (or whoever is nominated to receive notification of dealing intentions) as to circumstances where exceptions to the model code may be considered, always assuming that no breach of the statutory provisions would result; and

(ii) the statutory provisions do not specifically relate to other interests of a director, nor to the position of spouses or infant children. In this respect the model code has broader application than the statutory provisions.

The basic principles

1. Directors should not deal in their companies' securities on consideration of a short-term nature.

2. Directors will always be thought to be in possession of more information than can at any particular time be published. Accordingly they must accept that they cannot at all times feel free to deal in their companies' securities, even when the statutory provisions would not prohibit them from doing so.

3. Notwithstanding this general constraint there must be periods in the year when directors are in principle (but subject to the statutory provisions) to be regarded as free to deal in their companies' securities. The following model rules have been formulated on the basis that:—

(i) dealings should not normally take place for a minimum period prior to the announcement of regularly recurring information, particularly profits, dividends and other distributions, whether or not the information is price sensitive (this period being defined in rule 3.1); and

(ii) dealings should not take place prior to the announcement of matters of an exceptional nature involving unpublished price-sensitive information in relation to the securities of the company (or where relevant any other listed company).

4. Matters of an exceptional nature cause particular difficulty. A director who has knowledge of the exceptional matter in question will normally be prohibited from dealing by the statutory provisions but even if he is not so prohibited he should nevertheless not deal in the circumstances outlined below. Similarly, a director who has no such knowledge should be advised, when he notifies his intention to deal under rule 2.1, that it would be inappropriate for him to deal where the same circumstances apply. Those circumstances are where:—

(i) the matter in question constitutes unpublished price-sensitive information in relation to the company's securities, and
(ii) the proposed dealing would take place after the time when the likelihood of an announcement ultimately being necessary has become a reasonable probability.

An exhaustive definition of price-sensitive information is not possible. Nevertheless it should be assumed for this purpose that the matters referred to in paragraph 3(3) and 5 of the listing agreement are to be so regarded.

5. In principle, a director should seek to secure that all dealings in which he is or is deemed to be interested should be conducted in accordance with the provisions of the model code. Rule 4.1 sets this out as a general proposition. Nevertheless it is recognised that a director's duty in this respect will depend on the particular circumstances. A director who is sole trustee, for example, should follow the same procedure as for any dealings on his own account and should deal only if he would be personally allowed to deal under the code, even if he is excepted from the general prohibitions imposed by the statutory provisions by virtue of the special defences relating to trustees granted by such provisions.

Where a director has co-trustees who are not themsleves directors of the company, he may not be able to ensure that the procedure applicable to his personal dealings is followed in respect of dealings on behalf of the trust. The director/trustee has to avoid acting in breach of trust and at the same to refrain from divulging or abusing confidential information, and it may not therefore always be practicable to expect that trustees will refrain from dealing at a time when one of their number is not personally free to deal.

On the other hand if a director, whether or not himself a trustee, has, as settlor or otherwise, an important influence over the decision of the trustees, the procedure applicable to his personal dealings ought to be followed and the trustees should not deal when he personally is not free to deal. Again, the remoteness of some interests may be such as to make the imposition of any duty under rule 4.1 impracticable or inappropriate. Rule 4.2 and 4.3 indicate certain precautions which should be taken.

It is an over-riding principle that under no circumstances should a director deal where prohibited from doing so by the statutory provisions or make any unauthorised disclosure of any confidential information, whether to co-trustees or any other person, or make any use of such information for the advantage of himself or others — even those to whom he owes a fiduciary duty.

6. When a director places investment funds under professional management, even where discretion is given, the managers should nonetheless be made subject to the same restrictions and procedures as the director himself in respect of proposed dealings in the company's securities.

The following Model Rules should be used as Guidelines for companies in formulating their own Codes:

1.1 A director should not deal in any of the securities of the company at any time when he is in possession of unpublished price-sensitive information in relation to those securities.

1.2 The same restrictions should apply to dealings by a director in the securities of any other company which are listed on The Stock Exchange when by virtue of his position as a director of his own company, he is in possession of unpublished price-sensitive information in relation to those securities.

At other times, a director WHO IS NOT PROHIBITED FROM DOING SO BY PART V OF THE COMPANIES ACT 1980 can feel free to deal subject to the provisions of the rules which follow:

2.1 A director should not deal in any securities of his own company without first notifying the chairman (or other director(s) appointed for the specific purpose), and receiving acknowledgement. In his own case the chairman of the board should first notify the board at a board meeting, or alternatively notify the other director(s) appointed for the purpose and receive acknowledgement.

2.2 The procedure established within the company should, as a minimum, provide for there to be a written record maintained by the company that the appropriate notification was given and acknowledged, and for the director concerned to have written confirmation to that effect.

3.1 During the periods of two months immediately preceding the preliminary announcement of the company's annual results and of the announcement of the half-yearly results together with dividends and distributions to be paid or passed, a director should not purchase any securities of the company; nor should he sell any such securities unless the circumstances are exceptional, for example, where a pressing financial commitment has to be met. In any event he must comply with the procedure in rule 2 above.

3.2 Companies producing quarterly results should consult the Quotations Department on the formulation of modified dealing procedures appropriate to their case.

4.1 The restrictions on dealings by a director contained in this code should be regarded as equally applicable to any dealings by the director's spouse or by or on behalf of any infant child and any other dealings in which for the purposes of the Companies Act 1967 he is or is to be treated as interested. It is the duty of the director, therefore, to seek to avoid any such dealing at a time when he himself is not free to deal.

4.2 Any director of the company who acts as trustee of a trust should ensure that his co-trustees are aware of the identity of any company of which he is a director so as to enable them to anticipate possible difficulties. A director having funds under management should likewise advise the investment manager.

4.3 Any director who is a beneficiary, but not a trustee, of a trust which deals in securities of the company should endeavour to ensure that the trustees notify him after they have dealt in such securities on behalf of the trust, in order that he in turn may notify the company. For this purpose he should ensure that the trustees are aware of the companies of which he is a director.

5. A list of directors' dealings in the securities of the company since the date of the previous list should be circulated to members of the board with the board papers; alternatively the register maintained in accordance with Section 29 of the Companies Act 1967 should be made available for inspection at every meeting of the board.

6. The directors of a company should as a board and individually endeavour to ensure that any employee of the company or director or employee of a subsidiary company who, because of his office or employment in the company or a subsidiary, is in possession of unpublished price-sensitive information in relation to the market price of the securities of any listed company, deals in those securities in accordance with this model code.

7. References in this code to 'securities' have the meanings ascribed thereto by Section 73 of the Companies Act 1980.

DECLARATION WITH REGARD TO DIRECTORS

Notes

(1) Please answer all questions, and if a question is answerable in the negative, please answer "No". Do not leave any section blank.

(2) If insufficient space is provided for completion of any paragraph, additional information may be entered on a separate sheet of paper duly signed and attached.

1. State:—
   - (a) Present Surname and any former Surname(s).
   - (b) Present Forename(s) and any former Forename(s).
   - (c) Date of Birth.
   - (d) Residential address.
   - (e) Nationality and former nationality, if any.
   - (f) Professional qualifications, if any.

2. Are you a Director of any other Limited Companies or Corporations? If so, state:—

   Names of such Companies or Corporations, nature of business where this is not indicated in title and date of commencement of each Directorship.

   Note: Particulars are required in respect of all relevant companies, whether or not incorporated in the United Kingdom. Where a relevant company has securities listed on The Stock Exchange, the name of any subsidiary company of which you are also a director need not be stated.

3. (a) Have you at any time been adjudged bankrupt either in the United Kingdom or else-

where? If so, state the Court by which you were adjudged bankrupt and if discharged, the date and conditions on which you were granted your discharge.

(b) Have you at any time been a party to a deed of arrangement or made any other form of composition with your creditors? If so, give particulars.

(c) Are there any unsatisfied judgements outstanding against you? If so, give particulars.

(d) Has any company or other body corporate been put into liquidation (other than a members' voluntary winding-up) or had a receiver appointed during the period when you were (or within the preceding six months had been) one of its directors? If so, in each case state the name, nature of business, date of commencement of winding-up or receivership and the amount involved together with an indication of the outcome or current position.

4. Have you at any time been convicted in the United Kingdom or elsewhere of any offence involving fraud or dishonesty, or in the United Kingdom of any offence (whether or not involving fraud or dishonesty) under the Companies Acts, the Bankruptcy Acts, the Prevention of Fraud (Investments) Acts, the Protection of Depositors Act 1963, or the Income Tax or Finance Acts?

If so, state the Court by which you were convicted, the date of conviction and full particulars of the offence and the penalty imposed.

I .... of (Company)..........................

declare that the answers to all the above questions are true and I hereby give my authority to the Secretary to the Council of The Stock Exchange, or to any person authorised by him to disclose any of the foregoing particulars given by me to such Members of The Stock Exchange and with the approval of the Chairman or a Deputy Chairman of The Stock Exchange, to such other persons as the said Secretary in his absolute discretion may think fit.

Signature ....

Dated .... 19....

Appendix 4
Companies (No 2) Bill 1981, Part IV

Part IV

DISCLOSURE OF INTERESTS IN SHARES

Disclosure of interests in voting shares in public companies

58. Obligation to notify known interests in voting shares in a public company.—(1) Where a person either—

(a) to his knowledge acquires any interest in shares comprised in relevant share capital of a public company or ceases to be interested in any shares so comprised (whether or not he retains any interest in other shares so comprised); or

(b) becomes aware that he has acquired any interest in shares so comprised or that he has ceased to be interested in any shares so comprised in which he was previously interested;

he shall be under an obligation to make to the company the notification with respect to his interest in shares so comprised required by subsection (5) below in any case within subsection (2) below.

(2) That obligation arises where either—

(a) he has an interest subject to the notification requirement under this section in shares comprised in the share capital in question immediately after the relevant time but did not have such an interest immediately before that time; or

(b) he had an interest subject to the notification requirement under this section in shares comprised in that share capital immediately before the relevant time but does not have such an interest immediately after that time; or

(c) he has an interest subject to the notification requirement under this section in shares comprised in that share capital both immediately before and immediately after the relevant time but the percentage levels of his interest immediately before and immediately after that time are not the same.

(3) A person has an interest subject to the notification requirement under this section in relevant share capital of a public company at any time when he is interested in shares comprised in relevant share capital of any such company of an aggregate nominal

value equal to or more than the percentage of the nominal value of that share capital which is for the time being the notifiable percentage under this section, but all facts relevant to determining for the purposes of this section whether a person has such an interest at any time (or the percentage level of his interest) shall be taken to be what he knows them to be at that time.

(4) Where otherwise than in circumstances within subsection (1) above a person—

(a) is aware at the time when it occurs of any change of circumstances affecting any fact relevant to the application of the notification requirement under this section in relation to any existing interest of his in shares comprised in a company's share capital of any description;

(b) otherwise becomes aware of any such fact (whether or not arising from any such change of circumstances);

he shall be under an obligation to make to the company the notification with respect to his interest required by subsection (5) below in any case within subsection (2)(a) above.

(5) A notification required by this subsection with respect to a person's interest (if any) in shares comprised in relevant share capital of a public company must be in writing and must specify the share capital to which it relates; and any such notification must also either—

(a) state the number of shares comprised in that share capital in which the person making the notification knows he was interested immediately after the time when the obligation to make the notification arose; or

(b) in any case where the person making the notification no longer has an interest subject to the notification requirement under this section in shares comprised in that share capital, state that he no longer has such an interest.

(6) A person's obligation to make any such notification must be performed within the period of five days next following the day on which that obligation arises.

(7) Subject to the qualification mentioned below, in subsection (2)(c) above 'percentage level' means the percentage figure found by expressing the aggregate nominal value of all the shares comprised in the share capital there mentioned in which the person in question is interested immediately before or (as the case may be) immediately after the relevant time as a percentage of the nominal value of that share capital and rounding that figure down, if it is not a whole number, to the next whole number.

Where the nominal value of that share capital is greater immediately after the relevant time than it was immediately before that time the percentage level of his interest immediately before (as well as immediately after) that time shall be determined by reference to the larger amount.

(8) The reference in subsection (3) above to the percentage which is for the time being the notifiable percentage under this section is a reference to five per cent, or such other percentage as may from time to time be prescribed for the purposes of this section by regulations under section 59 of this Act.

(9) References in subsections (2) and (7) above, as they apply in relation to any person's interest, to the relevant time are references to the time of the event or change of circumstances relevant for the purposes of subsection (1)(a) or (4)(a) above or the time when he acquires the knowledge relevant for the purposes of subsection (1)(b) or (4)(b) above (as the case may require).

(10) For the purposes of this Part of this Act 'relevant share capital', in relation to any public company, means issued share capital of that company of a class carrying rights to vote in all circumstances at general meetings of the company.

59. The prescribed percentage.—(1) The Secretary of State may by regulations made by statutory instrument from time to time prescribe the percentage to apply in determining whether a person's interest in any shares in a company is subject to the notification requirement under section 58 of this Act, and different percentages may be so prescribed in relation to companies of different classes or descriptions.

(2) Where in consequence of any reduction in the percentage applicable for the purposes of that section made by regulations under this section a person's interest in relevant share capital of any public company becomes an interest subject to the notification requirement under that section, he shall be under an obligation to make to the company the notification with respect to his interest required by subsection (5) of that section.

(3) Subsection (6) of that section shall not apply in any such case, but a person's obligation to make any notification under that section by virtue of this section must be performed within the period of fourteen days next following the day on which that obligation arises.

(4) No regulations shall be made under this section unless a draft of the instrument containing the regulations has been laid before Parliament and has been approved by resolution of each House of Parliament.

60. Obligation to notify particulars of registered ownership of voting shares in a public company.—(1) A notification under section 58 of this Act with respect to a person's interest in relevant share capital of a public company (other than one stating that he no longer has an interest subject to the notification requirement under that section in shares comprised in that share capital) shall include particulars of—

(a) the identity of each registered holder of any shares to which the notification relates; and

(b) the number of those shares held by each such registered holder;

so far as known to the person making the notification at the date of the notification.

(2) A person who has an interest in shares comprised in relevant share capital of a public company which is subject to the notification requirement under section 58 of this Act shall be under an obligation to notify the company in writing—

(a) of any such particulars in relation to those shares as are mentioned in subsection (1) above; and

(b) of any change in any such particulars;

of which in either case he becomes aware at any time after any interest notification date and before the first occasion following that date on which he becomes subject to any further obligation to make any notification under that section with respect to his interest in shares comprised in that share capital.

(3) The reference in subsection (2) above to an interest notificiation date, in relation to any person's interest in shares comprised in relevant share capital of a public company, is a reference to either of the following, that is to say—

(a) the date of any notification made by him with respect to his interest under section 58 of this Act; and

(b) where he has failed to make any such notification, the date on which the period allowed under this Part of this Act for making that notification came to an end.

(4) A person who at any time has an interest in shares comprised in relevant share capital of a public company which is subject to the notification requirement under section 58 of this Act shall be regarded for the purposes of subsection (2) above as continuing to have an interest in those shares subject to that requirement unless and until he becomes subject to an obligation to make a notification under that section stating that he no longer has such an interest in those shares.

(5) A person's obligation to make a notification required by this section must be performed within the period of five days next following the day on which that obligation arises.

61. Notification of certain family and corporate interests.—(1) For the purposes of sections 58 to 60 of this Act a person shall be taken to be interested in any shares in which his spouse or any infant child or step-child of his is interested.

(2) For the purposes of those sections, a person shall be taken to be interested in shares if a body corporate is interested in them and—

(a) that body corporate or its directors are accustomed to act in accordance with his directions or instructions; or

(b) he is entitled to exercise or control the exercise of one-third or more of the voting power at general meetings of that body corporate.

(3) Where a person is entitled to exercise or control the exercise of one-third or more of the voting power at general meetings of a body corporate and that body corporate is entitled to exercise or control the exercise of any of the voting power at general meetings of another body corporate (the 'relevant voting power'), then, for the purposes of subsection (2)(b) above, the relevant voting power shall be taken to be exercisable by that person.

(4) For the purposes of subsections (2)(b) and (3) above, a person shall be taken to be entitled to exercise or control the exercise of any voting power if he has a right (whether subject to conditions or not) the exercise of which would make him so entitled or is under an obligation (whether so subject or not) the fulfilment of which would make him so entitled.

(5) In this section 'infant', in relation to Scotland, means pupil or minor.

62. Notification of group interests of persons acting together.—(1) Subject to subsection (1) below, an agreement between two or more persons which includes provision for the acquisition by any one or more of the parties to the agreement of interests in shares in a particular company ('the target company') is an agreement to which this section applies if—

(a) it also includes provisions imposing obligations or restrictions on any one or more of the parties to the agreement with respect to their use, retention or disposal of interests in that company shares acquired in pursuance of the agreement (whether or not together with any other interests of theirs in that company's shares to which the agreement relates); and

(b) any interest in that company's shares is in fact acquired by any of the parties in pursuance of the agreement;

and in relation to any such agreement references below in this section and in section 63 of this Act to the target company shall be read as referring to the company which is the target company for that agreement in accordance with this subsection.

(2) The reference in subsection (1)(a) above to the use by parties to the agreement of interests in shares in the target company is a reference to the exercise of any rights or of any control or influence

arising from those interests (including the right to enter into any agreement or arrangement for the exercise, or for control of the exercise, of any of those rights by any other person).

(3) Once any interest in shares in the target company has been acquired in pursuance of any such agreement as is mentioned in subsection (1) above, this section shall continue to apply to the agreement irrespective of—

(a) whether or not any further acquisitions of interests in that company's shares take place in pursuance of the agreement; and

(b) any change in the persons who are for the time being parties to the agreement; and

(c) any variation of the agreement;

so long as the agreement continues to include provisions of any description mentioned in paragraph (a) of that subsection.

References in this subsection to the agreement include references to any agreement having effect (whether directly or indirectly) in substitution for the original agreement.

(4) Subject to subsection (5) below, in this section (and in references elsewhere in this Part of this Act to an agreement to which this section applies) 'agreement' includes any agreement or arrangement; and references in this section to provisions of an agreement—

(a) accordingly include undertakings, expectations or understandings operative under any arrangement; and

(b) (without prejudice to paragraph (a) above) also include any provisions, whether express or implied and whether absolute or not.

(5) The application of this section to an arrangement which is not legally binding is limited to an arrangement involving mutuality in the undertakings, expectations or understandings of the parties to it.

(6) For the purposes of sections 58 to 60 of this Act each party to an agreement to which this section applies shall be taken to be interested in all shares in the target company in which any other party to the agreement is interested apart from the agreement (whether or not the interest of the other party in question was acquired, or includes any interest which was acquired, in pursuance of the agreement).

(7) For the purposes of subsection (6) above and section 63 of this Act an interest of any party to an agreement to which this section applies in shares in the target company is an interest apart from that agreement if he is interested in those shares otherwise than by virtue of the application of this section in relation to that agreement (and accordingly any such interest of his apart from that

agreement includes for those purposes any interest treated as his by virtue of section 61 of this Act or by virtue of the application of this section in relation to any other agreement with respect to shares in the target company to which he is a party).

(8) Any notification with respect to his interest in shares in the target company made to that company under section 58 of this Act by a person who is for the time being a party to an agreement to which this section applies—

(a) shall state that the person making the notification is a party to an agreement to which this section applies;

(b) shall include the names and (so far as known to him) the addresses of the other parties to the agreement, identifying them as such; and

(c) shall state whether or not any of the shares to which the notification relates are shares in which he is interested by virtue of this section and, if so, the number of those shares.

(9) Where a person makes a notification to any company under section 58 of this Act in consequence of ceasing to be interested in any shares in that company by virtue of the fact that he or any other person has ceased to be a party to an agreement to which this section applies, the notification shall include a statement that he or that other person has ceased to be a party to the agreement (as the case may require) and also (in the latter case) the name and (if known to him) the address of that other person.

(10) This section shall not apply to any agreement to underwrite or sub-underwrite any offer of shares in a company, provided the agreement is confined to that purpose and any matters incidental to it.

63. Obligation of persons acting together to keep each other informed of relevant facts.—(1) A person who is a party to an agreement to which section 62 of this Act applies shall be subject to the requirements of this section at any time when—

(a) the target company is a public company; and

(b) the shares in that company to which the agreement relates consist of or include shares comprised in relevant share capital of that company; and

(c) he knows the facts which make the agreement one to which section 62 applies and the facts with respect to the company and the shares mentioned in paragraphs (a) and (b) above respectively.

(2) Any such person shall be under an obligation to notify each other party to the agreement, in writing, of the relevant particulars

of his interest (if any) apart from the agreement in shares comprised in relevant share capital of the target company—

(a) on his first becoming subject to the requirements of this section; and

(b) on each occurrence after that time while he is still subject to those requirements of any event or circumstances within subsection (1) of section 58 of this Act as it applies to his case otherwise than by reference to interests treated as his under section 62 of this Act as it applies to that agreement.

(3) For the purposes of subsection (2) above, the relevant particulars of a person's interest apart from the agreement in question in shares comprised in relevant share capital of the target company are, in relation to any notice required under that subsection—

(a) the number of shares (if any) comprised in that share capital in which he would be required to state his interest if he were required to make a notification under section 58 of this Act with respect to his interest in those shares apart from the agreement immediately after the time when his obligation to give that notice under subsection (2) above arose; and

(b) the relevant particulars with respect to the registered ownership of those shares, so far as known to him at the date of the notice.

(4) A person who is for the time being subject to the requirements of this section shall also be under an obligation to notify each other party to the agreement, in writing—

(a) of any relevant particulars with respect to the registered ownership of any shares comprised in relevant share capital of the target company in which he is interested apart from the agreement; and

(b) of any change in those particulars;

of which in either case he becomes aware at any time after any interest notification date and before the first occasion following that date on which he becomes subject to any further obligation to give any notice under subsection (2) above with respect to his interest in shares comprised in that share capital.

(5) The reference in subsection (4) above to an interest notification date, in relation to any person's interest in shares comprised in relevant share capital of the target company, is a reference to either of the following, that is to say—

(a) the date of any notice given by him with respect to his interest under subsection (2) above; and

(b) where he has failed to give any such notice, the date on which the period allowed by this section for giving that notice came to an end.

(6) Any notice given by a person under this section shall include his current address unless that address has already been notified to the person to whom the notice is given by a previous notice under this section.

(7) References in this section to the relevant particulars with respect to the registered ownership of any shares are references to such particulars in relation to those shares as are mentioned in section 60(1)(a) or (b) of this Act.

(8) A person's obligation to give any notice required by this section to any other person must be performed within the period of five days next following the day on which that obligation arises.

64. Application of section 58 in cases within section 61 or 62.—(1) References in section 58 of this Act to a person's acquiring any interest in shares or ceasing to be interested in any shares shall be read as including references to his becoming or ceasing to be interested in those shares by virtue of another person's interest.

(2) For the purposes of this section, a person becomes or ceases to be interested in any shares by virtue of another person's interest where he becomes or ceases to be interested in any shares by virtue of section 61 or (as the case may be) by virtue of section 62 of this Act, whether—

(a) by virtue of the fact that the person who is interested in those shares becomes or ceases to be a person whose interests (if any) fall by virtue of either of those sections to be treated as his; or

(b) in consequence of the fact that any such person has become or ceased to be interested in those shares; or

(c) in consequence of the fact that he himself becomes or ceases to be a party to an agreement to which section 62 applies to which the person interested in those shares is for the time being a party or an agreement to which both he and that person are parties becomes or ceases to be one to which that section applies.

(3) Where a person becomes or ceases to be interested in any shares by virtue of another person's interest he shall be regarded for the purposes of section 58 of this Act as knowing he has acquired an interest in those shares or (as the case may be) that he has ceased to be interested in those shares if and when he knows both—

(a) the relevant facts with respect to that other person's interest in those shares; and

(b) the relevant facts by virtue of which he himself has become or ceased to be interested in those shares in accordance with section 61 or 62 of this Act.

(4) For the purposes of subsection (3)(a) above a person shall be regarded as knowing the relevant facts with respect to another person's interest in any shares if he knows (whether contemporaneously or otherwise) either of the subsistence of that other person's interest in those shares at any relevant time or of the fact that that other person has become or ceased to be interested in those shares at any such time; and in this subsection 'relevant time' means any time when that other person's interests (if any) fall or fell to be treated as his by virtue of section 61 or 62 of this Act.

(5) For the purposes of subsection (4) above (but without prejudice to its application apart from this subsection), a person shall be regarded as knowing of the subsistence of another person's interest in any shares or (as the case may be) that another person has become or ceased to be interested in any shares if he has been notified under section 63 of this Act of facts with respect to that other person's interest which indicate that he is or has become or ceased to be interested in those shares (whether on his own account or by virtue of a third person's interest in those shares).

65. Interests to be notified.—(1) The provisions of this section shall apply, subject to section 66 of this Act, in determining for the purposes of sections 58 to 60 of this Act whether a person has a notifiable interest in any shares.

(2) Any reference to an interest in shares shall be read as including a reference to any interest of any kind whatsoever in the shares; and accordingly there shall be disregarded any restraints or restrictions to which the exercise of any right attached to the interest is or may be subject.

(3) Where any property is held on trust and any interest in shares is comprised in that property, any beneficiary of that trust who apart from this subsection does not have an interest in the shares shall be taken to have such an interest.

(4) A person shall be taken to have an interest in shares if—

(a) he enters into a contract for their purchase by him (whether for cash or other consideration); or

(b) not being the registered holder, he is entitled to exercise any right conferred by the holding of those shares or is entitled to control the exercise of any such right.

(5) A person shall be taken to have an interest in shares if, otherwise than by virtue of having an interest under a trust—

(a) he has a right to call for delivery of the shares to himself or to his order; or

(b) he has a right to acquire an interest in shares or is under an obligation to take an interest in shares;

whether in any case the right or obligation is conditional or absolute.

(6) For the purposes of subsection (4)(b) above, a person shall be taken to be entitled to exercise or control the exercise of any right conferred by the holding of shares if he has a right (whether subject to conditions or not) the exercise of which would make him so entitled or is under an obligation (whether so subject or not) the fulfilment of which would make him so entitled.

(7) Persons having a joint interest shall be taken each of them to have that interest.

(8) It is immaterial that shares in which a person has an interest are unidentifiable.

66. Interests to be disregarded.—(1) The following interests in shares shall for the purposes of sections 58 to 60 of this Act be disregarded, that is to say—

(a) where any property is held on trust according to the law of England and Wales and any interest in shares is comprised in that property, an interest in reversion or remainder or of a bare trustee or a custodian trustee and any discretionary interest;

(b) where any property is held on trust according to the law of Scotland and any interest in shares is comprised in that property, an interest in fee or of a simple trustee and any discretionary interest;

(c) an interest which subsists by virtue of an authorised unit trust scheme within the meaning of the Prevention of Fraud (Investments) Act 1958, a scheme made under section 22 of the Charities Act 1960, section 11 of the Trustee Investments Act 1961 or section 1 of the Administration of Justice Act 1965 or the scheme set out in the Schedule to the Church Funds Investment Measure 1958;

(d) an interest of the Church of Scotland General Trustees or of the Church of Scotland Trust in shares held by them or of any other person in shares held by the said Trustees or Trust otherwise than as simple trustees;

(e) an interest, for the life of himself or another, of a person under a settlement in the case of which the property comprised in the settlement consists of, or includes, shares, and the conditions mentioned in subsection (3) below are satisfied;

(f) an exempt interest held by a recognised jobber;

(g) an exempt security interest;

(h) an interest of the President of the Family Division of the High Court subsisting by virtue of section 9 of the Administration of Estates Act 1925;
(i) an interest of the Accountant General of the Supreme Court in shares held by him;
(j) any such interests, or interests of such class, as may be prescribed for the purposes of this paragraph by regulations made by the Secretary of State by statutory instrument.

(2) A person shall not by virtue of section 65(4)(b) of this Act be taken to be interested in any shares by reason only that he has been appointed a proxy to vote at a specified meeting of a company or of any class of its members and at any adjournment of that meeting or has been appointed by a corporation to act as its representative at any meeting of a company or of any class of its members.

(3) The conditions referred to in subsection (1)(e) above are, in relation to any settlement—
(a) that it is irrevocable; and
(b) that the settlor (within the meaning of section 403 of the Income Tax Act 1952) has no interest in any income arising under, or property comprised in, the settlement.

(4) A person is a recognised jobber for the purposes of subsection (1)(f) above if he is a member of The Stock Exchange recognised by the Council of The Stock Exchange as carrying on the business of a jobber; and an interest of any such person in shares is an exempt interest for those purposes if—
(a) he carries on that business in the United Kingdom; and
(b) he holds the interest for the purposes of that business.

(5) An interest in shares is an exempt security interest for the purposes of subsection (1)(g) above if—
(a) it is held by a person who is—
  (i) a recognised bank or licensed institution within the meaning of the Banking Act 1979 or an insurance company within the meaning of the Insurance Companies Act 1974 to which Part II of that Act applies; or
  (ii) a trustee savings bank (within the meaning of the Trustee Savings Banks Act 1976); or
  (iii) a member of The Stock Exchange carrying on business in the United Kingdom as a stock broker; and
(b) it is held by way of security only for the purposes of a transaction entered into in the ordinary course of his business as such a person;

or if it is held by the Post Office by way of security only for the puposes of a transaction entered into by the Post Office in the ordinary course of that part of its business which consists of the provision of banking services.

67. Supplementary provisions.—(1) Where a person authorises any other person ('the agent') to acquire or dispose of, on his behalf, interests in shares comprised in relevant share capital of a public company, he shall secure that the agent notifies him immediately of acquisitions or disposals of interests in shares so comprised effected by the agent which will or may give rise to any obligation on his part to make a notification under section 58 of this Act with respect to his interest in that share capital.

(2) An obligation to make any notification imposed on any person by any provision of sections 58 to 60 of this Act shall be treated as not being fulfilled unless the notice by means of which it purports to be fulfilled identifies him and gives his address, and in a case where he is a director of the company, is expressed to be given in fulfilment of that obligation.

(3) A person who—

(a) fails to fulfil, within the proper period, an obligation to make a notification required by any provision of section 58 of this Act; or

(b) in purported fulfilment of any such obligation makes to a company a statement which he knows to be false or recklessly makes to a company a statement which is false; or

(c) fails to fulfil, within the proper period, an obligation to give any other person any notice required by section 63 of this Act; or

(d) fails without reasonable excuse to comply with subsection (1) above;

shall be guilty of an offence under this section.

(4) A person who is guilty of an offence under this section shall be liable—

(a) on conviction on indictment, to imprisonment for a term not exceeding two years or a fine, or both; and

(b) on summary conviction, to imprisonment for a term not exceeding six months or a fine not exceeding the statutory maximum, or both.

(5) It shall be a defence for a person charged with an offence under subsection (3)(c) above to prove that it was not possible for him to give the notice to that other person required by section 63 within the proper period, and either—

(a) that it has not since become possible for him to give the notice so required; or

(b) that he gave that notice as soon after the end of that period as it became possible for him to do so.

(6) Where a person is convicted of an offence under this section, other than an offence relating to his ceasing to be interested in shares in any company, the Secretary of State may direct that the

shares in relation to which the offence was committed shall, until further order, be subject to the restrictions imposed by section 174 of the 1948 Act.

(7) Subsection (6) above shall apply in relation to shares in any company notwithstanding any power contained in the memorandum or articles of the company enabling it to impose similar restrictions on the shares in question itself.

(8) Subsections (3) to (7) of section 174 of the 1948 Act shall apply in relation to any shares subject to the restrictions imposed by that section by virtue of an order under this section as those subsections apply where the restrictions are imposed by virtue of an order under that section.

(9) Proceedings in respect of an offence under this section shall not, in England and Wales, be instituted except by, or with the consent of, the Secretary of State or the Director of Public Prosecutions.

Register of interests in shares

68. Register of interests in shares.—(1) Every public company shall keep a register for the purposes of sections 58 to 60 of this Act, and whenever the company receives information from a person in consequence of the fulfilment of an obligation imposed on him by any of those sections, it shall be under an obligation to inscribe in the register, against the name of that person, that information and the date of the inscription.

(2) Without prejudice to subsection (1) above, where a company receives a notification under section 58 of this Act which includes a statement that the person making the notification or any other person has ceased to be a party to an agreement to which section 62 of this Act applies, it shall be under an obligation to record that information against the name of that person in every place where his name appears in the register as a party to that agreement (including any entry relating to him made against another person's name).

(3) An obligation imposed by subsection (1) or (2) above must be fulfilled within the period of three days next following the day on which that obligation arises.

(4) The company shall not, by virtue of anything done for the purposes of this section, be affected with notice of, or put upon inquiry as to, the rights of any person in relation to any shares.

(5) The register must be so made up that the entries against the several names inscribed in the register appear in chronological order.

(6) Unless the register is in such form as to constitute in itself an index, the company shall keep an index of the names inscribed in the register which shall in respect of each name contain a sufficient indication to enable the information inscribed against it to be readily found; and the company shall, within fourteen days after the date on which a name is inscribed in the register, make any necessary alteration in the index.

(7) Where the company ceases to be a public company it shall continue to keep the register and any associated index until the end of the period of ten years beginning with the day next following that on which it ceases to be such a company.

(8) The register and any associated index—

(a) shall be kept at the place at which the register required to be kept by the company by section 29 of the 1967 Act (register of directors' interests) is kept; and

(b) subject to subsection (9) below, shall be available for inspection in accordance with section 75 of this Act.

(9) Neither the register nor any associated index shall be available for inspection in accordance with that section in so far as it contains information with respect to a company for the time being entitled to avail itself of the benefit conferred by section 3(3) or 4(3) of the 1967 Act (exemption of a company from requirement to disclose in its accounts particulars of substantial shareholdings in subsidiaries or other bodies corporate incorporated or carrying on business outside the United Kingdom in circumstances where disclosure would be harmful to business).

(10) If default is made in complying with subsection (1) or (2) or with any of subsections (5) to (7) above, the company and every officer of the company who is in default shall be liable on summary conviction to a fine not exceeding one-fifth of the statutory maximum or, on conviction after continued contravention, a default fine not exceeding one-fiftieth of the statutory maximum.

Investigation by a company of interests in shares

69. Power of company to require information with respect to interests in its voting shares.—(1) Any public company may by notice in writing require any person whom the company knows or has reasonable cause to believe to be or, at any time during the three years immediately preceding the date on which the notice is issued, to have been interested in shares comprised in relevant share capital of that company to confirm that fact or (as the case may be) to indicate whether or not it is the case and, where he holds or has during that time held any interest in shares so comprised, to give such further information as may be required in accordance with subsection (2) below.

(2) A notice under subsection (1) above may require the person to whom it is addressed—

(a) to give particulars of his own past or present interest in shares comprised in relevant share capital of the company (held by him at any time during the three year period mentioned in subsection (1) above);

(b) where the interest is a present interest and any other interest in the shares subsists or, in any case, where another interest in the shares subsisted during that three year period at any time when his own interest subsisted, to give so far as lies within his knowledge such particulars with respect to that other interest as may be required by the notice;

(c) where his interest is a past interest, to give so far as lies within his knowledge particulars of the identity of the person who held that interest immediately upon his ceasing to hold it.

(3) The particulars referred to in subsection (2)(a) and (b) above include particulars of the identity of persons interested in the shares in question and of whether persons interested in the same shares are or were parties to any agreement to which section 62 of this Act applies or to any agreement or arrangement relating to the exercise of any of the rights conferred by the holding of the shares.

(4) A notice under this section shall require any information given in response to the notice to be given in writing within such reasonable time as may be specified in the notice.

(5) Sections 61, 62 and 65 of this Act shall apply for the purpose of construing references in this section to persons interested in shares and to interests in shares respectively as they apply in relation to section 58 of this Act (but with the omission of any reference to section 66).

(6) This section shall apply in relation to a person who has or previously had or is or was entitled to acquire a right to subscribe for shares in a public company which would on issue be comprised in relevant share capital of that company as it applies in relation to a person who is or was interested in shares so comprised; and references in the preceding provisions of this section to an interest in shares so comprised and to shares so comprised shall be read accordingly in any such case as including references respectively to any such right and to shares which would on issue be so comprised.

70. Registration of interests disclosed under section 69.— (1) Wherever in pursuance of a requirement imposed on any person under section 69 of this Act a company receives any information to which this section applies relating to shares comprised in relevant share capital of the company it shall be under an obligation to inscribe against the name of the registered holder of those shares in a separate part of its register of interests in shares—

(a) the fact that the requirement was imposed and the date on which it was imposed; and

(b) any information to which this section applies received in pursuance of the requirement.

(2) This section applies to any information received in pursuance of a requirement imposed under section 69 which relates to the present interests held by any persons in shares comprised in relevant share capital of the company in question.

(3) Subsections (3) to (10) of section 68 of this Act shall apply in relation to the part of the register maintained in accordance with subsection (1) above as they apply in relation to the remainder of the register, reading references to subsection (1) of that section as including references to subsection (1) above.

71. Investigation and report on requisition of members.—(1) A company may be required to exercise its powers under section 69 of this Act on the requisition of members of the company holding at the date of the deposit of the requisition not less than one-tenth of such of the paid up capital of the company as carries at that date the right of voting at general meetings of the company.

(2) The requisition must—

(a) state that the requisitionists are requiring the company to exercise its powers under section 69 of this Act;

(b) specify the manner in which they require those powers to be exercised; and

(c) give reasonable grounds for requiring the company to exercise those powers in the manner specified;

and must be signed by the requisitionists and deposited at the registered office of the company.

(3) The requisition may consist of several documents in like form each signed by one or more requisitionists.

(4) On the deposit of a requisition which complies with this section it shall be the duty of the company to exercise its powers under section 69 of this Act in the manner specified in the requisition.

(5) On the conclusion of any investigation carried out by a company in pursuance of a requisition under this section it shall be the duty of the company to cause a report of the information received in pursuance of that investigation to be prepared, and that report shall be made available at the registered office of the company within a reasonable period (which shall not exceed twenty-eight days) after the conclusion of that investigation.

(6) A report prepared in pursuance of subsection (5) above shall not include any information with respect to a company entitled to avail itself of the benefit conferred by section 3(3) or 4(3) of the 1967 Act (where disclosure of substantial holdings in bodies incorporated or carrying on business outside the United Kingdom would be harmful) but where any such information is omitted that fact shall be stated in the report.

(7) The company shall within three days of making the report available at its registered office notify the requisitionists that the report is so available.

(8) An investigation carried out by a company in pursuance of a requisition under this section shall be regarded for the purposes of subsection (5) above as concluded when the company has made all such enquiries as are necessary or expedient for the purposes of the requisition and, in the case of each such inquiry, either a response has been received by the company or the time allowed for a response has elapsed.

(9) The report of any investigation carried out by a company in pursuance of a requisition under this section—

(a) shall be kept at the company's registered office from the day on which it is first made available there in accordance with subsection (5) above until the expiration of the period of ten years beginning with the day next following that day; and

(b) shall be available for inspection in accordance with section 75 of this Act so long as it is so kept.

(10) If default is made in complying with subsection (4), (5), (7) or (9)(a) above the company and every officer of the company who is in default shall be liable—

(a) on conviction on indictment, to a fine; and

(b) on summary conviction, to a fine not exceeding the statutory maximum.

72. Penalties for failure to provide information under section 69.—(1) Where a notice is served by any company under subsections (1) and (2) of section 69 of this Act on any person who is or was interested in any shares in the company and that person fails to give the company any information required by the notice within the time specified in the notice, the company may apply to the court for an order directing that the shares in question shall be subject to the restrictions imposed by section 174 of the 1948 Act.

(2) An order may be made by the court on an application under subsection (1) above notwithstanding any power contained in the memorandum or articles of the applicant company enabling it to impose similar restrictions on the shares in question itself.

(3) Where an order is made under subsection (1) above directing that shares shall be subject to the restrictions imposed by section 174 of the 1948 Act, the company or any person aggrieved by the order may apply to the court for an order directing that the shares shall cease to be subject thereto.

(4) Subsections (3A) to (7) of section 174 shall apply in relation to any shares subject to the restrictions imposed by section 174 by virtue of an order under this section but with the omission in subsections (3A) to (6) of any reference to the Secretary of State or the Board of Trade.

(5) Subject to subsections (6) and (7) below, any person who fails to comply with a notice under section 69 of this Act, or who, in purported compliance with such a notice, makes any statement which he knows to be false in a material particular or recklessly makes any statement which is false in a material particular shall be guilty of an offence and liable—

(a) on conviction on indictment, to imprisonment for a term not exceeding two years or a fine or both; and

(b) on summary conviction, to imprisonment for a term not exceeding six months or a fine not exceeding the statutory maximum or both.

(6) A person shall not be guilty of an offence by virtue of failing to comply with a notice under section 69 of this Act if he proves that the requirement to give the information was frivolous or vexatious.

(7) A person shall not be obliged to comply with a notice under section 69 of this Act if he is for the time being exempted by the Secretary of State shall not grant any such exemption except after consultation with the Governor of the Bank of England and unless satisfied that, having regard to any undertaking given by the person in question with respect to the shares held or to be held by him, there are special reasons why that person should not be subject to the obligations imposed by that section.

Removal of entries from register

73. Provision for removal of certain entries in register.—(1) A company may remove an entry against any person's name from its register of interests in shares where more than ten years have elapsed since the date of its inscription, and either—

(a) that entry recorded the fact that the person in question had ceased to have an interest subject to the notification requirement under section 58 of this Act in relevant share capital of the company; or

(b) it has been superseded by a later entry inscribed under section 68 of this Act against the same person's name;

and in a case within paragraph (a) above the company may also remove that person's name from the register.

(2) Where any person in pursuance of an obligation imposed on him by any provision of this Part of this Act gives to a company the name and address of any other person as being interested in shares in the company, the company shall, within twenty-one days of the date on which it was given that information, notify that other person that he has been so named and shall include in that notification—

(a) particulars of any entry relating to him made, in consequence of its being given that information, by the company in its register of interests in shares; and

(b) a statement informing him of his right to apply to have that entry removed in accordance with the following provisions of this section.

(3) Any person who has been notified by a company in pursuance of subsection (2) above that an entry relating to him has been made in the company's register of interests in shares may apply in writing to the company for the removal of that entry from the register; and the company shall remove the entry if satisfied that the information in pursuance of which the entry was made was incorrect.

(4) Where a person who is identified in a company's register of interests in shares as being a party to an agreement to which section 62 of this Act applies (whether by an entry against his own name or by an entry relating to him made against another person's name as mentioned in subsection (2)(a) above) ceases to be a party to that agreement, he may apply in writing to the company for the inclusion of that information in the register; and if the company is satisfied that he has ceased to be a party to that agreement it shall record that information (if not already recorded) in every place where his name appears as a party to that agreement in the register.

(5) Where an application under subsection (3) or (4) above is refused (in a case within subsection (4), otherwise than on the ground that the information has already been recorded) the applicant may apply to the court for an order directing the company to remove the entry in question from the register or (as the case may be) to include the information in question in the register, and the court may if it thinks fit make such an order.

(6) Where any name is removed from a company's register of interests in shares in pursuance of subsection (1) or (3) above or an order under subsection (5), the company shall within fourteen days

of the date of that removal make any necessary alteration in any associated index.

(7) If default is made in complying with subsection (2) or (6) above, the company and every officer who is in default shall be liable on summary conviction to a fine not exceeding one-fifth of the statutory maximum or, on conviction after continued contravention, a default fine not exceeding one-fiftieth of the statutory maximum.

74. Prohibition of removal of entries in register.—(1) Entries in a company's register of interests in shares shall not be deleted except in accordance with section 73 of this Act.

(2) If default is made in complying with subsection (1) above the company and every officer who is in default shall be liable on summary conviction to a fine not exceeding one-fifth of the statutory maximum or, on conviction after continued contravention, a default fine not exceeding one-fiftieth of the statutory maximum.

Inspection of register and reports

75. Inspection of register and reports.—(1) Any register of interests in shares and any report which is required by section 71 of this Act to be available for inspection in accordance with this section shall, during business hours (subject to such reasonable restrictions as the company may in general meeting impose, provided that not less than two hours in each day are allowed for inspection) be open to the inspection of any member of the company without charge and of any other person on payment of such reasonable fee as the company may prescribe, for each inspection.

(2) Any member of the company or other person may require a copy of any such register or report, or any part of it, on payment of such reasonable fee as the company may prescribe; and the company shall cause any copy so required by a person to be sent to him before the expiration of the period of ten days beginning with the day next following that on which the requirement is received by the company.

(3) If an inspection required under this section is refused or a copy required under this section is not sent within the proper period, the company and every officer of the company who is in default shall be liable on summary conviction to a fine not exceeding one-fifth of the statutory maximum, or on conviction after continued contravention, a default fine not exceeding one-fiftieth of the statutory maximum.

(4) In the case of a refusal of an inspection required under this section of any register or report, the court may by order compel an

immediate inspection of it; and in the case of failure to send a copy required under this section, the court may by order direct that the copy required shall be sent to the person requiring it.

Supplemental

76. Offences by bodies corporate.—(1) Where a body corporate is guilty of an offence under section 67 or 72(5) of this Act and it is proved that the offence occurred with the consent or connivance of, or was attributable to any neglect on the part of any director, manager, secretary or other officer of the body, or any person who was purporting to act in any such capacity, he, as well as the body corporate, shall be deemed to be guilty of that offence and shall be liable to be proceeded against and punished accordingly.

(2) Where the affairs of a body corporate are managed by its members, subsection (1) above shall apply in relation to the acts and defaults of a member in connection with his functions of management as if he were a director of the body corporate.

77. Interpretation.—(1) In this Part of this Act—

'associated index', in relation to any register, means the index kept in relation to that register in pursuance of section 68(6) of this Act;

'register of interests in shares' means the register kept in pursuance of section 68 of this Act including, except where the context otherwise requires, that part of the register kept in pursuance of section 70 of this Act; and

'relevant share capital' has the meaning given by section 58(10) of this Act.

(2) It is hereby declared for the avoidance of doubt that where the relevant share capital of a public company is divided into different classes of shares, references in this Part of this Act to a percentage of the nominal value of its relevant share capital are references to a percentage of the nominal value of the issued shares comprised in each of those classes taken separately.

(3) It is hereby declared for the avoidance of doubt that the temporary suspension of voting rights in respect of shares comprised in relevant share capital of any public company does not affect the application of this Part of this Act in relation to interests in those shares.

(4) In reckoning any period allowed by any provision of this Part of this Act for fulfilling any obligation, a day that is a Saturday or Sunday or a bank holiday in any part of Great Britain shall be disregarded.

78. Repeals, transitional provisions and saving.—(1) Sections 33 and 34 of the 1967 Act and sections 26 and 27 of the 1976 Act, which are superseded by the preceding provisions of this Part of this Act, shall cease to have effect.

(2) Subject to subsection (3) below, where on the appointed day a person has an interest subject to the notification requirement under section 58 of this Act in relevant share capital of a public company he shall be under an obligation to make to the company the notification with respect to his interest required by subsection (5) of that section.

(3) A person shall not be required to make any such notification by virtue of subsection (2) above in any case where—

(a) he has made a notification to the company under section 33 of the 1967 Act with respect to any interest of his in shares comprised in the share capital in question; and

(b) the percentage level of the interest notified (or last notified) by him under that section is the same as the percentage level of his interest on the appointed day determined in accordance with section 58 of this Act.

(4) In subsection (3)(b) above 'percentage level' means, in relation to any interest in share capital notified by a person under section 33 of the 1967 Act, the percentage figure found by expressing the aggregate nominal value of all the shares so notified as a percentage of the nominal value of that share capital as known to the person in question on the appointed day and rounding that figure down, if it is not a whole number, to the next whole number.

(5) Section 58(6) shall not apply in any case where a person is required to make a notification under that section by virtue of subsection (2) above, but a person's obligation to make any such notification must be performed within the period of fourteen days next following the appointed day.

(6) Section 62 of this Act shall apply in relation to an agreement notwithstanding that it was made before the appointed day or that any such acquisition of shares as is mentioned in subsection (2) of that section took place before the appointed day.

(7) Section 64 of this Act applies where a person becomes or ceases to be interested in any shares by virtue of section 61 or 62 of this Act on the coming into operation of either of the two last-mentioned sections as it applies in the other cases mentioned in subsection (2) of that section; and references in that section to a person's becoming interested in any shares by virtue of section 61 shall be read as including any case within this subsection notwithstanding that the person in question was interested in the shares immediately before the appointed day by virtue of section 28(3) of the 1967 Act.

(8) Any register kept by a company immediately before the appointed day under section 34 of the 1967 Act, and any part of any such register so kept for the purposes of section 27 of the 1976 Act, shall continue to be kept by the company under and for the purposes of sections 68 and 70 of this Act respectively.

(9) Notwithstanding the repeal by this Act of section 27 of the 1976 Act, subsections (1) to (4) and (7) to (10) of that section shall continue to apply in relation to any notice given to any person under that section before the appointed day (and further notices may accordingly be given under that section on or after that day by virtue of information received in pursuance of any notice given before that day or any further notice given by virtue of this subsection); and references in section 70 of this Act to a requirement imposed under section 69 of this Act shall be read as including references to a requirement imposed under section 27.

Appendix 5
Insider dealing

Insider dealing

Part V of the Companies Act 1980 which came into effect on 23 June 1980 makes it a criminal offence for individuals to deal in securities if they have 'insider information' which could affect the value of these securities.

PROHIBITIONS UNDER THE NEW ACT

(1) Any person who is or during the previous six months has been knowingly connected with a company (see Note 1) is forbidden to deal on a recognised Stock Exchange in the securities of that company if he has information which:
   (a) he holds by virtue of his connection with the company;
   (b) he would be expected not to disclose (except in the normal course of his duties);
   (c) he knows is unpublished information which if generally known would affect the share price of the company.

(2) It is also forbidden for an individual who is or during the previous six months has been connected with a company to deal in the securities of *another company* (with which he is not connected) if he has obtained his information through his position in the *first* company. The information concerned must be confidential, (i e unpublished) price-sensitive information (as in (b) and (c) above) and relate to an actual or contemplated transaction involving the two companies.

(3) Similar dealing is forbidden by any individual who *is not himself connected* but who obtains the information directly or indirectly from a person who is connected or has access in the manner described in the preceding paragraphs. The individual receiving the information must, however, have reason to believe that the information is confidential and price-sensitive and that the original informant acquired it by virtue of his company position.

(4) It is forbidden for an individual to deal in the shares of a company if *in some other capacity* he is contemplating making a

takeover bid for that company and knows that the information that this offer is (or is not) to be made is unpublished and price sensitive. This restriction applies to anyone having received the information from any person contemplating making a takeover bid.

(5) Any of the persons referred to above who are themselves prohibited from dealing *must not advise or procure* any other person to deal in the shares referred to on a recognised Stock Exchange.

(6) Further, persons debarred from dealing themselves under the above rules are forbidden to *communicate* the information referred to, i e offer 'tips', if they have reasonable cause to believe that it will then be used by *some other person* (the tippee) to deal in these securities on a recognised Stock Exchange.

Note 1

A person is considered to be *connected* with a company if:

(a) he is a Director or Officer or Employee or has a professional or business relationship with the company either directly or through his Employer or a company of which he is a Director; and

(2) any of these positions may reasonably be expected to give him access to unpublished price sensitive information about the company concerned which it would be reasonable to expect a person in his position not to disclose.

Note 2

Unpublished price sensitive information is defined by the Act as referring to information which relates to specific matters of concern to the company and is not generally known to those persons who are accustomed or would be likely to deal in its securities but which would, if generally known to them, be likely materially to affect the price of those securities.

Note 3

The restrictions referred to above hold good for any dealings in advertised securities which may take place other than on a recognised Stock Exchange or outside Great Britain.

EXCEPTIONS AND LIMITATIONS

The Act contains a number of provisions limiting the general penal liabilities set out above. These are mainly as follows:

(1) It is no offence to do any particular thing provided that the motive was not to make a profit or avoid a loss in the transaction. This will probably relate to situations where the

purchase or sale or securities was necessary to meet some particular obligation such as payment of tax.

(2) Any person acting in a professional capacity whether as liquidator, receiver or trustee in bankruptcy is excluded from the prohibitions under the Act as are jobbers, or trustees who are acting in good faith in the normal course of their duties and relying on professional advice.

(3) It is also no offence to take advantage of insider information to refrain from dealing or to advise another not to deal.

PENALTIES

Any person contravening the provisions of the Act will be liable on conviction to imprisonment for up to two years or a fine or both.

SUMMARY

To summarise, the significance of the new Act is that:

(1) It makes insider dealing a criminal offence for the first time.

(2) It creates a wide range of persons who may be liable for prosecutions extending to all employees, professional advisers, business associates or even members of the general public who may have access to unpublished price sensitive information in certain circumstances.

(3) It defines more clearly than in the past the circumstances in which insider dealing will be deemed to have taken place.

It is not yet possible to judge how rigorously the Act will be enforced, but until the situation is clarified it would be advisable for all directors and employees, not only to observe the rules of confidentiality which already apply, but to take particular care in discussing company affairs with third parties where matters having a significant impact on the company's results or future prospects may be involved.

RELATION TO MODEL CODE

The requirements to be observed by all Directors, Officers and Employees which are set out in this Memorandum shall be read together with the Model Code for Securities Transactions by Directors of Listed Companies [which has already been circulated to you].

Index